Mindfully Saving Myself

One Moment At A Time

Stephen McCoull

Stephen McCoull

Copyright © 2021 Stephen McCoull

All rights reserved.

ISBN: 979-84-92407-63-6

Mindfully Saving Myself – One Moment at a Time

For Marta and for my children

Stephen McCoull

Contents

Introduction 6

From Darkness to the Light.................................8

My First Meditations..24

Fantasy Chat – Unproductive Conversations in your Head 34

Loving Kindness Meditation..............................40

Attachment leads to suffering?..........................51

Facing yourself on the cushion...........................58

Counting Away from the Past as a Way to Escape the Present............66

Noticing Thoughts and then labelling them..................72

A Way to Calm a Busy Mind................................77

Acceptance is Key...81

Responsibility for Your Life is Yours Alone.............89

The News and Social Media – Do you need it? 102

Using Gratitude to Help You Find Wonder in Everything 111

Fixing your Spiritual Roof whilst the Sun is Shining.............122

Converting Loneliness Into Alone Time 127

Death or Forgiveness? 139

Why Trying to be a Good Meditator can be Counter Productive........146

Not Self..153

Accepting the Rain 163

Turning Nostalgia into a Useful Tool..................165

Mindfully Breaking my Attachment to Alcohol 172

What Other Addictions Can You Observe and then Escape? 183

Exercising Smart...188

What is this? A tool to bring you into the present moment...............192

Mindfully Saving Myself – One Moment at a Time

An Inferiority Complex is just a Collection of Thoughts 198

Every day is a New Day 206

Recognising Judgement 211

Mindfully approaching Grief 217

Confrontation does not lead to Peace 228

Life Unmindfully Passing You By 233

Being a Snob Harms You So Observe It 236

Distraction is not mindfulness 241

Triumphing over Fear 246

Benefits of Mindfulness – What you get out of it 255

Using the Inevitable Backwards Step as a Tool 268

What's Outside Doesn't Give You Peace 274

Life is What We Make it 279

Acknowledgements 281

Stephen McCoull

Introduction

Whilst I'd heard the term before, it was not until 2016 that I truly discovered a way of living that is called "Mindfulness". Living a mindful life was by no means something that I was able to immediately fall into and live in my life. It took great effort and faith that mindfulness could help me, but once I understood its power, I have never stopped practicing and learning. Slowly, the practice has enveloped me and mindful living has made a revolutionary change to my life. When I say revolutionary, I do not exaggerate that point, I could not imagine going back to my former way of life nor could I envisage surviving as I had done previously.

In my former life, despite how my personality may have appeared, I was an extremely reactive human being, filled with rage at life and myself. I was fearful, upset, depressed and anxious and no matter what I did to escape these emotions, my life was only getting worse. I never felt at home anywhere, especially inside my own skin. I was lost and my thoughts were extremely dark.

Yet, after only just under five years of practice, mindfulness has helped me learn how I can live in internal peace, which I sometimes find extraordinary, even when I have been surrounded by storms, storms that would have drowned me before. I can state without any doubt, that altering my life from reactivity to one of mindful living has helped me save my own life, a life that had formerly been blighted by years of mental torment. It is that powerful and it is utterly radical.

Why did I decide to write this book? One day, as I was out walking, I observed the thought that if the practice of mindfulness can help save me, then it could save anyone, if only they had the opportunity to discover mindfulness and apply it to their own lives. As I observed that thought, I realised that there was truth in it. Anyone could use the practice to move themselves towards peace. I knew then that I couldn't keep this to myself, I had to write about the practices that have helped me turn my life around.

The purpose of this book is to show you that mindfulness is a simple practice, one that anyone can do, but a practice that is as transformative as it is straightforward. I am no Zen master and I do not pretend to be. Instead, I want to encourage you to give mindfulness a try and show you that the practice can be applied to any life. I point out the pitfalls I came across, share lessons I have learnt from the way I have applied mindfulness to all aspects of my life, and the amazing outcome I have experienced.

Mindfulness can change your life for the better in ways that you could never imagine. Whilst I hope Mindfully Saving Myself - One Moment at a Time can be useful to a lot of people, if it helps just one person live mindfully and experience greater peace within their life, then it has been a success.

Stephen McCoull

From Darkness to the Light

I have used the words radical and revolutionary to describe the practice in relation to my own life, but to comprehend how it is both these things you need to understand where I came from. I need to show you how delinquent my mental state was before to help you really appreciate the magnitude of change that has occurred.

For much of my life I have surrounded myself with people. The people I chose to call my friends might have changed over time, but throughout my life there has nearly always been someone I could call up and arrange to meet for a chat, drink or even to go out with and party. I never had to be on my own if I didn't want to be. When I was younger, there was a time when I did enjoy my own company, but as I aged, I chose to not be alone more and more often, until I was rarely ever alone at all.

In addition to always wanting or needing friends around, I liked to go out and "get on it" as we say in the UK. Going out drinking and, very occasionally, taking recreational drugs and just being out of my mind for a few hours with whoever was there with me. In my late teens I used partying as a way to meet people and to come out of my very shy shell. As I moved into my twenties, whilst I rarely drank at home, I found more excuses to go out and have a drink with friends. Always having mates to see meant I could drink whenever and wherever I wanted to. Drinking is a big part of the British culture and what I did didn't particularly stick out. Whilst I drank often, my entire social life revolved around drinking, I was fortunate that I also had a fondness for exercise, to the point where I would workout in some form or another at least five times a week. It was only that love of exercise that stopped my drinking from going from excessively unhealthy to becoming a physical addiction.

In the second half of my twenties I met a Norwegian girl when I was briefly traveling in Malaysia. She was traveling for several months and when her trip ended, we met up again. Before I knew it, we were an exclusive item and I was flying to Norway once a month to see her. Once her studies in Norway were over, she moved in with me in the UK. I was very happy with her, I thought I had met the one and I would be with her for our entire lives and we got engaged. Yet, deep down, I always felt like my life was going to fall apart in some undefined way. I now see that as anxiety, but at the time the partying continued, because partying helped me ignore that feeling of impending doom. Suddenly, at the end of the summer of 2005, after over five years together, she came home one day and told me the relationship was over. She couldn't explain why it was over, just that she didn't love me anymore, and then she flew back to Norway, never to be seen again.

It was a huge shock and I broke on every level. At that point in my life I had never felt emotional pain like it. I was lost. For two or three days I didn't eat and I certainly didn't drink. Alcohol was something fun and I was having the opposite of fun. Life was torment.

The following weekend, a friend, who was concerned for my welfare, invited me to stay with her and her husband for the night. We sat down and discussed what had happened. I cried in front of her, expressed my complete and utter devastation and she opened a bottle of wine. Whilst I hadn't had the desire to drink since I'd been dumped, I drank the offered glass and I felt a bit better. Then I drank some more and I found alcohol provided me with a break from days' worth of agony I had been suffering. I woke up the next day and felt even worse than before. Remembering the escape from the previous night I embraced drinking like never before. My relationship with alcohol had changed. It no longer was just from a pick-me-up I used to socialise. For the first time in my life I consciously made the decision to turn to drink to escape emotional torture.

I knew my now ex-wife prior to my break up with my fiancée and, like many people I knew at the time, she immediately offered me support and closer friendship. She was a shoulder to cry on but, more importantly, she was someone who wanted to go out and drink and I really wanted to drink to not feel like my insides had been ripped out of me via my chest. Over a period of about three weeks I spent more and more time with her. Then one day I realised that the pain I felt after the breakup was no longer there, even when I wasn't drinking. All my emotions had turned away from the pain, almost as if a switch had been flicked, and were suddenly directed towards my wife. Less than a month after the end of my previous relationship I was in a new one, with my wife. She had a very young son, who quickly became my son, whom I loved and still love dearly. Almost a year after we got together we had

Mindfully Saving Myself – One Moment at a Time

another wonderful son, then got married in 2009 and, finally, we had a beautiful daughter in 2010.

Early on, if you had asked me what the best thing about my wife was, I would have told you it was the fact I could drink a lot and occasionally take drugs without any judgement at all. I didn't have to hide it and, in fact, she encouraged me to drink a lot because she loved to drink as well. As she had a son, going out was not always an option. If we wanted to drink we sometimes had to drink at home, once he was in bed. This meant that my home was no longer a place free of alcohol. Life became a crazy rollercoaster of fun and it appeared that she was great for me. However, I drank as I was still running from my anguish about my ex-fiancée that I wasn't brave enough to face or even acknowledge kept reappearing. Ultimately, the relationship with my wife enabled me to fully embrace all the damaging things inflicted on myself without ever having a reason to limit them. I welcomed this new found freedom.

Since I had begun my relationship with my wife, I was open about my love of exercise, it wasn't something I'd hidden from her. I worked out, I did it often and I needed to do it as it made me feel good. It had been my go to activity to help promote my own wellbeing and, in some ways, it was also a way to escape from life other than drink. After a brief honeymoon period things in our relationship began to change. Whilst my wife would encourage me to do things like excessive drinking, she started to get upset that I was working out. As time progressed, she became more and more hostile to the fact I worked out, even when I was exercising during my lunch break at work. She would try to discourage me by saying it wasn't fair when she couldn't work out, so, in an attempt to placate her, I would tell her she could go swimming in the evenings, her preferred exercise, and that she didn't have to worry about the kids. I said she could do it as often as she liked, which she did. Despite that, my wife continued to be annoyed that I was still exercising and she started to tell me that working out showed that I was selfish and only cared for myself. She'd do anything to berate me about my fitness. For instance, if I had my top off when I was changing in our bedroom and I happened to scratch myself she'd tell me how I had to keep touching myself because I was so obsessed with my body. The weird thing was that being drunk and hungover was completely acceptable in her eyes but exercise seemed to make me disgusting. I still wanted to keep fit, because it was the one thing holding me together, but now my anxiety around it grew because I knew it would bring with it arguments. It got to the point I started trying to hide the fact I had worked out at lunch.

During our relationship my wife liked to make the decisions. Whether it was how eggs were cooked or how we brought up the kids, we had to do it her way. When we first got together, she tolerated me having views different to hers but it was clear she thought she was right and it was better for me to fall in line. As the honeymoon period drifted into the past, she started to become angry if I didn't do as she pleased. When that happened it felt as if she'd withdrawn her love. After she got volatile, because I'd not matched her expectations, a whirlpool of suffering would appear deep within me, as if every single feeling I had been hiding from were immediately unleashed. I would do anything to make her love me again because it stopped the pain, but often whatever I did would be the opposite of what she wanted. The longer time went on, the worse her anger, and sometimes even hatred, would be towards me and I became ever more anxious that I would upset her and that my pain would reappear. I wanted anything but that hurt, and I would do whatever I had to do to stop it, so I gave up being my own person.

I never knew what to expect when I was at home. The longer I was with her the more I started to feel lost at sea and out of control of

Mindfully Saving Myself – One Moment at a Time

my life. I had become completely co-dependant. If she was angry at me, I hated myself and I felt extreme mental suffering. When she offered those brief glimpses of what I took for love, my anxiety would reduce to almost nothing. In the end, I would just do whatever she wanted to do in the hope that would be enough for her to love me but her mind was prone to change so agreeing with her one minute could mean I was against her the next. Whatever I did was never enough. *I* was never enough. And slowly I became extremely depressed and anxious. My work was affected as my mental health continued to decline and I was no longer able to do my job well. I felt uncomfortable whenever I was in the office, because I knew my work was poor and ultimately I didn't think I was good enough, yet I was never in any rush to get home because I had no idea which wife I would meet at the door. Mentally, I never had any peace in any place. My depression and anxiety became absolute.

To our party friends that we developed around us we looked like a great couple. We had beautiful children, good jobs, an amazing social life and we were always up to something. I didn't realise it at the time but we were rarely alone. In a way, we had managed to have a family without really growing up ourselves, which appeared to be quite a fantasy for some people. With one or two notable exceptions, what happened between my wife and I remained private and people didn't have any idea of what was happening behind closed doors. We were a party couple and on the outside our lives looked wonderful but inside I was slowly dying. My drinking increased. It helped to ease the pain I was feeling but it also brought more misery, more reasons to drink and there was nothing to stop me doing just that because I wasn't allowed to not drink.

Early in the last decade I started to feel that life was completely chaotic. I continued to smile, I continued to socialise. No one apart from my wife and a couple of close friends had a clue that there was anything wrong, until I had been suffering for some time and the façade I hid behind began to crumble. I was mentally ill and the sicker I got, the more my wife appeared to hate the weakness she felt I was showing. Rather than provide support, she got ever more combative, verbally attacking me at some of the lowest points of my life. She'd tell me that I was awful because I was off work due to depression, shouting at me that work would be good for me as she slammed the door in my face leaving the house for her own job. If I asked her for support, she'd tell me she wasn't my counsellor and demand I not talk to her about how I felt. If I tried again, I would get shouted at. She never made any attempt to understand the illness I was in the grip of. It was my problem and all my fault.

This went on during 2013 and 2014 and I had no escape at all, until I started to hook on to a thought in my head. There was a female friend from our group who my wife had known since school and we were very friendly with. Quickly, I started to fantasize that she would save me from my hell and I would save her from what I thought was her own. These thoughts weren't of sex, although I was interested in that, but actually of us being together and looking after each other as a couple. The fantasy sometimes made me really excited that things would change and, as far from reality as it was, the thoughts kept me from descending into a mental abyss, if only for a few minutes at a time.

One day, after a very drunken and wild party in my house, I went home with her and we slept together. I was very inebriated and it was all very blurry but after doing something this awful to my marriage, I saw that there was no way this woman could save me and no way I could save her. The spell was broken. I didn't want to be that kind of man that would cheat on his wife but it's what I was. I was a horrible, disgusting, selfish, failure of a human being. I took everything I'd been told for years

Mindfully Saving Myself – One Moment at a Time

as fact because it must have been true. Why else would I have done what I had done? I was filled with regret and guilt and thoughts of her were no longer a distraction. Instead, I fell fully into the hole of depression and 2014 began to swallow me up as if it were some great beast.

As the year marched on, I knew I couldn't continue living like I was. If I did, I would end up in an extremely bad mental place. Yet, I felt I was unable to leave the situation I found myself in because my co-dependency would not allow me to even think that was a possibility. In fact I still hoped my wife would change and she would save me. Maybe she would finally love me and maybe her love would make me whole again.

There were also my children. I loved them and I just couldn't imagine life without seeing them every day. I knew that they needed me and I couldn't put them through the trauma of a breakup. The idea itself added further to my depression as, whatever option I considered, I felt trapped. I was also well aware that, if I left my wife, all our friends would take her side when they found out about what I had done with her friend. The idea of losing my friends, on top of everything else, was also too much to bear. I didn't want to stay with my wife but I didn't want to leave because of what I would lose. So, I stayed and my life continued to darken and the story about myself my wife would feed me, and which I reinforced in my head, became ever more toxic. It was all my fault, I was the cause of all our problems. I was pathetic and selfish. I believed it all, what I had done with my wife's friend proved it. I started to approach the point where I felt that everyone would be better off without me. Everyone, including my children. I wanted escape for everyone else as much as for me.

On 5th December 2014 I had come to the end of my tether. I was married to someone who was never going to be satisfied with

15

Stephen McCoull

anything I did, and who could blame her? To say I hated myself is to simplify the feelings that ravaged me inside.

I wasn't just lacking in confidence, I was way beyond that. I no longer saw value in myself as a man. I doubted everything about who I thought I was, and I believed that everything was my fault because I had been emotionally beaten into the floor by a lifetime of being told I was selfish and not good enough. To make matters worse, I had become one of the loudest people berating me. I was a waste of space, a drain on the planet. I wanted to scream and physically rip myself out of my own body, if it were at all possible.

I remember it vividly. It was a Friday. I was "working" from home. Except working I was not. I was sobbing uncontrollably and in the morning my suicidal thoughts became a definite plan. I opened the cutlery draw and stared at the knives wondering which one would cut my veins and arteries the best. I remember the strange mixture of excitement and fear that enveloped me in that moment. I have never felt an emotion more extreme than in those moments.

Yet, before I could cut myself, one thing made me pause for a second. It was an uninvited question that popped into my head. What did I really want the outcome to be? This stopped me in my tracks and I thought about that question for a while. Then, I recognised the truth of what I was about to do. I wanted to be found, I wanted to be saved. I wanted people to see the pain I had been in for so long. I wanted people to understand everything I had been through, to love me for who I really was and I wanted them to save me. My wife was not one of the people I thought about then. After a moment, there was a realisation that this was an extremely unlikely outcome. What I was planning meant I was unlikely to be found alive and that, even if I was, it wouldn't change anything, no one would understand. As the realisation flooded through me, I learnt something incredibly important in that moment. I didn't want to die.

I decided to live.

Instead of slashing my arms, I drove to the doctor and I told him everything that had happened. He seemed out of his depth and wasn't able to offer me the support I needed but said he could provide a prescription for tranquilizers. I declined and, as I returned home, I knew I had no choice but to leave my wife to save myself. Nothing else would help.

Despite the fact it was clear to me that I had to leave, it still wasn't easy. I finally got up the guts to leave my wife a few days later. Realising that I was about to break free, my wife told me she'd forgive me for what I had done but I understood my only hope was to escape the relationship. I made the decision that I could only get better on my own, without her, and I told her it was over and left for good. It felt like a gigantic weight had been removed not only from on top of me but from deep within my being. I felt a lightness in life I had not felt for a very long time but it was a short lived high.

I knew I'd lose a lot of friends in the process. Even though I expected it, I was shocked with how many friends turned their backs on me. Whilst they didn't all disappear from my life all at once, I lost every friendship in the end with a couple of exceptions. Even though it was my decision for our friendship to end, my best friend from childhood was one of them (which was a mindful decision I took towards the end of 2017).

As I entered 2015 and the year started to progress, the lack of friends was like a hammer blow to the stomach that just kept slamming. I found myself suddenly without people to call up when my thoughts went through horrendous negative cycles that sometimes took me back to the thought of taking my own life. As time progressed, I tried to contact people - directly seeking support, and indirectly on social media but the outcome was always the same. Judgement against me or people telling me that they were still my friend but excuses as to why they could no longer talk to me. I had no one to talk me down from the ledge and I swayed on that ledge many times. Whilst I never again had a definitive plan to kill myself, the thoughts about wanting to die never went away in those early months of 2015.

I had started therapy back in 2013 and I periodically continued having sessions throughout 2015 and into 2016. It was during therapy that I first realised that I would never get better with my ex-wife, a thought I suppressed for a year or more. It was during therapy that I worked out I had done the terrible thing of cheating on my wife because I wanted to distract myself from my depression. I also discovered that, ultimately, I wanted that one lone act to take the decision to end my marriage out of my hands. It was through therapy that I learned that that was still no excuse for what I'd done, that I had to come to terms with it and try to make peace with myself. It was when I received therapy that I discovered that taking the decision to leave my wife, when she refused to kick me out, was the most positive decision for my own wellbeing that I had ever taken until that point.

Without therapy it may have taken me years to come to these conclusions or I may have never come to them at all. Therapy helped me learn so much about myself, my actions and how I thought. Without a doubt, therapy laid the ground work for what came next and I am forever grateful for the help I received. However, therapy never stopped me from feeling depressed and anxious, nor had it subdued my mind from offering me up thoughts about my own death. Therapy had taught me things about myself I had never understood before but even with all

Mindfully Saving Myself – One Moment at a Time

that knowledge I was still sick and still prone to making the same mistakes.

Being separated and without friends, I was lonely. It was a physical pain that I could not escape from. I remember this dreadful feeling slowly overcoming my entire body one day. A black cloud is often used to describe depression but that doesn't cover it. It was a feeling of panic without there being an attack, a feeling that my life was over, a feeling that no one would ever like me, let alone love me again. A feeling that I was utterly worthless and unworthy of care because, if I was worthy, my friends wouldn't have abandoned me like they had. I felt I had been swallowed alive by darkness. The feeling made me double over in pain. I cried more at that time of my life than I ever have done before or since.

I understood drinking was something I had to stop doing to get back some kind of mental stability. I wanted to get back control of my life after being out of control for so long. I knew drink was destroying me mentally so not only did I want out of my relationship with my wife, I wanted to break up with alcohol too. Despite that, I started to go out on my own to just pass the time. I would go to pubs, local gigs, bars and clubs and would occasionally find myself dancing on the dance floor alone and drunk. Other times I would make friends-for-the-night at these places as I drank with like-minded individuals. All I was trying to do was fill my time as best I could in the ways I used to but without my former friends. I look back now and it makes me grimace a little but at the time I sometimes thought that all this partying with strangers was fun.

I ended up living in a shared house as I couldn't afford to buy a place pre-divorce. I was lucky, as I ended up sharing it with good people. I was older than them and one of them was still in that early twenties stage of going out partying, drinking until the early hours, chatting to people and acting like tomorrow didn't matter. I got on well with him as I knew how to party and how to drink so we started going out drinking together. At the time, I thought I was moving forward, I was meeting new people, I was a free agent and I was "having a laugh". But I wasn't having a laugh. I was very lonely, not happy, and I was certainly not at peace. Peace was far from where I was at and my depression and anxiety had never been worse.

The partying filled my time but I couldn't do it all the time and I quickly got into another relationship. At first glance she appeared very different to my ex-wife but I realise now I was with her just to feel wanted, unconsciously taking another lover to help me escape myself. Another lover who saw my weakness and before long the relationship became toxic, as I tried to please her. Much like my ex she could never be pleased.

The final act of my second toxic relationship, with my then girlfriend, was going to Thailand early in 2016 for an almost three week break from dealing with the divorce. When I was there, I did all the same things I'd done before, although less intensely, but it was still all about the senses, about the distractions. Seeing the sights, good food, good drinks, and chatting to people, both tourists and locals, so that I didn't have time to be alone with my thoughts.

I didn't meditate when we were in Thailand or even really learn what Buddhism, where mindfulness comes from, was about at the time. Yet, Thailand made an impact on me that I could not shake off. Rightly or wrongly, my experience of Thailand was that the majority of the Thai people I met were so calm, had amazing empathy and they appeared only to want to do good, to be good. Many of them are poor by our western standards yet, despite this, the most striking thing I noted was that the

Mindfully Saving Myself – One Moment at a Time

people I interacted with seemed to be at peace. Considering how frantic my own mind was, Thailand made an impression on me in a way I find difficult to describe.

When I returned home from Thailand, I knew something needed to change and I slowly started reading about Buddhism and mindfulness. I didn't go overboard at first because religion, well the main religions we have in the Western world, never made sense to me. They seemed to push me away and not give me any peace at all, so I was wary. Buddhism and mindfulness did seem very confusing at first but rather than repel me, the more I read, it had the opposite effect. My distrust ebbed away and mindfulness drew me in. I became increasingly curious. I started to read as much as I could about mindfulness, swapping novels and books about 20th Century History for meditation guides and books about Buddhism.

My new toxic relationship ended in slow drawn out death throws, which led to my final breakdown in May 2016. I was almost in as much danger at that point as at the time at the end of 2014. Thoughts of my own death flooded my mind again, but I had already begun to live differently and, having learnt the lessons from my previous mental collapses, I was able to do things differently. I was very fortunate that, to use the cliché, it was more of a breakout than a breakdown, and was extremely short lived.

I started to meditate. Initially, only once or twice a week then, gradually, I started to increase the frequency and then the length of the meditations until I was meditating daily, often for half an hour at a time. It wasn't just during meditation that I was becoming aware of myself. I also began to live mindfully during the day. At first, I would be mindless most of the time but slowly I brought the awareness into certain moments of my daily life. Those moments became more frequent.

21

Finally, for the first time in many years, I started to see glimpses of light. Rather than continuing to look for explanations and fixes from external sources, the practice helped me look inside and start to understand myself. The more I looked inside, the more I understood myself and I started to realise I wasn't as bad as I thought. I also discovered that thinking I was an awful human being was a thought that I no longer had to follow.

I began to appreciate who I was, accept my faults and learn from them so that I could feel my own value and worth. The deeper I got into learning about myself, the more I realised that the only person responsible for me was me and I stopped blaming others for the negativity in my life. I was the person who was responsible for every aspect of my life. Accepting that truth empowered me to start to engage with others without needing them to fill the void of my own existence. My desire for my old friendships fell away and those remaining relationships I put time into were spiritually nourishing. As I learnt to love myself, I came across a person who would accept me for who I was, without any clauses. She didn't need me to make her whole and I didn't need her to complete me. Marta and I fell in love, but it was a relationship we wanted rather than one born of need.

Through living mindfully, I have learnt to be in the moment and accept things as they are, however good or bad the situation is. Mindfulness has enabled me to learn about myself, the human condition and how be at peace even when things aren't great. The thing that really strikes me the most about mindfulness, is that it is as if I am learning skills that I already had but had unknowingly ignored for my entire life. I think we all have them buried within us, if only we look. Life can mean that sometimes we turn to investigate what's inside us only when

Mindfully Saving Myself – One Moment at a Time

everything else in our lives has failed to bring us happiness, and we feel we have no other choice.

Stephen McCoull

My First Meditations

Before coming to mindfulness my mind was busy, noisy and nearly always filled with depressive thoughts about the past or anxious thoughts about the future. I was fed up with the way my head had been for years. All I wanted was for my mind to shut up for a minute or two and I thought that mindfulness could help with that.

You're probably wondering how someone whose poor mental health had built up over a number of years to having serious thoughts about taking my own life can use mindfulness to do a complete about turn in life. Well, there are many different aspects to mindfulness that can help a person step away from the darkness, but in my experience the best way to change your life through mindful living is to begin by practicing formal meditation.

What do I mean by formal meditation? Any meditation in which you deliberately stop to pause and be with what is in that moment. It can be anywhere and in any physical posture but you don't do anything else whilst you are meditating. You focus on the practice alone.

When I first started reading about mindfulness and taking it seriously as an option to nourish myself I didn't really have a good idea of what meditation was. I knew it had something to do with sitting cross legged and calming your mind but I hadn't really given it too much

Mindfully Saving Myself – One Moment at a Time

consideration before I started practicing myself. That meant that I didn't have any preconceptions and I had no idea what to expect. I didn't know anyone who meditated or practiced mindfulness so, like most people do nowadays when they don't know about something and want to learn, I turned to the internet.

As I was carrying out my research, I came across a mobile app called Calm. Although it was a subscription based service, I noticed that it had some free content. I downloaded the app and started to use it periodically. I also found some meditations on YouTube and even on Spotify. Wherever I could find a meditation to practice along to, I listened to it and then, after a while, I started to practice without external prompts.

The first type of meditations I came cross and practiced regularly was simply focusing on the breath. The second one involves paying attention to your whole body, a meditation known as the body scan. What does meditating on your breath or your body actually mean? In essence, both meditations are very straight forward. All the practice involves is paying as close attention as you can to either the flow of the breath or various parts of your body. You observe, without trying to change or react to what is going on. There's not much else to it really. It's quite simple, but at the same time it's not easy, as it can be a struggle because our pesky overactive brains get in the way. Whether it's thinking about when your colleague said he could do that job himself, was it really a dig at you? Or if you took the right college course back in 1993 or what you will have for dinner tonight, your mind will resist the meditation. So, the thing that makes it difficult is the very reason you want to practice in the first place, your head. However difficult you may find it, it is worth the effort because meditation can help you change your entire life.

Stephen McCoull

How do you meditate on the breath? First, you find a relaxed sitting position, make sure that you are sitting comfortably but with an alert and upright posture. Don't slouch but don't sit rigid either. Find a middle ground that allows you to maintain the posture for the duration of the meditation. It can be done cross legged, in that well known meditative pose but, depending on your flexibility, but that might not be comfortable for you. When I started meditating I had to sit in a chair using a cushion to help me sit upright. Some of you may have physical issues that make it difficult to even sit still for the duration of the meditation. If that's the case, you can meditate lying down, focusing on maintaining consciousness. Ultimately, the pose isn't that important as long as you're able to focus.

Once you've sat down and made sure you're in a position that you can remain in for the length of the meditation, you then close your eyes and bring your attention to your breath. Just observe what the breath naturally does without forcing it to be anything other than it is. It could be deep or shallow, it could be noisy or quiet. Just pay attention to how it is, in this moment, without trying to change it. Allow these first few seconds of focus to help you slow down. Then, as you feel that you may be settling into this moment, inhale as deeply as you can and then slowly release the breath and empty the lungs. Take between three and five deep breaths, all the while remaining in an alert but relaxed posture with your attention fully on the breath.

After you've taken the deep breaths, return to your normal breathing. Do not force it, just focus again on the breath, observing it as it is. It may have changed from before you took those deep breaths. It may be longer or shorter, deeper or shallower. Again, it doesn't matter how your breath is, just notice the flow without judging whether it is good or bad.

Mindfully Saving Myself – One Moment at a Time

You may find, even though you are only a minute or two into the meditation, that your mind will have wandered off. You'll find yourself thinking about the washing you have to do later, the fight you had with your partner, a problem you have at work, that fun night out you had last week, an annoying task you can't complete on a computer game and even a conversation you may have had 20 years ago that embarrasses you greatly whenever it pops into your head. As you get lost in whatever is occupying your mind, you will be doing anything but focusing on the breath.

Don't worry if that happens. It is perfectly normal especially if you're new to meditation. When you finally notice that you are thinking about anything and everything but the breath, you may feel as if you have failed in some way. You haven't. It's just the human mind doing what evolution has moulded it to do: thinking and resolving both real and fictional problems. So when you get lost in thought, all you need to do is notice your mind has drifted and return it back to the breath. Don't judge, don't think your mind is impossible to reign in, just fully accept that the mind has wandered and bring it back to the breath. Whilst this will happen less and less often, the more experienced a meditator you become, this is something you will find yourself having to do repeatedly throughout your life following this practice. During your first meditation you will almost certainly have to do it many times. That is exactly what happened to me early on during my mindfulness journey and it's not an unusual experience at all.

We now know that mindful observation of the breath, recognising that the mind has wandered off, followed by a return of focus to the breath is one of the best ways of mindfully meditating. If this is all you did for five, ten or however many minutes you can manage to commit each day then you would be mindfully meditating. That alone, without ever trying another style of meditation, is enough to put you on a path that will help you in ways that you will not have anticipated. As I've grown in experience, this type remains my go to meditation. I will meditate in this way on a cushion, in a chair, on a bus or stood in a supermarket queue. This type of meditation is so versatile that I use it pretty much anywhere that I find myself with a few seconds to spare.

I found just focusing on the breath to be quite difficult to maintain as a beginner so, whilst most mindfulness meditations will involve focusing on the breath for some, if not all of it, early on I found observing the body slightly easier than focusing on the ever present breath.

The body scan is not much different than meditating on the breath. You have to face what is, you need to accept whatever you find and do so without any judgement. The difference here is that, rather than on the breath, the focus is on the rest of your body.

To do a body scan, start the practice as you did for the meditation on the breath. Get settled into a comfortable position, bring your attention to the breath and take a few deep breaths to bring yourself into the moment. This will most likely include all the to-ing and fro-ing between the breath and thoughts that is bound to happen early on. Thoughts about whether raspberry jam is better than strawberry jam or the guilt because of that horrible thing you said behind someone's back five years ago. It's ok, just return to the breath. Once you've gone through that for a few minutes, you can then start the body scan.

First, take your focus away from the breath and then place it on one small part of the body, whilst observing it with your mind. Once all your attention is on that one part of the body, you can observe all sorts of feelings that you may not normally notice as you go about your day to day. You may feel heat or coolness, maybe tingling. There may be mild

Mindfully Saving Myself – One Moment at a Time

pain, there may be pleasant sensations or there may even be no feeling at all. You may notice, whatever feelings you have, that the sensations do not stay the same. As you put all your attention on the physical experience and really observe what is there, the perception will change. As you gain experience, you will find that sensations that you imagine to be unmovable will actually transform in some way nearly all the time. Sometimes the physical feeling will get more powerful, sometimes they will come and go and other times what you are physically experiencing will disappear as you watch your body. Occasionally what you perceive will change from unpleasant to pleasant and then back again. You will learn that the sensations that you physical feel are not fixed.

And here is the really important part - don't react or judge whatever is going on. If there's a pleasant sensation don't grasp on to it. If you hold onto your experience then, when it slowly dissolves before you, a disappointment will sweep through you causing you suffering, no matter how mildly. If you observe an undesirable sensation, don't do the opposite and judge it negatively, wishing it were gone and try and run from it. It's important that you don't react to what is happening but just remain a non-judgemental observer who is accepting what is happening fully. Keep studying your body's sensations, both the good and the bad. If you catch yourself thinking "this is bad", step back from that thought, acknowledge it and then let it go and return back to observing the physical sensations without judgement.

So that itch on your nose is there but you just leave it be, don't scratch it, just keep observing it. Really get into that feeling and look at it so that you can see everything that itch is made of. Maybe the feeling will go or, perhaps, it will continue for a while, but just keep observing without reacting. Do the same with any desire to scratch the itch that may arise. See what that desire is made of and watch it as it ebbs and flows, without doing anything about it. Non-reactivity doesn't mean you ignore everything though. Whilst this has happened to me just a handful of times in four years of meditating, if you note cramp in your leg and it's getting worse to the point where it's going to cause problems, then you know you need to stretch it out to get rid of it. Stretching the cramp out and observing yourself as you do it is a mindful response. A reaction would be thinking "damn that cramp I just want to sit still for half an hour" or swearing out loud as you jump around moaning. The cramp just is, and you've responded to it by stretching out, so sit back down again and continue the body scan.

You might think that it's impossible not to react to what is happening to that itch, to that heat or the odd feeling in your arm but, even early on, I found that most sensations were physical feelings that could be observed without reactivity or requiring an active response either. I was often amazed by how itches, which would have previously driven me to distraction, didn't do anything to me, as long as I openly witnessed them and accepted their presence.

As straightforward as the body scan is, like with breath focused meditation, it's very likely that thoughts will take over your attention as you meditate, because we are all still human after all. One minute your attention is in the right shoulder seeing that knot of tiredness and then you're wondering which teams played in the 1986 World Cup final. When that happens, and it will, all you need to do is one thing. Without judgement, note that you have been lost in thought, return back to the last bit of the body you were scanning and continue the practice. Each time you return to the meditation, after being lost in thought, it strengthens your ability to quickly spot where your mind has roamed. Remember, having your mind wander is not a failure but, instead, it is

Mindfully Saving Myself – One Moment at a Time

something you can use to practice letting thoughts go and returning to the meditation and direct observation.

The great thing about the body scan meditation is that it's extremely adaptable. You can make it as long or as short as you want. I usually start my scan with the top of my head and then slowly work all the way down to my toes. How you observe each part of the body depends on how long the mediation will be. For instance, if you've only got five minutes, you can simply focus briefly on a large area of the body, say your head or your arms, stay there for a while and see what is there at that moment and move on, and then before you know it you've scanned your whole body. Alternatively, you can make the body scan a very long meditation by doing the opposite and focusing on really small parts of the body, say a tiny bit of your forehead or a finger, at a time or by observing a part of the body for an extended period of time. I find it quite possible to do a body scan in under three minutes or well over 40 minutes at time. It's really up to you. The important thing is to observe whatever is going on without judgement, whilst witnessing as much as you can.

Towards the end of the meditation, once you have scanned each part of your body, you then telescope your attention out to cover your entire body from the top of your head to the tips of your toes. Just hold your whole body in your attention for a few seconds or even minutes. Observe it as you did each with individual part of the body, with acceptance and without judgement. Whatever is going on is just what is going on. Sit with that feeling and experience the peace of acceptance of what is. Once you have finished observing the whole body, slowly return your focus back to the breath, remain there for a short while, and finally open your eyes. You've just completed a body scan.

Mindfulness is about being present for the here and now and the body scan really helps you do that with your physical sensations. If we have any difficulties as we formally practice, we can put our centre of attention into that physical problem area, observe it and try not to get drawn into what is happening and react. I actually find when there's something that normally we could judge as negative, within the formal meditation, whether minor or not, this is when I learn the most as I have something ever changing to observe.

To give an example I got a cold and wondered how I would be able to meditate whilst I felt unwell. My nose was blocked, I was sneezing occasionally and felt achy but, rather than wanting to be well and being annoyed that I wasn't, I took this as another chance to see things as they really were. A cold gives you a lot of sensations within the body, most of which we perceive as negative. How many times in life have you had a cold and wished it away? Think back, did wishing it away change the cold or did it just add to the physical suffering the cold caused within your body?

The first time I did a meditation on a cold, I focused my attention right on my chest and my throat, both of which had been causing me issues that day. This still amazes me but, when I focused my attention on these areas, I observed and accepted whatever was there, I found that the sensations were neither negative nor positive and, suddenly, it was hard to hold on to the difficulties I had been experiencing. The power of the pain and discomfort was reduced greatly, if not completely. I saw that the less judgement I brought to the situation the more at peace I was with my physical situation.

That was not the last time I've meditated on the sensations of a cold. I've noticed with all physical sensations, both good and bad, that much of the suffering I may experience is actually mental, caused by my

Mindfully Saving Myself – One Moment at a Time

inability to accept things as they are. When we focus on the sensations directly in meditation we can see them for what they are. Their power is generated from our willingness to try and flee negative sensations, to escape whatever is happening and grasp some comfort. Or grasp our positive physical feelings, rejecting the truth that they are impermanent, rather than accepting the present moment as it is. When we accept whatever is happening then we see that our experience was not that powerful after all. Observing a difficulty doesn't really take the problem away, I still had a bad chest and sore throat, but the control the sensations had over me was gone because I didn't want things any other way than they were.

What you will likely find out, as you develop your practice, is that what is true for physical sensations is also true when you observe emotional difficulties. Later in the book I talk about facing our emotions in the same manner in the chapter, Facing Yourself on the Cushion.

Stephen McCoull

Fantasy Chat – Unproductive Conversations in your Head

Before all this, when I was sick, my head was busy. I was always thinking. Always. There was never any mental space in which I could relax. I'm sure this is something that a lot of people experience when they have mental health issues. Some people may wonder how people with mental health problems are affected by them. Overthinking can, in some cases, be a huge part of the problem. Although I can't tell you what other people think, I can explain some of the thought processes that have affected me.

Quite early in my mindfulness practice I spotted one type of unhelpful thinking that I was engaging in. I was cleaning the kitchen one day and, after doing some dishes, I put some plates away in the cupboard. A thought appeared out of nowhere. I realised I wasn't ordering the cupboard how my Dad would. I started to think that, if I was at my parents' house and had placed the plates in their cupboard like that, my Dad would ask me to move them, or would have taken the plates out of my hand and placed them himself. The next thing that I experienced was the feeling that I was not good enough and that, I had let my father down because I wasn't packing away dishes as he would. I was in my own flat, on my own and somehow, in about half a second, I

34

Mindfully Saving Myself – One Moment at a Time

had managed to convince myself that my Dad would frown upon what I had just done. He wasn't there and it was all in my head.

Maybe other people have thoughts like these. Our parents have such a big impact on us that it wouldn't surprise me if, even people without mental health issues, every now and then had similar thoughts. It didn't, however, stop there. Instead of laughing at myself for having that thought and for allowing it to have an impact on me, I started to have a conversation with my Dad in my head. I started explaining to him why I'd packed the cupboard the way I had and why that was the way it should be done in my flat. It was almost as if I were putting him straight, but I wasn't satisfied with that. My fantasy Dad told me I should do it his way, it was better. In my head I started to argue with him. The argument went back and forth, and feelings of inadequacy and anger swept through me like a powerful storm. This made up argument, all in my imagination, was having a physical impact on my body, as if I were having a real argument face to face with my dad.

As the argument continued to rage, I abruptly stopped. I don't know what triggered the change in me in that moment but, suddenly, I was able to step back from what was happening and observe this fantasy argument. Rather than mindlessly being involved with my thoughts, I had awareness of what was happening, which I hadn't a second before, and, whilst it still continued for a while, on one level I was no longer part of the argument. It was as if I were observing a film rather than being an active participant in the drama that was unfolding within me. As I watched on, I realised how utterly ridiculous this all was. For one, my Dad wasn't arguing with me, he wasn't even in the flat with me, so my anger that had been building towards him was unjustified. Also, I realised that the anger was hurting me right in that moment and it was making me suffer for no reason whatsoever. My heart was racing, I was stressed and it felt like my blood pressure was through the roof. I was full of anxiety about a simple task of putting the washing up away.

Suddenly, I became very curious as to what the hell was going on with me. Not unlike with the body scan, I put all my focus into the thoughts and the powerful physical sensations that were raking through my body. As my focus zeroed in on what was happening, the thoughts quickly dropped away and soon the argument stopped altogether. The argument vanished in the same way it arrived, without any effort at all.

I had been standing up, alert, in my kitchen. Almost as if I had been ready for a fight. I walked over to the living room and sat myself down on my sofa and just observed my body and watched it as it settled down into a peaceful rhythm and then I thought. *Who on earth has pretend arguments in their head with someone who wasn't there?* Whilst I wanted to engage with the negative thoughts in my mind, I just watched those thoughts and then, slowly, I let them go too.

As my negative self-talk disappeared, I thought back and examined what had happened a little more. As embarrassed as I felt, I knew, without doubt, that I was having full blown conversations with people in my head. If I didn't do it all the time, I was having those chats at least several times a day. Those internally invented conversations would be for a variety of reasons, sometimes good and sometimes bad, and these discussions were often based around real events or issues that I'd been through or things that could happen in the future that I was worried about.

The fantasy chats, as I started to call them, generally weren't triggered by something completely unreal but could be an extension of very real issues with my family, friends or colleagues. On other occasions, the conversations could be with people I didn't know and could be someone I half heard being rude to another person. I would

Mindfully Saving Myself – One Moment at a Time

imagine what the person's response would be and I would respond to their imaginary reply and so on and so forth. Sometimes the conversation would be enjoyable but, more often than not, it would be an argument in my head and it would have as negative an impact on me as if it were a real argument. These conversations would go around and around over the same ground and sometimes they would repeat multiple times over the days, weeks and even months that followed. On rare occasions even years. Worst of all, these conversations, that no one in the real world was aware of or involved with, could sometimes affect my relationship with the person in real life.

I know that sometimes, when you have issues in life that you need to work out strategies for handling them in advance, you need to think through your options and what you will do in specific circumstances, that's normal. But I wasn't strategizing on how to handle a certain situation, I actually imagined the conversations. None of what I was doing in my head was helpful to me in my real life because the reactions of the people in my fantasy chats weren't real and often weren't even remotely like what the people would really do.

If I ever did get into a situation where the topics of my fantasy chats were broached in real life, even though I'd had a similar conversation in my head many times before, I wasn't even present for it now it was really happening. Instead, I was too busy working out how to use what I had already deployed in the arguments in my head. Worse still, the people involved would act in a completely different way to what I'd imagined they would, meaning I was ill prepared and not even listening to them properly.

When I recognised what I was doing and realised how long I'd been allowing this behaviour to go on, many years and probably decades, I asked myself how I had not spotted it before. How had I not seen how counterproductive those thoughts were to my quality of life before that day?

After giving this some thought, I realised how I had missed something so obvious. When most people follow a path or a road that they go down every day, the majority of people don't stop and take a look at their journey with a child's mind, a mind of interest and wonder. They may pay attention to traffic to avoid it but for much of the journey they don't slow down and think about everything around them, because they know the road and they just do what they've always done. I had been having those fantasy chats, for so long that I was treading on such well-worn mental pathways which meant I just couldn't recognise what I was doing, never mind question my behaviour. I wasn't looking at what was happening with even a miniscule amount of interest, I just kept repeating it because that was what I always did with any anxious or depressive thoughts. When something was troubling me, rather than stop and look around, I would end up having a fantasy chat.

There was another way the fantasy chat damaged me. Whenever I was thinking in that way, I wasn't living in the present moment. I was either in the past, discussing events that could never be changed, getting depressed, angry and guilty or whatever, or I was in the future, getting anxious, fearful and nervous and fantasy arguing over things that were very unlikely ever to happen in the way I was scared about. I really got wound up and it was very real and very out of control until that day I finally spotted what I was doing.

I finally noticed it because I'd been practicing just concentrating on my breath or the sensations in my body without any expectation or judgement. Those hours of just noticing things as they are taught me a skill: the ability not to attach to what is going on within my mind. Which

Mindfully Saving Myself – One Moment at a Time

meant that, finally, I could see my fantasy chats as they were and face them without acting my habitual patterns out.

Now that I live my life mindfully, it doesn't mean that this doesn't happen to me anymore. It's difficult to get away from mental reactions that have developed over decades but since that day I am able to recognise when I'm starting to think that way. Now, instead of joining the battle in my mind, all I do is become curious about what is brewing up, step back and observe the experience without aversion and trying to force it away. Then the old thought pattern slowly ceases without any real effort.

The wonderful thing with this practice is that the more you practice non-reactivity and non-judgement to what is, even fantasy chats appearing in your head, the easier it becomes to not attach to that thinking the next time it arises. The more you don't attach to fantasy chats, or any non-mindful behaviour, the less often you think in that manner. With regular practice it can become a virtuous circle. Behaving in that way means I've got to the point now where I have no idea when I last had a fantasy chat. Probably in the car when I believed someone had transgressed in my unmindful moments. I really can't be sure, but the important thing is that I no longer suffer because of something made up in my own mind.

Stephen McCoull

Loving Kindness Meditation

Early on, my goal remained to calm my mind. I had no other expectations about meditation. I just wanted to be more at ease with life, even if only for the time I was meditating. I was willing to try anything to achieve that goal.

Through the Calm app and reading books by Theravada Buddhist monks, I discovered a new type of meditation: the loving kindness meditation or Mettá, as Theravada Buddhists call it. Loving kindness meditations were a welcome addition to my usual practices as it introduced some much needed variety in my meditations. Meditating on the breath and body scans were great but I wanted to try something else. Loving kindness additionally struck a chord as at the time, when I first discovered this meditation, I felt my life lacked any loving kindness at all. I had very few people to give it to and a small number to give it back to me.

As with the body scan, the loving kindness meditation itself is quite straightforward. You begin by putting yourself into a comfortable but alert posture and, when you're ready, you close your eyes and bring your attention to the breath. As before, you observe your breath for a period of time, noting the out breath, noting the slight pause, then

Mindfully Saving Myself – One Moment at a Time

noticing the in breath. Repeat. Once you've focused for a while, you take three to five deep breaths, observing each one without judgement or expectation, breathing slowly in and then slowly out. Once you've completed your deep breaths, you let your breathing return to normal without forcing it in any way.

All my meditations start in this way, because taking the deep breaths is a ritual, a great way of separating yourself from whatever you were doing beforehand. It brings you into this moment. Once you are feeling grounded, you can then move on to the loving kindness part of the meditation.

First, focus completely on yourself. In the West, especially, we're often brought up to believe that focusing on ourselves is selfish and it's impossible to do so without being self-centred. But is it? I'm a first aider and one of the first things you are taught during training, is that you cannot look after someone else if you haven't looked after yourself first. When attending to someone, you need to make sure you are OK and you will remain safe at all times before you do anything else to help the person in need. That is because if you're out of action, you're of no use to anyone. Instead of one casualty there will be two. In first aid, looking after yourself is not selfish at all but absolutely essential for making sure you can help others.

I believe the same applies to your emotional and mental well-being. How can you be good and empathetic towards others, especially those in distress, if you've not looked after your own wellbeing and you are not in a good place yourself? It's difficult, and anyone who tries will add further burden to their own mental state, which can have negative long term consequences.

Whilst it may seem counter-intuitive initially, the first part of the loving kindness meditation is directed inwards, to yourself. Once you are settled, you move your focus away from your breath and bring your attention into your heart centre and offer yourself positive feelings. Some people create a positive happy non-thinking feeling in their heart centre. I tend to do that now-a-days, but early on I would tell myself something that I knew was true but that I often didn't feel. "Stephen you are good enough, you are a good person, you've made mistakes but you are determined to learn from them and be better. You deserve a peaceful heart." I would really focus on what I was telling myself and being positive in that way would generate an optimistic feeling towards myself within my body. More importantly, in the beginning, as I focused on the loving kindness thoughts, my mind wasn't jumping all over the place being depressed and anxious. Generating and offering yourself this kind of emotion may well feel odd at first but stick with it because it does get easier with practice.

Offering yourself positive thoughts and emotions may only take a few short moments and it is just the start of this meditation. Once you've generated loving acceptance of yourself, you then move onto the more formal section of the meditation. What you do next is say in your mind three or four loving kindness phrases to yourself. The phrases I often use are "May I be happy, may I be fulfilled, may I be healthy, may I have a peaceful heart".

I will sit on my cushion alert with my eyes closed and slowly think "May I be happy" followed by a mindful breath or two. "May I be fulfilled", more fully aware breaths, "May I be healthy" and then, finally, "May I have a peaceful heart". Like the body scan, this is also quite a versatile meditation because, if you've only got a small amount of time, you only offer yourself the phrases once. If you have time, you can say the phrases as many times as you want. Sometimes. I will say the phrases

five or six times, pausing for three or four mindful breat'
round.

One danger of this meditation, especially onc'
few times, is that you can start repeating these phrases in you.
automatically. It's really important to be present and to focus on each
word and what it means, but again, without judging what you are saying.
You stay aware of the phrases you are thinking and accept each one of
the expressions as they are with an open heart.

By the time you have completed as many rounds as you plan to,
you have offered yourself loving kindness and that is quite a radical thing
to do. Generally, the thoughts that I directed at myself before then were
anything but loving, quite the opposite. In my thoughts, I would say
terrible things to myself about myself. Things that no one should say
about anyone, let alone about oneself. Offering myself loving kindness in
such an open and accepting way, really was one of the most impactful
things I had done at that point.

I've already mentioned that this goes against a lot of what we are
taught about looking after yourself and you may find this difficult the
first few times you do it. If that happens, notice the difficulty, the
thoughts and body sensations around the emotions you're experiencing,
yet do not judge yourself for what is happening, just sit with it all with
acceptance.

The loving kindness meditation doesn't stop with you. Now
you've offered yourself loving kindness and are in this present moment,
you can move onto offering it to other people. The first person you offer
loving kindness to is someone you have positive feelings towards. It's
best to work out who you will offer the meditation to before you start, so
that you can avoid stimulating the thinking mind too much mid-
meditation. The person you choose could be your husband or wife, one

your children, a good friend or one of your parents. It can really be anyone at all, as long as you feel positively about them.

The first thing you do is think about the person you have chosen. I usually think about the person's face and imagine them smiling or doing something they enjoy, or I just settle on the sense of them in a less defined way. It may take you a few breaths to do that, there is no time limit. Once you've settled on the person, you offer them exactly the same loving kindness that you offered yourself. "May you be happy", breathe, "May you be fulfilled", breathe, "May you be healthy" and "May you have a peaceful heart".

Offering this person the loving kindness phrases may feel far easier than offering yourself loving kindness. It may seem effortless. In my experience, it's because you like or love them and want them to be happy and, most of the time, your thoughts towards them will be of a positive loving nature outside of the meditation. Again, depending on time, you can offer them the phrases once or more times, if you're planning to sit for a longer meditation. I usually offer the people in my meditation the same number of rounds that I offer myself. If I offered myself loving kindness over four rounds, everyone else gets four rounds.

After offering loving kindness to the person you have positive feelings towards, you move onto the next person. This person should be someone you don't have any particular feelings for at all. Maybe it's someone you pass in the street each day, a bus driver you see every now and then when you travel or a person who silently but diligently serves you coffee each morning. It doesn't matter who the person is, as long as you are aware of them and have no positive or negative feelings for them. This is likely to feel stranger than offering loving kindness to someone you have overtly pleasant feelings for because we often don't give this type of person too much thought on a normal day. It did feel slightly stalkerish every now and then but this is a really important part of the practice because it prepares us for something more difficult later on.

As before, you imagine the person you have chosen and offer them loving kindness as you did during the two previous cycles. "May you be happy", breathe, "May you be fulfilled", breathe, "May you be healthy" and "May you have a peaceful heart". Just like before, depending on time, you can just do this once or go through several well-paced cycles.

Once you come to terms with the oddity of offering loving kindness to a known stranger, this part of the meditation becomes quite natural. The next part, however, can become a challenge, because the next person you offer the loving kindness to is someone you have negative feelings for.

People can find this really tough, I know I did, because generally, offering people you don't like loving kindness isn't what we have learnt or want to do. Normally, we offer them anger or other negative emotions. Don't underestimate how much of a struggle this may become. To ease into this practice, early on, it's best to pick someone who you don't dislike a lot, it's better to go with someone who may have irritated you just a little. It could be a friend who's treated you badly but not so badly that they are no longer in your life, someone who's not pulling their weight at work or maybe a shop assistant who's always short with you and other customers and who winds you up. Pick someone who challenges you, but not to the extent that it stops you carrying out this practice.

This stage is no different to the previous three, you bring that person into your mind and focus on them briefly. With the difficult person in this meditation, I think it's really important to try and imagine them smiling. Not a spiteful smile, but a kind one because it's likely, despite your feelings towards them, that deep down that they are a good person who is in pain too. Once you have settled on the person in your mind, offer them the loving kindness phrases, concentrating on each word as you think them.

This is a practice and there is no time limit for moving on, but once you've carried out this practice for a while, try and see if you're ready for someone more difficult to offer loving kindness to. Once you are at that stage when you can face a person who is connected to deeper negativity and pain in your life, start to make them the focus of this part of the meditation. It's really important not to set any kind of expectation with that section of the meditation. Some people will offer loving kindness to the worst people from their lives the first time they carry out this practice, whereas others may take many attempts before they can truly offer loving kindness to anyone who, they feel, has really hurt them deeply.

Finally, once you've offered yourself, a person you like, a person you have no thoughts about and a person you have negative thoughts about loving kindness, you offer it to a large group of people. This can be any large group of people. It could be all the people that work for your company, the people who live in your street, all the people in the town or city where you live or, if it feels right, even the entire planet, all seven billion of us.

For this final segment of the meditation, I offer loving kindness to the whole world. I don't spend too much time doing this but I bring to mind images of people in deserts, in forests, in cities, on farms, on boats, people in Africa, people in Asia, Americans, Australians, Ethiopians, many different people with different cultures and then I zoom out and imagine the Earth in front of me, as if I were looking down upon everyone from the international space station.

"May all beings be happy", breathe, "May all beings be fulfilled", breathe, "May all beings be healthy" and "May all beings have peaceful hearts".

Once you have finished, settle your attention back in your heart centre and observe whatever feelings you have, without getting involved with them. Then return to the breath for a minute or two to bring the meditation to a close and, finally, you open your eyes.

The first time I practiced loving kindness meditations, it generated a lot of emotions in me. Firstly, there was the realisation that I never used to say nice things to myself. Recognising that I hadn't loved myself at any point during my life was eye opening. Then, there was the difficulty of saying such nice things about someone who, I felt, was deliberately making my life difficult, someone who was trying to hurt me as much as they could humanly do so. Did they really deserve me saying and feeling these things about them even if no one else on the planet was aware I was saying them? Was there any point in doing this when no one would know I was doing it? What did offering loving kindness really mean? Did positive vibes somehow travel through the ether to the person I was focused on? If so, how? It was impossible, so I questioned whether it was worthwhile continuing with the loving kindness meditations, when I felt as though it would have no impact.

Despite my initial doubts and questions, I carried on, because the important thing was whether my mind was calm or not, and when I carried out this type of meditation my mind was like a flat sea in summer. Focusing on the loving kindness phrases stopped my mind from thinking. In some ways it was even more effective in doing so than the body scan. Initially, despite the strangeness of the meditation, that was enough for me.

Then, with time, I learnt something from this meditation. I learnt to be able to offer loving kindness for everyone I came across. Sometimes, I'd be at work and someone would be nasty and I would think a loving kindness phrase in my head and direct it towards them. Other times, someone would be unhappy, so I'd offer them one as well. When you start feeling loving kindness for the world and the people in it, ultimately you begin to learn to love life, your life, whatever it is made up of. You really start to find unconditional love for things and people.

You may have found through life, that it is so difficult to have loving kindness for the random person who sticks their finger up at you when you are driving, for a person who is shouting at their partner in the street, the person mistreating their pet, or the neighbour who always causes issues in the area you live in. However, through offering loving kindness we learn that each of these people we come across, the people that can and have caused aversion in us, have their own pain, which they have not dealt with, and that is often the reason they are the way they are. Offering loving kindness when on the meditation cushion to people in our lives can help us to go from dislike for many different individuals to realising they need loving kindness too, even if they would reject that very notion if it were ever explained to them. We learn that, in fact, these people are often the people who need loving kindness more than most.

If a person offers you negativity, in the myriad of forms that negativity can be presented, and we respond to that person in kind, or even just think spiteful thoughts in our head, then we help perpetuate hostility and even hatred in society. We may feel that the person does not deserve anything else from us but what would happen if you offered that person unconditional love instead? It does not mean we say to them "I

Mindfully Saving Myself – One Moment at a Time

love you" or anything of that nature, but unconditional love can just be not expecting any specific behaviour from a person. Or, when a person does behave badly, understanding that their behaviour is rooted in their own pain and then just being nice to them, no matter how they are with us. Sometimes, offering a person unconditional love is not allowing emotion to interfere with how you react or respond to them and sticking to the facts, setting boundaries if necessary, and forgiving them for their behaviour.

Whilst this hadn't occurred to me when I first started the loving kindness practice, after a while I started to wonder if we can change the world through mindfulness. Currently, in the world there's a lot of uncertainty and terrible events of one sort or another. I'm sure the same will be true at the time when this book is read, which leads me to question, what can I do to make this world better than it currently is? What can we, as individuals, do? These types of questions can often end up with the answer "nothing". Most people aren't the Prime Minister of a nation, or a CEO of a multi-national corporation, they feel powerless to make a positive change to the world so they don't bother to do anything.

Yet, I actually think we're already changing the world through our mindfulness practice and through offering loving kindness to people. As we practice, we learn to be more mindful with each passing day. We begin to observe our inner voice more regularly rather than react to it. Importantly, we're accepting ourselves and people around us without so much judgement, accepting that they have their own inner voice and demons.

When we regularly practice mindfulness, we slowly become calmer and, hopefully, more capable of real unconditional love for our fellow humans and life in general. As people begin to practice, they'll

Stephen McCoull

wake up to seeing things as they really are. More and more of us will live our lives in awareness and there may be some of us who are even enlightened. Surely, as practitioners increase, the more people who don't react to other people's mindless behaviour, the less negative there will be as we instead offer unconditional love?

Our improved state will slowly become obvious to those around us. When it's noticed, people will ask what we are doing and the more daily practice will spread amongst the population of the world. Even those people who aren't mindful, who are reactive, who want drama and arguments will have difficulties maintaining that level of hostility when faced with people who do not react to their behaviour in kind but, instead, respond with unconditional love. The growing numbers of people that practice mindfulness and loving kindness, the less people in the world will react to life, instead just being in the here and now. Maybe then the world's society will slowly improve?

I'm not delusional. I realise that, no matter how many people start to awaken on some level, it will be a very slow process and that any worldwide change will not be that noticeable within my lifetime and, most likely, for many future generations. Yet, by you sitting on the cushion and learning to offer loving kindness to everyone you are making a difference to the world around you.

On one level, the practice of loving kindness is simply a tool for calming the mind, but on another level, it is so much more. It can take a long time to get there, but through regular and sustained practice, it teaches the meditator the ability to offer unconditional love to the world, to be in the present, to accept the present moment as it really is, to accept fellow humans with all their faults. Loving Kindness can change the world one person at a time, that person can be you.

Attachment leads to suffering?

As my practice developed, I realised that the more I meditated the better I felt. The calm I felt during meditation, whilst not filling every moment of my life, far from it, was certainly transferring away from my formal meditations into moments of my everyday life. I noticed the change and it pricked the curiosity in me further. I already knew that mindfulness and meditation was a big part of Buddhism and I'd already read a book by Pema Chödrön before I had started practicing meditation. I'd known a little bit about Buddhism but I wanted to know more, so I started googling about anything Buddhist.

To my surprise I found out that there is a Buddhist monastery in Hertfordshire, UK called Amaravati. It's a Theravada Buddhist monastery in the Thai forest tradition and their religious text is the Pali Canon. At the time that didn't mean anything to me, I just knew they were Buddhists and they may be able to help me learn more.

I decided to email them, asking for advice on reading material for someone like me, a person who was interested in Buddhism but really didn't know much about it. One of the helpers at the monastery replied the following day and told me that a good place to start was to read works by a monk called Ajahn Sumedho, specifically a piece of work called "The Four Noble Truths". Conveniently, the work was on their website and free for anyone wanting to read it. I printed it off at work and took it home to read that night.

At first glance, it all seemed so simplistic, the four Noble truths are the Noble Truth of Suffering, the Noble Truth of the Origin of Suffering, the Noble truth of the Cessation of Suffering and the Noble Truth of the way leading to the cessation of Suffering. I know that to some people all the talk of suffering sounds quite negative, as if Buddhism is a religion of pain but that isn't the way I took it. I'd already experienced an improvement in my mental health situation based upon my meditation practice, so I was extremely open to learn.

I'm not going to explain the Four Noble Truths in detail as there are many extremely experienced monks, lay practitioners and meditators who can explain them infinitely better than I can. I will, however, explain the difficulties I had with parts of them, the concepts, what I took away from working through those complications and how that new knowledge helped me.

What I have found with Buddhism is that I can read about a concept that I struggle with, one that initially doesn't make sense, and I can't move onto other parts of Buddhism until I have come to my own understanding of that concept. After reading Ajahn Sumedho's book, the thing that stuck in my head was that one of the causes of suffering is attachment. That was my first block. I listened online to some speeches about Buddhism, called Dhamma talks, that Ajahn Sumedho and other monks from the monastery gave and the concept of attachment leading to suffering regularly came up. What they were teaching is that if you stopped being attached to things then suffering could be extinguished and you could have peace. You might even find Nibbāna, which is the Pali word for Nirvana, if you focused on your practice of non-attachment and brought it to every part of your life.

Mindfully Saving Myself – One Moment at a Time

How could attachment be the cause of suffering? I am attached to my family, I love them. How could not being attached to them ease my suffering? Like many families, we may bicker every now and then but surely not being attached to my family would have the opposite effect to ceasing suffering? When I needed the support of my family, or they needed mine, I or they would not be able to rely on it and we'd all suffer more. Initially, the idea that attachment leads to suffering didn't make much sense.

I imagined the whole world and thought nearly everybody in the world was attached to someone, be it their partner, their friends, family, colleagues and even their pets, amongst many other things. If non-attachment was the path to the cessation of suffering, it didn't sound very pleasant. It sounded like something that would cut a person off from the world and that wasn't something I wanted to experience. I wanted to be in the world and be part of it.

It really didn't make sense for some time, but I stuck with it. As I continued reading and listening to Dhamma talks, slowly, the idea of attachment being the cause of suffering began to crystallise. It was as if a veil was being slowly peeled back and I was able to see the truth. I can't say that the way I see it is the Buddhist way of viewing it, not that there's a single Buddhist way of viewing anything, but it's how I understand attachment and it has certainly helped me ease some of the suffering of life.

Non-attachment doesn't really have anything to do with the people you like or dislike, or the pets in your life, or the football team you support, or your favourite pub, or beer or whatever. Attachment is not love. Instead, it has everything to do with how you view those things. How you view everything. Attachment is holding on to what is right now, usually people or events we judge to be good for us, and an

53

aversion to change. You focus so much on what you could lose, that you end up not being present for the person or what is happening right now that you do not want to change.

The easiest way is to explain how attachment actually causes suffering, is to explain how it caused me suffering in my previous life, the life in which I often partied far too hard. Say I was having a great night out, there were great people to interact with, great conversation, nice drinks and maybe I was dancing to beautiful music with these amazing people I was with, maybe I met someone I really fancied, who seemed to like me and it would all seem amazing. Yet deep within me, almost unconscious, was the thought that I didn't want this wonderful moment to end. That feeling was attachment and, whilst not immediately obvious, it did cause suffering right there and then.

It may have been the best night of my life, truly, but my reaction to it would make me suffer. I had desire for things to remain as they were, attachment to that present moment, so there was a lack of acceptance of the ultimate reality. I was attached to a world that would not exist in the next moment and the truth was that the night would end, it was impossible for it not to. Now, this may sound obvious, because of course I'd suffer as I would have a hangover the next day, especially as I had those extra drinks to make the night last longer, but mentally I'd suffer on another level because I didn't want things to change when change they would.

By not wanting a specific moment to end, being attached to it, I was doing two things. I was grasping onto the present moment, wanting to hold on to it because I found it delightful and I wanted to feel those wonderful feelings forever. I held on to them knowing full well they would end. I didn't want that moment to change at all when it can do nothing else but change as nothing is permanent. So when it changed, as

Mindfully Saving Myself – One Moment at a Time

all moments do, I felt a sense of loss. But worse still, because, deep down, I didn't want the good times to end, I wasn't actually fully present for that moment, my head was somewhere else and I didn't really experience that moment at all.

I experienced that feeling of attachment for how things are right now many times. Not just on nights out but when friendships ebbed away, when I finished a particularly good book, watched an emotion inducing film, saw a magnificent sunset, had a great trip and, most acutely, when my romantic relationships came to an end. I said attachment is not love but, before my view of attachment changed, I thought it was love. That was the case of my relationship with one former partner; I wanted to be with her all the time and I travelled a lot to see her, as we lived in different countries. It was exciting, we were always on the go but I was attached to the situation in that moment. With hindsight, I now recognise that my attachment was stronger than my real love for her. I didn't want how things were in those moments to change, as I perceived it all as so exciting, so good. Yet change did come and she developed and moved forward in life and I felt loss because I did not accept that things alter and some things end. I attached myself to what I judged to be positive. As a result, I felt a sense of doom in the new moments I had with her, rather than being present for those new times.

Another thing I was doing was having an aversion for the things I don't like. In the case of a night out, it was cold light of day I never wanted to arrive, the loss of the sense of belonging that I had attached to, and the hangover that tomorrow would bring. Worst still, maybe I had to go to work feeling rough, or paint a wall in my house, maybe I had agreed to help a friend with a task I really didn't want to do. I wanted to push these things away so they never happened. In the

55

moment of saying "I never want this night to end", I was rejecting the reality that would be my life the next day, the next week or the next month. Even if my night was the best night I'd ever experienced, the experience was tarnished because, deep down, I didn't want it to end. Thus, it wasn't as good as it could have been as I was suffering even during the good moments because I wanted it to last forever. Then, when the next day did arrive and I had to go to work or paint that wall, I would mentally fight against it. "I wish this wasn't happening", "I really don't want to help like this today". It's beyond physical. I was suffering because I did not accept that good things end and that sometimes in life you have to live through less than positive things. I suffered not only because of what life threw at me, but also because I desperately attached to everything I saw as positive. Result? Double the suffering, all due to attachment.

It seems so obvious now. As I write about attachment and how it affects your well-being, I feel like I'm just saying what everyone knows. And the fact is, we do all know that the good times end and that, at times, things won't be great but we never think about it like that because we're not programmed to do so. Our programming in the modern world is nearly always that we should seek out the good things and find pleasure, whilst avoiding the bad experiences. We should do whatever we can to hold onto the positive aspects of life with all our might and reject the negative ones with an equal amount of force. This is why so many people who are lucky enough to go on a two week holiday spend the second week of the holiday not present in the moment and dreading the fact they have to return home to work at the end of it. Most people are constantly grasping on to the positives and feeling aversion for the negatives in one way or another.

What does that mean in reality, though? Does it mean we shouldn't have good times as they will end and we will suffer? Should we avoid getting into relationships? Should we not bother trying in life at all because everything ends? Not at all. Everything changes, good times become bad but then bad times become good, in an endless and, often, unpredictable cycle. That is life. But once you recognise your own thought processes, you can step back from your thoughts and observe what your mind is doing. Get into that romantic relationship, take that course, go on that amazing trip you've always dreamt of and enjoy them all that much more by being entirely present in those moments, without wishing them to never change. Become the observer of this second right now and immerse yourself in your relationship, your course or that trip.

I use this word a lot but meditation practice is truly a revolution in thinking. Just simply noticing that you are attached to the moment and don't want it to change means that you can let that clinging to the present go and just be in it instead. Without that grasping or aversion towards what may or may not come next, you are fully present. You can enjoy your time with your friends and family, enjoy that holiday or whatever, without your attention being elsewhere. Just notice how engaged you can be with reality when you let yourself truly do that.

Stephen McCoull

Facing yourself on the cushion

Whilst I've explained about meditating on the breath in My First Meditations, I didn't actually practice on the breath at all at the beginning of my practice. Instead, my early meditation regime consisted of body scans and loving kindness meditations for the first few months. Both these meditations brought me calm for the time I was meditating and also some tranquillity away from my formal practice but at the time it appeared that was the main benefit the practice gave me.

At about the same time as I started wanting to try new meditations, I was randomly gifted a full subscription to my meditation app, after I posted a comment on their online community. Perfect timing, almost as if the universe had been listening to what I needed.

The app was full of meditations, with various teachings provided at the end of them by the experienced meditator, Tamara Levitt and, suddenly, I was overwhelmed with choices. The one thing I noticed, though, was that most of the meditations used an anchor and that was, more often than not, your breath.

Now, for anyone who's tried mindful meditation at all, the fact that the vast majority of meditations utilise the breath isn't a big surprise. The breath, whilst not being the only thing you can use, is generally the go to focus point to secure your attention for the period of meditation.

58

Mindfully Saving Myself – One Moment at a Time

For me, however, who had only used Body Scans and Loving Kindness meditations until that point, it was a big eye opener.

At first, I found it really difficult to use the breath as an anchor because I viewed the breath as boring. I mean, it's just your breath, so what gives? Body scans weren't boring because you slowly move your focus over your whole body. Even if you do a long meditation and settle on very small parts of your body, it's not long until you move onto something new. The loving kindness meditations are similar, new things are happening all the time so it stays interesting and fresh but with the breath nothing new is happening. It's just the breath. In and out.

When I started to practice meditations that used the breath, I would sit there and all sorts of things would steal my attention away. I'd find myself ruminating over past events, things people had done to me and what I'd done to them, sometimes good things that would make me happy and other times the opposite. On the cushion, I'd get sad or angry at peoples' past behaviour and more regularly I'd get angry with myself. Sometimes there would be thoughts about things I'd done twenty years ago and I'd be embarrassed or I'd feel nostalgic or whatever, as if it had just happened and was not an event from the early 90s. When it wasn't the past affecting me, I'd think about what I was having for dinner, other times I'd be thinking about when I was next going to the gym, or the pub, or when I was next going to get paid. Time and time again, when I was meditating, I would realise I'd been thinking and I'd return to the breath, only for my attention to be dragged away almost immediately afterwards. During some sessions, I'd return to the breath what felt like a hundred times.

I found I was sitting on the cushion with all these thoughts flooding my head and that was not what I wanted. I just wanted a break from me, which was why I had taken up meditation in the first place.

But, at that point, meditation had paid me back incredible dividends, just by giving me the moments of calm I'd already had, so no matter how difficult it may have felt, I stuck with it because, whilst I was not a man of faith, I had faith in the practice. One skill I had already developed, which helped me avoid getting too disheartened during this period of time, was the knowledge that judging what was happening didn't help. I could have beaten myself up: "Why can't I stay focused?" but I just accepted that was how it was at that moment. I just kept at it.

As I continued with this tug of war between thoughts and breath, I started to figure out that the brain is like a muscle and you need to train it like one. The more I lost concentration, got lost in thought, the more practice I got at returning my awareness to the breath, the easier that became. It was a total concentration work out that was helping prepare my mind. As time progressed, I started spotting the thoughts if not when they were arising but shortly after I'd got distracted by them and then, more importantly, I noticed that fewer thoughts interrupted me.

Whilst I was getting better at returning to the breath, I noticed that, when I was lost in thought, I was still becoming reactive to whatever thoughts came up. Negative thoughts brought about what I would judge as undesirable emotions and positive thoughts desirable emotions. I realised that although I was able to escape thoughts that would arise, in some way, by returning to the breath, I was running from the thoughts. Running from the thoughts wasn't going to help me face up to everything that had previously brought me to the edge of contemplating taking my own life. I didn't realise quite what a revelation that was at the time, but it turned out that that realisation, in a few months' time, would help me a great deal in my recovery from depression and anxiety.

Mindfully Saving Myself – One Moment at a Time

Despite this new understanding, I felt pretty confused about how to proceed. Luckily, early in 2017 I was fortunate enough to get a place on an NHS Mindfulness Course. What I learnt there, combined with the teachings of Ajahn Sumedho, Tamara Levitt and information I have read elsewhere, was revolutionary. Instead of letting my thoughts go and returning to the breath, I could become the observer of the thoughts. In my practice, I was able to stop running back to the breath and pushing the thoughts or emotions away so I no longer was giving the thoughts any fuel by dwelling on them or going down the rabbit hole of negative thinking that would occur when I allowed the thoughts to take over. Instead, I just simply observed any mental activity, like a spectator of a film or a play. In the mindfulness course, it was pointed out that all strong emotions have physical effects as well. Whether that's in your chest, your belly or somewhere else, you have a physical reaction to what you emotionally feel. Try it yourself the next time you have a strong reaction to anything, stop and notice what your body is doing. Everyone is different, so how the body reacts may not be the same for everyone, but it's almost without fail that your body will physically react to any emotions that you experience.

How does observing thoughts and emotions work in practice? Once you notice that there is a thought, you step back from it. You don't run from what is happening by getting distracted or focusing on your breath, you just accept it's there, without any judgement at all. If you think "oooh that's a horrid thought", then you are judging and reacting and you're going down that rabbit hole. You just accept the thought, whatever it is, as it is. Then you move your attention to your body and identify where your body feels the thought, then place your centre of attention in the location of this physical sensation and observe what is happening. This is where the body scan comes in, because you already do

61

Stephen McCoull

this for normal physical sensations. Do the same again, but, this time, with the sensations triggered by the emotional reaction.

I have noticed something remarkable happens when I do this. The more I directly observe a thought or an emotion and the physical sensation attached to it, without interacting with either, the less I am able to identify what any of it actually is. I don't grasp and hold on to my experience firmly, determined to identify it. Rather, I scrutinise everything I can about it, just to see what is there without judging the experience. It's an action beyond thinking, it's knowing. I found that the more I focused on anything emotional with all my awareness, the less that emotion would become. The emotion can become almost like a thin vapour that slips through your fingers and disappears as you try to be fully conscious of what is going on.

Previously, when I was depressed and anxious, I would have followed the thoughts into depression, feeding the negativity and feeding the flames of my own mental illness. With experience of really seeing what is going on within, understanding that you don't need to follow a thought or push it away, as long as you non-judgementally observe whatever is there, I find that the emotions will vanish before me. It's as if direct observation means that whatever mental object exists, becomes weaker, until it's almost nothing and was never really made of anything in the first place. Amazingly, incredibly strong emotions can lose all their strength and pass without having an impact on me.

I am very lucky that I've never had major physical issue since becoming mindful but I have noted the same with strong physical pain too. If I observe the pain directly, really try to see it for all it is, then suddenly it is as if it has no substance at all. If the pain is connected to something that requires a response, I am aware that I need to move or whatever but its emotional power against my mental stability is lost. So pain, whether emotional or physical, has greatest strength when we try to avoid it in some way. We suffer more when we try to escape, rather than turn towards an experience. Lean into the present moment.

It's impossible to be perfect at this all the time. Sometimes, I still get lost in thought and that can have a negative impact on me, if I don't step out of it. I still might find myself swearing in my head for something I have judged as utterly stupid I did twenty five years or go or find myself full of fear about the future, but the moment I become aware, I finally step back and watch, things change. I disassociate myself from the thoughts. If I do that, the thoughts and emotions are shown up for what they are. Powerless.

Early in my practice, that worried me a little. We're human beings and our emotions can have a purpose. I did not want not to feel them. Not always, but sometimes, when I was sad, there was a real reason for it, and the same when I was happy. I didn't want not to feel those emotions when I had them but facing them and becoming their observer doesn't have to stop our humanity. When there is sadness, we can see it for what it is and respond to it, rather than react automatically. If the sadness is caused by the loss of a loved one, we can face our sadness and grief and accept that it may be our companion for some time, without any aversion. With aversion, we'll do anything to get rid of the sadness and grief. We'll drink, we'll dive into work, or constantly distract ourselves in other ways and we'll never truly experience what the person we lost really meant for us and work through our pain. Instead, the grief remains in the background of our lives, slowly eating away at us, as we fight with ever more vigour to escape it.

The same applies to observing your feelings of happiness. You're happy, maybe it's your wedding day, everything is perfect, you're surrounded by loved ones and you're marrying the person you have a deep connection with. Step back and observe all your emotions and become present with them. Becoming an observer doesn't stop you being happy, instead you witness your life in this present moment and experience that happiness as fully as you ever have. The next morning, when the great day is over, you don't feel bad it has gone. Instead, you are present with the memories but you are also awake in the new day. If you don't do that, if you don't step back and witness the emotion and experience what is happening right now, you get attached to this positive moment instead. You may think that, of course you are attached to the positive event, that's normal, but that starts you wanting the day never to end. Instead of experiencing the happiness of that present moment, you spend your time fretting that this great day will be over and you don't want it to end so you suffer because there is no way it will not. Worse still, you don't experience any of it directly because your attachment to it has separated you from the present moment. The next day you suffer more, because that fantastic day is over and it will always be in the past. You feel down because it's gone. This is something I talk about more later in the book.

Having a lack of awareness of the present moment is how most people live their lives, it's certainly how I lived most of my life, and it generates suffering, whatever is happening in our lives. I didn't have a terrible life, but I certainly suffered greatly because of how I attached to thought and experiences and, when I started to practice mindfulness, my suffering was eased greatly. I'm not the first person who's learnt this, it's nothing new, many generations of people have discovered this and other truths through mindfulness.

I say all this to encourage you to practice but beware of trying to run before you can crawl. Practice meditating on the breath, practice noticing your thoughts and then letting them go and returning to the

Mindfully Saving Myself – One Moment at a Time

breath. Practice the body scan and loving kindness meditations in the same way. Early in your practice, these are excellent meditations that can help you learn to develop equanimity, that calmness and composure in any moment, as well as concentration and acceptance. I still use them today, as do many meditation practitioners. If you stick with just these meditations and never try any others, you will still get amazing results from them. Practice for as long as you need, before you try to use the practice to focus on the emotions that may arise. Facing emotions mindfully was a step on the road to recovery from depression and anxiety for me, a huge step, but trying it before you have developed mindful skills can be counterproductive. This is a journey of a lifetime and you can take the next step to face what is happening inside head on when you are ready.

As you will see throughout this book, accepting and facing each and every thought and feeling you have directly, is the most mindful thing you can do. If done with an open, accepting and non-judgemental heart, it is the action that can free you from suffering and help you to experience your life in a way you would never have done without mindfulness. It just takes practice and patience.

Stephen McCoull

Counting Away from the Past as a Way to Escape the Present

When people talk about mental health, it's sometimes difficult to understand precisely what it is or what they mean. Mental health isn't like physical health. Take a broken arm for instance. Even though people break their arms in different ways, the injury tends to be treated in the same fashion, the arm is set in a cast and the patient may have that cast in a sling. We know how it affects the person, or can guess, because we can see it right in front of us. The physical impact can be very similar for everyone who breaks their arm.

The same is not true of mental health. Even well-known mental health issues, such as depression or anxiety, aren't easy to understand for someone who hasn't experienced that condition themselves. Mental health issues, and the impact they have on the people affected, are difficult for outside observers to comprehend. Sufferers may look like there is nothing wrong at all. Even a person who does have a mental health condition may not fully understand how another person experiences the same mental health condition. It can be a very different experience for each person.

One person with depression may not be able to get out of bed. Others can get out of bed but don't want to engage with anyone. There

Mindfully Saving Myself – One Moment at a Time

will be people with depression that can still work and some will go through life and, externally, appear completely normal, whatever normal means. Some of that latter group may be thinking about ways to take their own life whilst out partying with friends or chairing a business meeting. It's almost impossible to see that they are depressed, because they just motor on with their life whilst feeling like they are slowly dying inside. When I was depressed I have been all of those people.

Part of the reason I started writing was not only to help people reduce their suffering but also to explain what being mentally ill can be like. I've already explained how fantasy chats were a big part of my life. Something else I was doing was working out how long it's been since something had happened in the past. Although it was very often good events, like festivals or gigs, holidays, or something that I really enjoyed, it might occasionally be bad events or even events that didn't really mean much at all. I'd count away from the point in time that event had happened and would occasionally have it in mind.

It may not sound too unusual so far, but I'd actually do that for years, in fact decades, after the event. There were so many time markers in my head, that at any time I was likely to think "Oh, I can't believe that happened two years and three weeks ago".

For example, I know went to Malaysia and the Philippines 20 years and three months ago and I could tell you what my friend and I on did on each day of that fantastic holiday. I've been to a lot of music festivals and I can tell you what bands I saw on what day of the festival, what stage they were on, the time of the day, what I was drinking and maybe some random people my friends and I spoke to, how old they were, and sometimes even their jobs or what they were studying etc. I can do that all the way back to 1994 or even before, especially for my favourite festival, Glastonbury. Some of my old school friends laugh at

67

me because we can talk about festivals we've been to and they can't remember any of the acts but I'll tell them that Saint Etienne was on the Glastonbury pyramid stage on the Friday afternoon in 1994 and they'll google it and find out I'm right.

Whilst these are good events, remembering them in this manner didn't fill with me joy. Instead, I felt sad that it's been so long since those times had happened. The more time had passed since that point in my life, the worse the feeling of loss I had.

I didn't just do this with good events. I know my ex-fiancé ended our relationship on 16th August 2005. Another one is that I know I failed the medical, due to a dodgy eye, after passing all the extensive testing and interviews for becoming an air traffic controller in November 1998. To give one that doesn't really mean much at all, I know I opened my first bank account on 24th February 1990. This is just a small sample of the things I counted away from. There are so many of these events in my head and I have been constantly counting away from them.

Although I no longer remember precisely how long ago the first time I remember doing this was when I was 11 years old. When I first started secondary school, I used to love drama and, in one of the lessons, we did a class wide improvised play in which we were meant to act out what we'd do if we'd been on a plane that came down on a deserted island. I became absolutely absorbed in that lesson, it was before I became negative towards school, and it just filled me with joy. I remember months later riding on my bike to go and meet a friend and thinking to myself that that lesson had been so many weeks beforehand and feeling quite sad that so much time had passed since that day.

Keeping tabs on life experiences in this manner wasn't a "oh, wasn't that a lovely holiday" reminiscing or "wasn't that horrible", but it was a pathological way of me thinking at all times. I used everything as a

Mindfully Saving Myself – One Moment at a Time

yardstick. It was always so many weeks, months or years away from something that had happened in my life. So much time since that excitement that I felt, that made me feel alive. I lived for all those memories and when things I didn't like, that I wanted to run from, were happening in my life in the present I would try to escape what was happening in my present by working out how long it had been since something else had happened. I'd been behaving in that way for so long, it became an automatic response. It was almost completely unconscious and I never questioned whether recording my life mentally in that way was a good or bad habit to have.

This is really a lifelong behaviour. Or, should I say had been, until I found mindfulness.

Since I've been meditating, I've slowly stopped chasing thoughts about past events down a bottomless rabbit hole. I spot what I am doing and I use my ability to observe my mental life to disengage from it. Now I don't tend to do it at all unless I'm talking about the past with others. It doesn't mean I forget what I've been remembering for years because I've forged these memories into my being but it means I don't need to return to those thoughts or make such strong memories about what is happening in my life right now. Since I began to cease this behaviour it has tied in very closely with my depression and anxiety lifting, which ties in closely with me starting meditating.

When I contemplated this ability to hold random dates in my mind for so long, it gave me a greater understanding of how my mind had been functioning, when it wasn't working well both as a precursor to my mental health issues and also when I was depressed and anxious.

Nearly all of the events I remember were either really great events, in which at the time I got lost in the now and felt freedom to be me as I was, so what I was really remembering was actually being present during my life in one way or another at a specific point in my life. Or they were linked to the really bad memories. The bad memories usually meant the end of something good or of a lovely period of my life. Remembering a specific time and knowing it was so many years and months ago, felt like I was being propelled away at ever increasing velocity from when I had good times with my ex-fiancée, since I'd seen my late grandparents, since the time when I didn't feel bad more often than not. The counting gave me a distance from these experiences, which made my grief so much stronger, feeding my depression whilst removing me from my life. Mentally counting in this manner made time anything but a great healer.

I don't know for sure, but I strongly suspect that when I first started this habit at the age of eleven the present moment slowly stopped existing for me. From that point I slowly lost touch with living in the moment and learnt to hide from it. That behaviour was key in steering me towards depression and anxiety later in my life. I was doing this to escape the present moment. This behaviour didn't give me peace, instead, I would feel down because that amazing festival I went to with so many great people, was so many months or years ago. I didn't accept the present moment, but also that the great times had moved into the past either. I would miss them, I would want the feelings these events triggered in me to return but those feelings can never return because that moment will never exist in that precise configuration ever again. The feelings and experiences I remember probably didn't even happen precisely as I remembered them in the first place. Yet, attaching to the past in this way would make me feel like darkness was spreading over my life because the times when things were good were so far away and fading all the time.

Mindfully Saving Myself – One Moment at a Time

I was stuck in a vicious cycle. The more I counted away from my life, the worse it made me feel about my life right now, so I was more likely to use the behaviour to attempt to escape how I felt. Counting away from events, like many things with mental health issues, was a mental behaviour that got more rancid with time. By studying myself, both on the cushion, during meditation, and off the cushion, during the day I came to understand what I had been doing. As a result, that pattern of thinking lost its power over me and I let the habit go. How did I even spot this so that I could step away from this pattern of behaviour? By no longer running from myself and looking at everything that was going on inside without fear or shame.

Mental health issues can have so many layers to them. A person doesn't have to have gone through anything specifically traumatic to become ill, and this way of thinking was one layer of my poor mental health behaviours. It was a normal behaviour, occasionally thinking about the past, turned abnormal, a symptom of me not being conscious in the moment. Now, when I look at this, it was an odd thing to do, an odd way to look at my past, a behaviour that blocked the light that life in the present moment could have brought, if only I stopped and looked around. I'm really grateful that I can recognise that I have this habit of thinking about the past in that way and use that knowledge to step back into this moment, right now.

Stephen McCoull

Noticing Thoughts and then labelling them

I'm sure there are some people who have tried meditation, the body scans, loving kindness and with the breath as the focus point, who just don't think they can remain present, let alone sit with your emotions. Maybe you're one of them and every time you sit down on a cushion or a chair to meditate the mind wanders off into endless thought. You get frustrated with yourself, you think you can't do this, that it's just not for you.

In meditation the one thing we can all be sure of is that thoughts will steal into your mind as you sit in silence. Even the most experienced meditator will experience thoughts interrupting their sit. Thinking during meditation doesn't mean you're a bad meditator, if there is such a thing. What it means is that you're human and your mind is doing precisely what it has evolved to do - evaluate risk and try to protect you from it. To gauge dangers, your mind can review previous events in your life to learn from them. Then your mind will devise future strategies based on the learnt experiences. A great process if you're a hunter gatherer with constant physical dangers but not so useful in the modern world.

What is important in meditation is not that we don't think, because we all will think at some point during meditation, it's

Mindfully Saving Myself – One Moment at a Time

unavoidable. The significant aspect is how we respond to thoughts when they do appear.

The first step, and often the most difficult early in your practice, is simply recognising that you are lost in thought. It may sound easy but if you've spent your entire life living in your own mind planning, reviewing, worrying, imagining, then you've had zero practice at spotting you've been lost to the present moment. Considering how your mind has been trained, if you do recognise you've been lost in thought is a huge achievement.

Once you've realised that you've been lost in mental activity don't judge yourself for having been unaware of the present moment. Don't think that you're a bad meditator or berate yourself in some other way, just accept that it happened and continue with your sit. Now that you've recognised you've been thinking, try to observe the thought without grasping it and following it down the rabbit hole of more thinking or, alternatively, having aversion for it and trying to make it go away. If you're early in your meditation journey then that observation may be brief, just a recognition the thought is there before you return back to your point of meditation, but if you've been meditating for a while this might be a time to deeply observe everything, related to the thought with acceptance, followed by returning to your point of meditation.

In some ways there's not too much more to meditating than that, just observing what is going on without judgement or attachment of any kind. It sounds so incredibly simple but in practice, especially when you are new to meditation, it's an extremely difficult thing to do.

If you're finding it difficult to step back from mental activity there's a really helpful way of separating yourself from the distracting thoughts that you experience that has been known by many meditators over the centuries. That is to label the thoughts as soon as you notice you are lost in them.

You might be thinking about a negative event in which you were upset or you did something that now makes you feel miserable. Once you realise what you're doing, label the emotion in some way - using "sadness" might be appropriate. Perhaps you're stressed about an interview you've got next week and you find yourself worrying about it, you might label what is going on as "anxiety". If you're scared about how a friend is going to react to news that you're moving town, you might label the thoughts "fear". If a strong emotion arises about another person that you don't get on with, you could label the thought as "dislike" or, possibly even "hate". There's also my former regular visitor, mentioned earlier in the book, "fantasy chat".

So far I've dwelt on negative thoughts and emotions because they're the kind of thoughts that people trying to beat depression, anxiety or some other mental difficulty will most likely face. I know that was true for me and I suspect true for others.

The labelling, however, isn't designed to help you judge the thought that has disturbed you and put it into a negative box in your head. The purpose of it is to help you separate yourself from what is going on in the mind so you can observe that mental activity without reacting to it. Therefore it's important to do the same for all thoughts, even ones that away from the cushion we would judge to be positive. A thought that you're looking forward to seeing a friend you've not seen in five years appears, you could label the thought "excitement" and then return to your breath. Perhaps you remember a funny joke a colleague told earlier in the day or an amusing situation in a supermarket queue - you could label those thoughts as "amusement".

Mindfully Saving Myself – One Moment at a Time

It's also probable that thoughts you would consider neither good nor bad arise. Thoughts about what you need to buy for dinner could be labelled as "planning", thoughts about when that meeting with one of your customers can fit into your diary could be described as "scheduling".

It doesn't matter what label you use. It's not something that should generate more thought as that would defy the point so don't overthink this suggestion, just note the thought. Normally the first description that enters your mind is the right one. You cannot observe a thought if you are right in the centre of the thought, therefore labelling helps you step back. When you label a thought you might find separating yourself from it much easier. Then, once you're able to view what is going on, you may find that the thought will slowly disappear of its own accord.

Labelling is a really great device, and the more you use this tool during meditation the stronger your ability to become uninvolved with the thoughts in your head will become. Over time you might find you don't need to do this as often as you did when you first started. If that happens, you should consider simplifying the labels you use and merely use one, "thinking". Whatever comes up, however powerful or weak, just label it as "thinking", observe without judgement and return to your point of meditation once that thought and emotion disappears. It is likely that this simplification will be a natural process that will happen when you are ready. After a while, experienced meditators may not even need to use this tool at all when they find that their mind is hectic on the cushion. After practicing with the labelling of thoughts and becoming experienced with that aspect of the practice, you may begin to notice the thoughts at a deeper level in which no label is required, there is simply the understanding thought has arisen and you begin to observe. That's

Stephen McCoull

when your practice can fill you with equanimity as you sit and that could be when you find that your practice on the cushion starts to spill over into your everyday life, allowing you the space to respond to what happens to you rather than react to what is.

A Way to Calm a Busy Mind

There may be some who think that labelling thoughts and facing them is all very well and good but their minds are just too busy during the normal day for what they learn on the cushion to be of any use in the real world.

It's true that some people may find that, very often, their mind doesn't give them a break even once they've started meditation. The moment their mind has a mental pause it is filled with thoughts about the past, things they wish they had done differently, conversations that get replayed down the decades wishing past events had had different outcomes, curious as to why relationships had failed, berating themselves for not doing well enough at school or university or depressive thoughts that can spiral if not checked. Alternatively, their mind may be filled with judgements or worries about the future. Their boss was snapping at them last week so what will happen if they lose their job? Will their child be happy or even safe at school? What will happen if the boiler breaks down just before Christmas or if they unexpectedly break a leg and can't look after themselves properly? Anxious thoughts can lead to very real physical stress and even panic attacks. The thoughts that can fill our minds, that generate pain, is why a lot of people try to never allow their minds to have an opportunity to be empty even for a second.

Even though I hadn't recognised it as a problem until 2013, that was how my mind had been for decades, probably since I was in my mid-teens, if not before. Even once I'd started on my mindfulness journey, which is exactly how my mind remained most of the time. Always thinking, constantly filled with depressive or anxious thoughts.

I only ever started this Mindfulness malarkey to get some periods of time when my mind was quiet and if not quiet then at least calmer than usual. As I described in the last chapter, I had already been labelling thoughts and emotions during meditations and it had become a key part of my early practice. One day, without me consciously trying to, I used that same labelling process away from the cushion.

I was getting changed after a workout at the gym and I was overwhelmed as my mind was being extremely noisy that day. Even though I recognised what I was doing, I couldn't step back from the thoughts as they engulfed me. I remember thinking that even trying to live mindfully wasn't helping me and this enormous feeling of being a failure swept over me. I was on the verge of being overcome with reactive frustration at myself and life when, all of a sudden, I just stopped and I started labelling what I was physically doing in that gym changing room. Unzipping my bag. Getting out my towel. Taking off my t-shirt. Finding my shower gel. Zipping up the bag and so on and so forth. I didn't consciously think about doing it but the habit from meditation unexpectedly spilled over into my daily routine and created a new way of calming my mind.

Once I had started, my focus zeroed in on each task with minute detail. I felt every tooth of the zip in my bag as I closed it. I heard every small note of the noise generated by that action and I was in that moment. No matter how small a task I was performing, each action was labelled and then mindfully undertaken. As I walked to the shower I thought "walking" and felt each step and how it affected my whole foot as I crossed the tiles. As I showered, I thought "showering" and I put all my concentration into the feeling of the water, noticing how my body was impacted by the temperature. I did the same as I dressed afterwards, labelling each activity and putting all my concentration into my experience and being there fully. I left the building in the same manner and, as I got into my car, I realised that the whole time I had been doing that my mind had ceased its endless chatter.

Out of nowhere, the skills I had been learning on the cushion helped me to find peace away from it. I started to use this practice of labelling away from the cushion whenever I needed to and, as with my practice on the cushion, gradually I labelled less. As I had done on the cushion when my mind became busy, I focused on the activity I was undertaking in a deeper way that didn't require mental labels. It was more a pure awareness of what I was doing. That awareness, that focus, can sometimes be all I need to step away from a mental storm.

So here's my suggestion. If you are overcome with anxiety or depression and you feel trapped within your mind, set yourself a task if you aren't already in the middle of one. It can be anything at all, it could be something simple like washing the dishes or something a little more complex. It's not the task itself that's important but how you undertake it. Whilst you carry out whatever task you've assigned yourself, tell yourself precisely what you're doing. If you're washing dishes, it might be saying to yourself: "I'm turning on the hot tap, I'm turning on the cold tap" and then "I'm squirting the detergent into the washing up bowl", "The water is too hot so I'm turning up the cold tap" and "I'm picking up the plate and moving it into the washing up bowl". Allow your concentration to envelope everything in your present experience. Get in the flow of even the simplest activity. If you can do this, then your mind

Stephen McCoull

is no longer able to continue whatever anxious thoughts you were having and you can reset yourself in that moment.

I've used this practice many times and I still do on occasions when I need to. It is an excellent way of quieting those thoughts that you've spent a long time listening to. It gives you a pause, a space for you to discover yourself in.

Acceptance is Key

One of the main things I've learnt from following a mindful path is that acceptance is key. Whatever is happening, good or bad, if you can accept it then your suffering is reduced. You may think that you are an accepting person but when people really give the matter some thought many find that they may not be as accepting as they believed.

How many people say "I wish it was Friday" and really mean it? Many parents long for the days when their kids will sleep through the night or when their kids will be able to walk themselves to school or even when their children can cook and feed themselves. Things will be easier then. Other people think that life will be better when they finish their training, when they get promoted, or when their boss moves on. People think their dream house will be the thing that changes their lives and they look forward to the day that they can afford to move up the housing ladder. There's always something in the future that will make life better but grasping for some time when things will improve, means a lack of acceptance of what is happening right now. Whatever else it does to you, it takes you out of the moment and propels you into a future that exists within your mind and stops you being present for your life.

Then there's people who never want things to change. On the Sunday people dread the fact Monday is approaching. They want to hold onto the weekend not wanting the freedom it brings to end. Some parents love their young children and fear what they will become when they enter their teens, wishing that these wonderful early childhood times will never change. Why do the good times have to end? People don't want to get that promotion that is on the horizon as they don't want the extra responsibility, or they really love their boss' easy going way and don't want her to leave. There's often something in this present moment that we never want to change because life will change and that impact of that change may not be positive. Everything changes. It's unavoidable, and fighting against it is to have an aversion for what is in the future, Hanging on to the current moment takes you out of it because your focus is also on the future.

Whether you are wanting the world to change or are desperately wishing it not to, both equate to a lack of acceptance of what is. Without having an acceptance of life as you find it right now it is impossible to be in the here and now. You either wish things were different than they are or you want them never to change at all. You spend your life living in the past or the future and you are dissatisfied with both.

No matter how strongly you yearn for things to remain the same or to change for the better, no matter what God you pray to demanding for better times, does thinking that way change whatever it is that you have no control over? Does it change this present moment and bring you peace? No. This lack of acceptance can turn you reactive rather than responsive to life. Anger, frustration, jealousy, and greed arise and you end up attaching to those feelings and getting drawn into negative thought patterns and ultimately you suffer. Whilst there are many things we are not in control of we are in control of our own destiny. We have it within our power to stop the mental suffering that is of our own creation. If you accept the here and now exactly as it is, understand that

Mindfully Saving Myself – One Moment at a Time

there are parts of life that are outside of your control and that everything is impermanent, then you can settle into this moment and see that it is what it is and be OK with that. Even when things are really tough and you have strong emotions you will find that acceptance will bring you peace. A kind of peace is possible, during life's storms, if you learn to have acceptance of what is. I've experienced times when there has been sadness but I have also been at peace.

Some people may question this and wonder if I'm talking about being passive about life and almost letting what happens wash over you with a shrug of indifference. What I am saying has nothing to do with stepping away from life or inaction. Accepting things as they are doesn't mean you do nothing. It means you mindfully engage with the world and with reality as you currently find it.

If things aren't right in your life you don't ignore them and do nothing. If you need new skills to get a job, there is no point wishing you had more skills right this second, or wishing you'd taken that course last year, because that won't change the fact you don't have those skills in this moment. Wanting how things are right now to be another way will lead to suffering. A response to that situation would be to investigate what training opportunities are available, and, once you're set on what you need to help you, booking the course. If during that process you start wishing that you could get on the course sooner than the available dates, because you really want to start training right away, then you've become reactive again and are creating more suffering for yourself. Understanding that it takes time from first thinking about training, to booking the course, and to finally starting the course.

Acceptance is about being present throughout your journey in life, seeing it for what it is and engaging with your life in a very active way in each moment.

83

Stephen McCoull

All that is easier said than done because we are taught from a very early age that life gets better just around the corner. It's something we've learnt from our parents, our schools, the media and our peers. We've all been told the next thing will always make life better, if only we grin and bear this moment. Life becomes something to get through rather than live. Conversely, many of us have been taught that change is scary and should be avoided because it leads to insecurity. When you realise that then it's completely understandable that we have seen the present moment as something to escape from.

If you've been taught not to embrace the present moment, what can you do to counteract your lack of acceptance? If you've been meditating, then you are already practicing accepting things as they are. Meditation is about exactly that, about embracing the present moment without judgement. When you carry out a body scan meditation, whether you are healthy or sick you just scan the body and whatever you find in that scan you accept it all as it is without judging anything good or bad. The same is true when thoughts enter your mind as you meditate. Mental conditions, thoughts, emotions, appear in your mind, you recognise they have distracted you, so you step back from them and you don't judge that as either good or bad. Simply observe it and let it go. That is acceptance. This is a skill that we can take away from the mediation cushion and use in our everyday lives when previously we would cause ourselves suffering by not accepting things as they are.

In addition to your formal meditative practice, you can also look for things in your day to day life that you struggle to accept to work on. It can be anything, big or small. For instance, I love running. A couple of years ago I had a few niggles which meant there were periods of time when I couldn't run for a few months.

Mindfully Saving Myself – One Moment at a Time

If I were to mentally process my inability to run for such an extended period of time with my old mind-set, after a couple of months away from running, I would have really wanted to run, thus demonstrating a complete lack of acceptance. I would have probably been so anxious to start running again I'd run on that slight niggle and made the injury worse. On top of the slight physical issues I would have had, I would have also been mentally suffering because of how I was processing my life. In fact, this is exactly what used to happen when I got injured. I felt rotten about everything until I finally got back to running.

Now, when I get a slight injury I know I need to take things easy. I just shrug. It is what it is, and my response is to accept the situation. I rest my legs or switch to a low impact routine. I only exercise in a way that protects my body and if that means I can't exercise my legs at all then I don't. Okay, so it's not what I really want but desires do not change how things really are. So now I approach these niggles as new opportunities to practice acceptance of the here and now.

I adopt the same mind-set when I'm confronted with more serious matters, like my divorce. When I felt the divorce was financially punitive towards me and I couldn't see my children as much as I would have liked to, especially after my ex-wife told me she was going to use the divorce for revenge, I was frustrated and angry about how everything had turned out. I thought it wasn't fair and I longed for a different outcome with all my might. The divorce was finalised early in 2016 and I remained angry and resentful about it for some time afterwards. My fury was re-ignited every time my ex-wife decided to play mental games with me. Yet, did any of that change the outcome? Being angry didn't change the result of the divorce. I still lost what I lost. Being overcome with rage just made me suffer more than I already had. Reacting to my ex-wife's provocations had the same effect. Meeting her in verbal battle, often over text messages, did nothing for me other than cause further distress and make the situation harder to cope with.

Once I was some way down the mindfulness path, a few months after my divorce was finalised, I came to the realisation that my distress about the divorce and the way my ex-wife continued to act was a lack of acceptance of what is. I saw that, rather than keep reacting, I had a new choice. One I had not made before: acceptance.

With my newfound mindfulness practice, I began to use those negative emotions about the divorce and my ex-wife as a focus of meditation so that I could practice acceptance of what is. Every time they appeared, I welcomed them and sat with them to see if I could learn to accept the reality of the situation and over time I did, not only on an intellectual level but also deeper within. I saw that the outcome of the divorce would never change and that my ex-wife's rage against me was not within my control. It may ease with time or it may not, that is under her control.

Have things changed since I had that realisation? Well, the outcome of the divorce hasn't. What has changed is that I am at peace with it because I no longer mentally rally against it. I've accepted it and the additional suffering has gone. When my ex-wife tries to emotionally manipulate me it no longer affects me. Previously, by trying to fight her I actually just fed arguments which led to worsening relations and more suffering for me (and probably for her too). My response now is to ignore the hurtful comments. I rarely make any attempt to counter them at all beyond asking that we speak to each other with respect. Now I only speak to her when it's something constructive about the children and let everything else go.

I don't want to give a false impression. It's not a perfect road, it takes time becauseit's a lifelong journey. When I don't get it right straight away I accept that too so I can really feel at peace with the situation most of the time, even if I've had a brief moment of reactivity.

Of course this doesn't all come at once, you can't just announce to yourself that now you're going to instantly accept everything that happens. Again, it takes practice and you start small to begin with. The first step could be to accept how you feel at any given moment. Accept that there's a feeling of aversion in you about whatever it is that you cannot change. You don't have to do anything else at first, you don't even have to step back from the feeling, just acknowledge it and accept that it is there and that is how it is right now.

Another step along the path could be that, once you've learnt to accept the feelings that arise, you can move on to accepting whatever has generated those emotions in the first place. To start, practice acceptance on something minor in your life rather than on something that can affect you on a deep level,. For instance, if someone gets on a machine at the gym seconds before you were about to, accept the feelings it brings up and that you need to find another machine to work out on. If you drop a plate in the kitchen, accept the anger that arises, that the plate is gone and you have to clean up. If the traffic light turns red before you have a chance to cross the junction that's another opportunity to flex your acceptance muscles. Once you've learnt to accept what comes up in your mind when minor things occur, the next step is to sit with the feelings, observe them and let your judgement and your attachment to them go.

Aversion, like everything that happens within the mind, is actually just a temporary condition of the mind. Once you've got used to accepting what is, you can start to use any aversion in you that you notice as something to practice with. Now you can start to learn to accept the feelings you have had for years about the fact your father left your mother as well as the fact that this separation did happen and there's

Stephen McCoull

nothing you can do to change that. When grasping or aversion occurs it becomes an opportunity to practice acceptance of whatever has been making you want reality to be different. Keep practicing and use everything that you come across. You can even use those negative thoughts that appear when you realise you didn't accept what happened an hour ago. Acknowledge the thought, accept it and accept whatever has transpired and let it all go.

This is not the first time I have said this and it certainly won't be the last but mindfulness, living in the moment, is a lifelong practice. It's not easy and some days are harder than others, but as in the name it's all about practice. From one breath to the next, exercise acceptance of everything within you and, with time, you will find that more often than not that this will become your base instinct.

Then, one day when you do get hit by something more substantial, as we all will, you may find that you're able to avoid adding to the pain of that event through a lack of acceptance. It doesn't mean you will achieve a state of constant happiness. Bad things will still upset you, you are human after all. It does mean, however, you won't follow those feelings and add to an already unpleasant situation. In fact, you may even be surprised to find yourself feeling unexpectedly at peace in terrible moments of life if you manage to practice acceptance consistently.

Responsibility for Your Life is Yours Alone

Accepting responsibility for your actions is the attitude of someone who is emotionally mature and at peace with who they are. I may have doubted myself in many ways but one thing I was always sure of was that I was someone who accepted responsibility for my actions.

If I made a mistake at work, I wouldn't hope that no one would notice, instead I would own up to it and apologise. Not only that, I would work out why I made that mistake and come up with solutions, maybe a change in routine or a process, and then let everyone know about it because I didn't want it to happen again. I've always tried to be transparent.

Assuming responsibility for your mistakes is something I value highly in others. I have struggled through life with people who are the opposite, who make a mistake at work or elsewhere and deny it had anything to do with them. They get angry that anyone has even questioned them or noticed their mistake and will react to anyone doing so very aggressively. They point at someone else and blame them, their work station, the fact the coffee machine isn't working properly today, that the moon is in Virgo or a myriad of other excuses that they use to deflect from their responsibility for their own actions. It's always someone or something else's fault and nothing to do with them.

Stephen McCoull

I'm sure you know one or two people in life that are like that and I guess, like me, many of you will get a little frustrated by their behaviour.

Until I started down the mindful path, I was living my life believing that I owned my mistakes and the responsibility for them. It was one thing I was proud about. Yet, when I found mindfulness I was surprised to find the reality was somewhat different.

If I accepted responsibility at work, then what was it in my life that I wasn't accepting responsibility for? It certainly wasn't anything minor. I didn't take responsibility for my reactions to almost everything that had happened to me. My reactions were always someone else's fault. When it came to emotions, I was the person who pointed at others and blamed them for how my life was. I blamed my school. I blamed my parents. I blamed some of my friends. I blamed my ex-wife. Whilst I realised I had problems, and deep down I understood that only I could deal with those problems, I believed it was not my fault my life wasn't great, and it was always caused by something outside of my control. I suspect a few readers might think something along the lines of "hey, but if someone treats you extremely badly and you get upset, then it's their actions that are to blame so that it is their responsibility" and I understand that thought process. But ask yourself, is that really true?

Let's explore that question. Imagine you've got a partner who after an initial honeymoon period becomes verbally abusive towards you, telling you that you're worthless, selfish or just a pain in the backside with no worthy features. They repeatedly tell you the same thing but make sure no one ever hears them tell you this. You start to doubt your self-worth, you wonder if they're right in saying you are an awful human being. You may even spot that what they're saying doesn't seem true and appears nasty but they turn it back on you telling you that you're the one

Mindfully Saving Myself – One Moment at a Time

causing all the problems, you're the nasty one. You question yourself even more and ultimately stay in the relationship.

Then suddenly your partner changes their tune and reverts to telling you how great you are, how much they adore you. They do lots of nice things for you and make big public gestures about their feelings towards you. People tell you that you are a lovely couple, so happy, so lucky, leading such a fantastic life. You get hooked onto the fact that occasionally life is good with them, they make you feel really special, and you don't want things to change and return to the bad times.

Yet there's fear that the nasty version of your loved one is going to reappear, pointing out your weaknesses and telling you how vile you are. You want the good times to stay, so you try to please them, because you want the loving version of them to stay. Life is good until, suddenly, the abusive version of that person resurfaces and, in shock, you try and please them more, try to be what they consider 'good', so that they'll adore you again and stop being horrible. It doesn't work. In fact, it makes them despise you even more causing you to get down about yourself and how awful you are. You retreat internally or use substances to try and ease the agony. Just as you're about to hit rock bottom, their affection returns and you feel alive again, but before you know it the hate returns and the same cycle repeats itself over and over again. You experience anger, disgust, and even hatred directed at you for the majority of the time with rare moments of respite when your partner acts like you just may be a human being worthy of their love. You feel awful most of the time and even when things are in the good phase you are full of anxiety concerned with when the terrible treatment will start again.

Each time you go through the cycle you feel worse at the end. You stop thinking about leaving but instead, your hatred for yourself grows until you wonder if you are even worthy of a life and whether anyone would miss you if you were gone. You believe everyone would be better off without you. Because you start to believe your partner is right. You are a terrible person who brings everyone pain. It, whatever it is, is all your fault. Then one day you feel like you can't stay in this world anymore. A world in which you do not fit. A world in which you cause everyone around you emotional agony. And the idea that you will take your own life arises.

Except you don't. Because something down in the very core of your being starts fighting. You suddenly comprehend that you want to live, but you don't want to live in pain. You realise you cannot live a life of peace in the relationship you have lived in over the years. The choice is live and leave or stay and die, so you decide to live and you leave your partner.

Your partner, who has worked tirelessly never to let anyone see how they treat you in private, goes on the attack. All the bad decisions you made when you were having breakdown after breakdown, and there were many, are used to show everyone that it was you that wrecked the relationship and a harem of friends support your ex-partner and rarely speak to you, or tell you what a horrible sod you are.

As the finances are separated, you lose much of what you have worked for in life and you find yourself alone and not particularly well off. You're still getting messages from your ex telling you how selfish and terrible you are, demanding more money, that you no longer have, and you get angry and respond in kind. You feel fury about what you see as injustice and how you've been emotionally abused yet you're the one who's been judged and abandoned as people flock to your abuser.

That is a world of hurt and it can crush you if you let it. Yet who is responsible for all that pain that you feel? Most people would say that the partner who was emotionally abusive is responsible for everything in

Mindfully Saving Myself – One Moment at a Time

this scenario. But are they really responsible for *all* of how you feel? The abusive, manipulative person is definitely responsible for their actions but, as terrible as their conduct is or was, are they responsible for anything else? Namely, are they responsible for how you felt and how you may continue to feel?

What I've discovered through my practice is that all human beings are responsible for their actions and those actions include how you react to and deal with others, including people who may treat you badly. How can the abusive partner be responsible for the behaviour of the victim of their abuse if we're all responsible for own actions? It flies in the face of many peoples' wisdom, but I've found that the abuser cannot be responsible for how their partner feels. I appreciate, that some people will find that a hard concept to accept but please bear with me as I explain further.

If you are in a relationship with someone who makes you feel bad we will often say things like "she hurt me", "he's made me feel awful" and so on. The same is true of lesser friendships or interactions with other people. Yet, we have a choice as to what we do in these situations. We have the choice to not listen or believe the person who is manipulating us. If we recognise the situation is bad, really stop and see it for how it is, then we have the choice to stay or leave. Yes, the person manipulates us, but if we listen to them and ignore everything our instincts are telling us and if we stay and allow them to continue their behaviour unchecked then we allow them to remain in our lives hurting us. That is no one's responsibility but our own. If we do stay with them then we are also responsible for the emotions we feel because, whilst the manipulators in the world may hope they cause a certain reaction within their victims, the victim has the choice to say "no bloody way, I'm not listening to or accepting this anymore, I'm off".

Stephen McCoull

But how can you not be affected by this whirlwind and not get sucked in? Firstly, it's important to understand that the fact that the emotions arise in the first place is not up to us, we can lay that one on evolution. But we do have a choice in what we do with those emotions. Those emotions are there for a reason. Your life with that person sucks, therefore, how we respond to those emotions is our responsibility. For instance we can accept whatever nasty emotion appears fully and follow it into whatever dark hole of self-loathing it may take us to or we can step back from the emotion and instead examine it without judgement, just as we would any experience on the cushion. We can see it as just a passing mental condition, even if it's a very understandable mental condition, which we can move away from and respond to in a positive manner. If we do that, there's a chance we can respond to the feelings by recognising that the person we are with is toxic and taking the hard decision to leave (or escape in some cases).

All this might sound pretty harsh and I can understand why. The longer you are being manipulated the harder it is to realise what is happening. But what I've described has happened to me so I've learnt that lesson first hand and the hard way.

I had a choice on that first cycle when the relationship turned nasty. I could have seen the hurt and fear that it created within me and decided that I would ignore my heart, which wanted the relationship and really just wanted to be loved, and instead I could have used my head and recognised the situation was toxic and left. I didn't, instead I reacted to the fear of losing her and started to become needier. That is my responsibility and no one else's. When I was told awful things about myself, that created great feelings of worthlessness within me I could have stopped and questioned them and examined whether they were true statements or not. Deep down I always felt I was a good but imperfect bloke so, if I had paused to reflect, I may have tapped into that and realised that what I was being told was all rubbish. I would have been ok, maybe even laughed it off as I packed my bags and got out but instead I followed the emotions and I allowed myself to believe them without any examination at all. Over a ten year period I made the same choices on each round of the cycle and each time I made those decisions it was my responsibility. It took me standing in my kitchen making a life or death decision to finally realise I had no choice but to leave the toxic situation I had allowed to fester.

Whilst I realised I had the choice to leave, I still didn't recognise that I had any other choices about my reactions, so outside of the relationship I was still reactive to the continued and intensified hostility. I still blamed my ex-wife for how I was feeling, I still rejected the responsibility for my own life.

Whilst I think it's clear that we are wholly responsible for ourselves, I understand how it can be almost impossible to appreciate that from a non-mindful perspective. From the moment we are born we are taught that if someone hurts us not only are they responsible for their actions but that they are also responsible for how we feel, so when we feel emotional pain we habitually blame others.

Starting to understand the social programming that had been taught that made me blame others made me begin to question the fact I held my ex-wife responsible for what I was feeling. Was it really her fault that I felt the way I did, both now and during the relationship? The more I became the observer of what was happening in my head the more I could see that the decisions I took when strong emotions appeared in my mind were taken by me alone. I decided whether I followed what was happening in my head or not and the more I practiced mindfulness the more I could step back, think "nah, not today" and not get involved in the toxicity. I accepted that it is only me that is accountable for what I am feeling.

I don't want to give the impression that becoming responsible for your internal life is an easy thing to do. Years of emotional abuse, even if minor, will take its toll on a person and the reactive mental pathways will be well worn within the mind and can be extremely easy to slip back into. It was far from a simple thing to do, it took dedication to the practice, acceptance that sometimes there would still be reactivity and blame of others, recognising what was happening and accepting again that I had control over what goes on within. Yet, no matter how tough the challenge accepting responsibility was, I started to appreciate that I really was liable for myself and whether I gave into negative emotions whatever external forces I was subjected to. I began to understand that my reactions to life could be completely within my control if I wanted them to be and that the choice was a never ending one.

Taking responsibility for my actions, all of them, not just in the relationship mentioned but every single thing I ever reacted to and ever held on to emotionally is another step on the path towards a peaceful inner life. Taking responsibility for yourself helps in that process of removing yourself from the pain that you held close to you. You can finally appreciate that you are in control of your inner world. You can choose to step away from the control of others and find peace. It's an exciting and empowering discovery.

Once you have fully accepted that you are responsible for your behaviours in response to both negative and positive external situations then something else happens. You can see which of your behaviours can cause suffering within you. Maybe you cling to your partners in a needy fashion and your relationships always fall apart. Now you've accepted responsibility for your behaviour you're in a position to accept that

Mindfully Saving Myself – One Moment at a Time

behaviour as part of who you have been, investigate its causes and then make different choices. That means, rather than avoiding emotions, you can now work on that part of yourself to help improve your life so that in the next relationship, if you start being needy, you can step back from it and recognise what you are doing before more damage is done.

I'll give you another, less emotional, example of how being responsible for your own actions can make a difference to your life. In the summer of 2019, I went on holiday with Marta to Poland to go to her sister's wedding and then spend a few days with her dad and his partner in the Polish lake district.

Whilst my fiancée, her sister and her sister's husband and a few other people at the wedding spoke good English there were many people who didn't. Not Marta's parents, nor her step mother. Me being stereotypical English, I have not put in the greatest effort into learning Polish so I am just happy, ecstatic in fact, that I can say "hello" and "cheers". There's no way I can even guess at what is being said when listening either, because Polish is a completely different language group from English. So on the language front I'm clueless.

In normal circumstances usually Marta and her sister translate often enough to make things flow with her Dad and her step mother but it was a wedding and I wanted Marta to catch up with her family. I told her not to worry about translating for me too much, just when she could, as I knew this was an extremely important day for her and her family. For large periods of time during the more formal parts of the wedding meal I would sit there not having any way of communicating beyond body language as Marta spoke Polish with people. After the wedding when we went and stayed by the lakes there were times when occasionally I was with her dad or her dad's partner without Marta being

Stephen McCoull

there as well, so we couldn't converse that easily then either. Yet despite not understanding that much I enjoyed my time on that trip immensely.

Now to explain how being mindful has created in me a responsibility for my own well-being I need to explain that I've been in that almost precise situation before many years ago. In the early 2000s I had a Norwegian girlfriend. I had made a small amount of effort to learn Norwegian so I could order food, get around on trains, even answer basic questions and I was comfortable out and about on my own. I didn't have conversational Norwegian but I could occasionally guess what was being said as some words were similar or could be connected to English in some way. Back then, surrounded by Norwegians who would intermittently speak English but would also talk a lot in Norwegian, I'd sit there often not able to converse for periods of time. During those periods of time, whilst not showing it, I would become quite withdrawn or frustrated. I was a very chatty person back then, chatting was a way of escaping myself, and I couldn't use that. Whenever the conversation switched to Norwegian I'd begin to feel really excluded and I would definitely become what I now recognise as depressed. I'd generally feel sorry for myself, I'd really feel despondent so when the conversation did switch back to English I'd not quickly engage with it, it would take me a moment to get into it and I'd not get as much out of the conversation as I could have done. I enjoyed going to Norway and really liked the people but actually it wasn't great for my mental health because of the way I viewed the situation. I didn't exactly blame anyone else for how I was feeling, I had no problem with them speaking their own language in my presence, but I never even considered the possibility that how I felt in those moments, how I interacted with people whether they were speaking English or not, was completely my responsibility.

Mindfully Saving Myself – One Moment at a Time

Fast forward a decade and a half or more to Poland and it was completely different. Whenever I'm there as people talk in Polish around me I take responsibility for my own welfare and I really focus mindfully on what they are saying without any judgement. It's easy to listen to the words without judgement when you don't understand, so that is what I do, I just soak it all up. I'm concentrating on their voices almost as if it were a point of meditation. Whilst I still don't recognise what they are saying, I'm fully engaged with them and, because I'm completely involved with the conversation despite not speaking almost any Polish, I pick up their body language and I am part of the conversation. I get a feel for what is going on without understanding a word. When the conversation switches back to English for a brief or long moment I am instantly engaged and involved, I'm an active participant because I've taken and accepted responsibility for myself within those moments. Despite not always being able to chat in the conversation, I feel completely included in it all. I won't say that I don't have the odd negative feeling coming up about not being able to jump in with the chat, of course I do, I'm human, but I know these feelings aren't me, they're just feelings that will take me downwards if I follow them. When that happens take full responsibility and just note the feeling, watch it disappear and then return to my point of concentration, the conversation before me. I have to say I always really enjoy my time in Poland.

So what has changed? Well, actually the way I was treated in Norway wasn't dissimilar to how I am treated in Poland. My former Norwegian girlfriend and Marta were both home and wanted to converse with their family and I was and still am glad for them to do so. In both Norway and Poland I was welcomed into their homes and the lives of their families with open arms. If the external stuff isn't too dissimilar, what has changed? I'm mindful now. I'm aware of the negative emotions that can come up and I don't attach to them. The focus mindfulness has given me means that I am part of the conversation even when I don't understand it. What has changed is me! I take responsibility for myself. In other words, in almost the same situation in Norway I didn't take responsibility for my inner life and I felt bad mentally, I would suffer quite a lot, but now in Poland, I take responsibility for my own well-being and it's a wonderful experience.

I think this is true about most things. It's how we view something and realise that we are always responsible for ourselves that is important, not so much the events that affect us. Some people have terrible things happen to them, it wrecks their lives and they never recover. Other people experience terrible things and they may take some time, sometimes years, but in the end they then get up and continue their journey stronger than before because they accept responsibility for their inner life. Some people have wonderful things happen to them and still are really depressed, other people bask in the great thing that's happened to them but then crash down later on because nothing lasts forever, and others still accept the positive points of their life without attachment to it and understand that whatever happens, it is them who ultimately are responsible for everything that goes on inside.

I hope that, by explaining my experiences of being responsible for my own reactions, I haven't upset people who have suffered after the terrible actions of others, that is far from my intention. I confess, that becoming responsible for my inner life was something I worked on very intensely over a couple of years. Whilst the idea is simple, actually following through can be one of the hardest things you can ever undertake, especially if you've been manipulated for years or decades. If I'm completely honest, because of the difficulty of stepping away from blaming others for what only I am in control of is something I still have to work on today. I find myself having to do it time and time again but I always end up owning my inner world. I imagine if you were to take this step, taking the power away from others and accepting responsibility for yourself, you will have to work on accepting accountability for the rest of your life too and that is no bad thing. Accepting responsibility for your own life will lead you to experience a liberation of sorts, one that lets you live the next chapter of your life without the past holding you back.

Stephen McCoull

The News and Social Media – Do you need it?

For as long as I can remember I've been a news addict. If I had half an hour or less to kill then my go to entertainment was the news. I didn't just listen to any news, though, my main fix was international news. News that had worldwide impact, news that affected possibly millions of people around the globe. If there was a conflict going on I was especially interested, keen to witness history as it happens. If a president was being stupid, belligerent, timid, or revolutionary, compared to their peers, I wanted to know more. International news was something I could never get enough of.

When I was a student I had a part time job in a restaurant within a well-known UK supermarket chain. We'd get an lunch hour during which I'd sit with my colleagues as we ate but the moment they would leave to play pool or watch whatever was on the TV in the staff room I would grab a newspaper. I would immediately jump to the international pages of whichever broadsheet newspaper was in the staff room and I read every single column within that section. The pages I didn't manage to read I'd go back to on one of my twenty minute tea breaks later in the day.

Mindfully Saving Myself – One Moment at a Time

I was the same at home, reading newspapers or watching the news. I especially enjoyed the in-depth news, such as Channel Four News and Newsnight, that did more than just skim the surface of a story.

I wanted to be informed. It was important to be knowledgeable, I told myself often. I was being a good citizen of the world knowing what was happening around the globe. The problem was I just couldn't get enough. I always wanted to understand more about a situation, have as well rounded a view as I could possibly get. No matter how much news I digested, having a full understanding of world events was just one more news article or one more political documentary away. When I couldn't consume any more news, because the news cycles meant there was nothing new to be said, I would end up reading history instead. I preferred 20th century history because then I could link that history through to the current affairs happening right now.

During my decades of news consumption I never once questioned what I hoped to gain by having so much information about world events. Deep down I felt that it was extremely important to understand what was happening so, as a voter, I could hold the government to account. Yet I never once asked what I was hoping to achieve for me. What did I really get out of it?

Did it help me in my day to day life? I had interviews with the Royal Air Force and then the Air Traffic Control service in the 90s, and it helped me within those interviews to demonstrate my understanding of current events, but during the average day there was no benefit. It didn't help me in my IT job and it didn't help me with my friendships, although occasionally we'd chat and even argue about current events. Other than knowledge for knowledge's sake, it didn't really improve my life that much.

Stephen McCoull

Whilst there were no positives from my news consumption, beyond an awareness of what has happening in the world, that doesn't mean my little habit was benign. Far from it. The news could be extremely upsetting for numerous reasons. Maybe there had been a natural disaster and thousands of people had been hurt, displaced or worse still, killed. I would feel sorrow for the families that were on the screens and occasionally it might even bring a tear to my eye. There were times when my country was involved in conflicts or wars that I strongly disagreed with. Along with horror and shame, I would feel rage at our politicians for putting our soldiers in harm's way whilst deliberately destroying another nation, often using lies for excuses. I would get extremely angry about it, so much so that I would occasionally write to my MP or the Prime Minister of the day berating them for allowing such savage things to be done in our name.

Then there were other times when I had the opposite thoughts, when there were people systematically being ethnically cleansed in Europe in a way unlike anything seen since 1945 and our government didn't take sides. I was quite young, I still had a lot to learn, and I raged that the government of the day stood back and allowed thousands to be killed on what seemed like on a monthly basis without any real action from our own armed forces. In some cases our armed forces stood aside whilst it happened. I felt horror, disgust and resentment. I wrote at least one letter calling our Prime Minister a coward for his inaction as people starved and were slaughtered.

There were times when the news was about man-made disasters caused by poorly governed international organisations, who were more interested in giving their shareholders a good profit than giving any thought for other people and the planet. More revulsion was felt and directed towards the perversion of international leaders.

Mindfully Saving Myself – One Moment at a Time

I could go on but I think you can see that, whilst there were no benefits, there was an impact - a very negative one. I would often be filled with negative emotions which were topped off with the feeling that I was helpless. It didn't matter how much wrath was generated within my head, it didn't matter how I attached to that negative power, I was powerless to make a change. Shouting at the TV or tutting with irritation as I read an article didn't change a thing, but it made my world a darker, less happy place. Writing letters, sending emails or even joining peaceful demonstrations didn't help either. The lack of impact on any policy just highlighted how much influence we as individuals actually had. All in all, the news made me upset, aggressive and aggravated with a generalised feeling of helplessness.

Then, halfway through the first decade of this new century, social media started to morph into its current form. As more and more people joined social media, our ability to interact with others, many of whom we would have never met before, increased. We could talk to people in the US with the same interests as us or interact with a hostel we'd like to stay at in Australia next year, all from our desks and, increasingly as time passed, via our phones. More importantly for the news addict who wants to put his understanding to good use, increasingly media outlets, journalists and then politicians started to join up to sites such as Facebook and Twitter. Hashtags and twitter handles started to appear on screen as news reports were being presented and lo and behold we could interact with the news in real time.

Now, in the new world, we can read about a news story from ten different news sources in the space of as many minutes. Better still, we can see how other people are reacting to it. We could add to the Twitter noise, trying to turn people's opinion to our way of thinking, determined to finally have an impact on the world. We could message politicians and congratulate them on a job well done or, more likely, tell them what a mistake their actions were. Whilst I was never a troll, someone engaging with others online purely to wind them up, I would get frustrated with trolls. I would still engage with them, as if explaining to them one more time that human rights are important would finally change their ways as they cheer another bombing.

These online battles leave you deflated. You want to get away from people with views unlike your own as you learn that they don't change, no matter how much you shout at them that they're wrong. You start to gravitate to other social media users who think similarly as you. You feel a comfort that you're not the only person who views the world the way you do. It makes you feel like you've finally got power. But then you look at the news and nothing changes. That two million signature petition that went around Twitter and Facebook, is ignored by a health secretary who tells the country how well his party is doing, whilst waiting lists go up and nurses become ever poorer, leading to many of them leaving the country in search of better opportunities.

We all have so much access to the news, to its sources, to the key players, all of whom we can directly interact with, but most of the time nothing really changes. hat feeling of helplessness that our lack of control over events generates has long since joined in with a general feeling of depression and anxiety. We feel bad because of the news, there is nothing we can do but we still want to consume, make one more comment because then everything will be better. But it's not. The negativity of it all just keeps piling up and nothing alters out there but inside you sense the darkness getting darker.

But you don't give up. You hook onto a worthy cause. You join a specific campaign because well supported campaigns can occasionally change the course of our oil tanker-like political process. Even then, when things do change, you're annoyed they don't change fast enough. That they didn't alter when you first wrote to your MP ten years ago. That they didn't get amended when that government report, that took five years to complete, concluded that things had to be improved. Worse still is when there is a change, often in a way you hadn't anticipated, it's usually in a way that you consider will make things worse. Whatever you have done, the end result is still just the biggest load of frustration that does not dissipate even when there are improvements in life. Because really it's never enough and salvation is just the next issue around the corner.

It doesn't matter whether you watch the news, like me, for international stories, or whether you want to find out about national or local news, or whether you just watch whatever is on. It's very likely that on occasions you have felt all the things that I have described. Stop and think about it. Really try and remember a time when the news was helpful to your life specifically, when you felt better for having watched it.

It's quite possible that there have been a rare time when it's been useful but for the amount of news that we've watched and the negative impact it can have on our mental health, you have to ask yourself, is it worth it?

News consumption, or rather overconsumption, was actually the last bastion of unmindful behaviour in my life. Even as I closely studied my inner world and came to realisations about how I made myself suffer, no matter how good or bad the world was, I still kept watching the news as often as I could. No matter how mindful I was being elsewhere I still got annoyed and I would sometimes tweet politicians about why their policy was wrong/evil/thoughtless/stupid/whatever.

Stephen McCoull

Then one day, without planning to, my focus came to rest upon this habit of mine and I realised that it hid a huge lack of acceptance of what is within my life. I made a decision to investigate this pattern of behaviour further. I looked back at the last few years when I knew the news had impacted me and I tried to remember all the events that I had heard, read about or seen on TV. Perhaps unsurprisingly, there were very little specifics I could remember. There were the odd big stories that bridged several months or years but even then I couldn't remember the precise details beyond the headlines. Was it really worth getting so worked up about subjects that I only had vague memories of a few months or years later?

Once I realised that, over about six months, I stopped following many of the news channels on Facebook. I would unfollow one news source and when another one that affected me negatively appeared, I would stop following that one as well. Soon, I'd given up following about 95% of the news sources I had been obsessively reading for years. In addition to that, rather than watching the news multiple times every day, especially first thing in the morning, I started to watch the news once a day. Then that reduced to a couple of times a week until there was a news story I felt was worthy of more time, then I'd revert to once a day. I decided that listening to the news in my car, as I drove to work, wasn't helpful either and I started to turn to Audible books or Spotify. Twitter was something that had turned very ugly and negative for me and I wanted to make it something more positive in my life. It was, however, impossible as it remembers all your interests, so I deleted my Twitter account as well with a plan to re-join and follow positive people at some point in the future, once I managed to get a handle on my news addiction.

Mindfully Saving Myself – One Moment at a Time

What happened when I did all this? Well the news didn't stop and the world just kept on turning. There's still war, there's still famine, there are still governments who look out for the rich and not everyone in their society. All that horrid stuff still happens just as before, the world hasn't changed one iota, but for me, not watching the news was revolutionary.

There was no longer anything to react against. I didn't get angry all the time about things that I couldn't change, I didn't feel useless or guilty because I couldn't change the world. I felt lighter. There is a deep peace in accepting that the world is not under your control, that it is certainly not perfect, and that no amount of mental negativity and effort from me, you or anyone else is going to change that. Once I had fully accepted that, the peace descended upon me almost immediately.

Whilst not all the time, I still do watch the news. I still think it's important to be informed but I can stay informed by watching the news two or three times a week. Now I don't get frustrated, because it doesn't help. If negative emotions do arise, as they still do, I just step back and observe what is going on within, without attachment. It means that now I can use the knowledge I do have to vote the right way or to make decisions about charities or lobby groups I wish to donate to. yet I don't hold on to any desired outcome from my vote or donation. I accept that I am not the only person doing that, many millions in this country and around the world do the same and some will vote and donate the opposite way to me. I accept that whilst I've done what I can, things may not always work out the way I want them to. That's perfectly fine because in a few years' time I probably won't remember any details anyway. What I will remember, though, is that peaceful heart that I've cultivated which will certainly help my life and in turn may help others too.

Stephen McCoull

In the current pandemic having this relationship with the news means I don't get drawn into what is a very difficult situation any more than I have to. I don't hold on to what I can't control but I take away the practicalities that I need to be aware of so that I can keep myself and others safe.

Using Gratitude to Help You Find Wonder in Everything

I heard a masterclass, an online talk by an expert, about gratitude by Shawn Achor, arranged by the Calm app. Shawn is described as a Happiness Advocate and the goal of his masterclass was to help anyone who heard him be able to make some simple changes to their lives that would skew their life towards a happier mind-set.

As my mindfulness practice had already helped me become more content with life, I wondered if there was more I could do and whether gratitude would help.

Shawn had several ideas for gratitude. Rather than recount them all I'll tell you about the two that really stuck in my head and from which my gratitude practice has developed.

The first gratitude practice is to think about three things that you are grateful for and tell yourself why you are grateful for them. It can be anything. I often carry out this practice first thing in the morning in my car as I drive to work, so occasionally there will be something car or journey related to be grateful for. It might be the person who let me out of the road I live on onto the main road in heavy traffic. I'm grateful for them as it makes my journey to work easier, quicker and it just shows me there are other kind people in the world. Sometimes it can be the sunrise as I drive along the motorway. I'm grateful to be reminded of the beauty of nature and that our lives are part of a wider universe.

Carrying out this practice at the beginning of the day, or at any time, can improve your mood. The important thing is to be completely mindful when you carry out the practice. Really observe and pay attention to the words you are saying or thinking and also the emotions that appear as you say them.

As I carry out the practice when I'm driving, events related to my journey often come to mind but Shawn also explained that gratitude practice doesn't work as well if you're grateful for the same things each time. If I always picked being grateful for being let into the busy traffic the practice would almost become an unconscious habit and it would lose its power. I'd stop carrying out the practice mindfully and I would no longer be present for how it affected me. The positive effect would be lost.

So it's important to really think about something new each day. It doesn't have to be difficult, it could be being grateful for your children, your partner, your parents or even a good friend who helped you out of a sticky situation the previous day. Or it could be just because your favourite brand of toothpaste really cleans your teeth like no other. Maybe you're grateful because that packet of Wine Gums had more black and red sweets than greens. It really can be anything, just mix it up and stay mindful as you carry out the practice to get the most out of it.

The next practice I carry out is not dissimilar from the first. To start, you think back over the last day or over the period of time since you last carried out a gratitude practice and pick a single event. It can be absolutely anything that you've experienced. It could be a meeting you had the previous day at work, a night out with friends, a great film you

Mindfully Saving Myself – One Moment at a Time

saw or even helping an elderly neighbour across the road. The sky is the limit but it has to be something that has happened to you.

Once you've picked an event, you find three things to be grateful for that are related to that event. If you had a night out with your friends it might be being grateful for having some time away from work and home, a change of scenery. You could be grateful for being able to keep the relationships you have with people positive and friendly. It could even be because you got to try a new dish at the restaurant you dined at that you'd never tried before and you ended up loving. This practice can really help you to find gratitude for absolutely anything in your life. The more you find gratitude for in your day to day existence the more you find in your life that there is to be grateful for. The more you are grateful the happier you will feel, and that feeling of happiness will make you feel even more thankful. More importantly, you will slowly become more peaceful within your heart.

When I first started the second practice I tended to look for positive events that had happened in the past day and then find three positives from that single event. Once you are used to the practice you can start applying it to anything that happens to you at all, even something negative. Here's an example of the very first time I used a negative event to find positives to be grateful for.

There was a person at my work who I used to be very friendly with. We were close enough that she'd seen me at some of my darkest points at work when I'd snuck away in our first aid room trying to hide the fact I was breaking down. I attended her wedding reception and I considered her a friend, and definitely someone I could trust. Then, for reasons I've never understood, she just stopped talking to me. She blocked my number and blocked me on social media. I was confused,

113

but I never got an answer as to why she'd shut me out, so I ended up leaving it and letting it go.

One day at work she called me up asking for my help with an Excel problem. I told her to send me the file she was struggling with and said I would look into it when I was next free. I worked out the issue, updated the file and sent it to her. I offered to talk her though how I fixed it when she had some time. There was some hope that if I helped out, unexplained tensions between us would ease. But that's not what happened. In fact nothing happened at all. There was no thanks, I got nothing back at all. Later in the day, when I noticed she hadn't replied I realised feelings that used to haunt me were resurfacing. There was mild anger at the way she'd treated me in the recent past and the lack of gratitude for my helping her with Excel. I remembered my gratitude practice so, instead of following the anger or trying to be its witness, I decided to do something else instead. This was another radical move for me.

I asked myself what I could be grateful for in this situation. Firstly, I was grateful because I had a small but interesting problem to solve and I could use my skills to do so whilst learning a little bit extra in the process. Secondly, I made her work life a little easier, so she could present her graphs in a way that would make sense to her audience. Whilst I didn't get a thanks, I'm sure it lightened her mood a little by reducing her work pressures and therefore her interactions with the world were likely to be that much more positive than before, so everyone won. Finally, I was grateful that this situation demonstrated to me that there was nothing left of our friendship. There was no respect, so I was able to let it go for the last time.

From that point on I have always tried to find positives. To be grateful for the experiences that many would define as negative.

For instance, one Friday I was finishing work at 1pm with no further responsibilities for the day. For various reasons I'd not had that amount of free time for myself for months, maybe even a year. I was really looking forward to taking a long run and pushing myself to see what I was currently capable of. Afterwards, I'd planned to write for a couple of hours and once my girlfriend, now fiancée, returned home from work we were going to go out for a meal.

It was going to be a lovely afternoon into evening and I was really looking forward to 1pm that day. Unfortunately, halfway through that Friday morning I had a migraine. I don't get them that badly, compared to some. I get some visual disturbance for an hour or so followed by a mild headache and nausea. However, the worst thing about them is that after the visual auras wear off my head feels like superglue has been injected into it and I'm left feeling exhausted. I just can't think or do too much for the rest of the day once I've had one.

So that Friday morning I was forced into the dark of the first aid room until it was safe enough for me to drive home to my bed. I got into bed and all the plans I'd been thinking about for days couldn't be fulfilled.

Old me would have definitely grumbled about it. I wouldn't have accepted that my day was not going to happen as I had planned. I would feel the day was ruined. Instead, I was grateful for the chance to practice acceptance of what is, the chance to practice self-care and do what was right for me at that moment. I was grateful for the fact that despite the fact I felt sick and spaced out that my headache is never anything as near as bad as experienced by some migraine sufferers. I was grateful for that luck. And, finally, I was grateful for Marta who is a loving human being who had no problems with the fact our plans had to be altered because I wasn't well. It was a situation that in the past could have led to anger, frustration and even self-pity but instead I felt truly grateful in that moment.

The amazing thing is that research has shown that if people keep up a daily gratitude practice for three weeks that their overall mood improves and they have a more positive outlook on life, which has been my experience. Having gratitude for everything that happens in your life generates more appreciation for what you experience during your life.

To use gratitude to help with bringing out an appreciation for life, often in moments when you feel anything but grateful, is something that you can start to do at any time. It will feel weird and possibly difficult at first and it's very likely that you'll forget to step into that gratitude mind-set more often than not but the more you do it the easier it will become and eventually it may become second nature.

Early in 2018 there was a guided meditation on the Calm app about being grateful for friends in your life, especially those ones who've always been there and have been with you through thick and thin. I did the meditation, observed my thoughts and my breath and got off my cushion and headed off to work for the day.

Unfortunately, the subject matter was not left on the cushion, though, and the idea about friends in life who'd been there through thick and thin stuck in my mind. The problem was that, apart from a couple of friends, I didn't have any mates who'd been there through the hard times. In the first few months of my separation from my ex-wife I ended up without many friends at all. The guided meditation had stimulated thoughts about those people who were no longer in my life. I started to think about the friends who had immediately judged me, those who just didn't bother one way or another, those who liked the drama and added petrol to the flames and also my former best mate. All these negative feelings about my lack of friends started to swirl around and I wasn't

Mindfully Saving Myself – One Moment at a Time

feeling that great about life. I remained that way for some hours. Previously, if I'd stayed on that course, I would have ended up going down the rabbit hole of thinking that I've lost all these friends, therefore I'm not good enough or worthy of love, that I didn't do enough to please people and that somehow it was all my fault. Instead, I avoided reactivity to the depressed emotions that arrived. Fortunately, my practice kicked in. I saw it as a great opportunity to develop the skill of observing and not reacting to the emotions that are generated.

As I watched the thoughts, I realised that they will pass and nothing is permanent. These negative emotions are not me but purely mental formations. As I became the observer of what was happening and stopped reacting, I turned my attention to what I could be grateful for. I was grateful that I had lost those friendships that weren't actually positive for me. Grateful that it gave me the space to find out all about myself in a way that I would have never been able to before. If those friends had remained in my life it is unlikely I would have ever written this book.

I had gratitude for the great people I did have in my life. Those from outside of my ex-wife's and my circle of friends, some of whom I had been close with, as well as those who I hadn't known that well yet who were there for me when I was at my worst and also now that I was feeling much healthier. Those who I'd met through my involvement with mindfulness both face to face but also the hundreds of people I had spoken to online, who had encouraged me and also respected me enough to learn from the experiences that I shared, who would also express gratitude to me. I was grateful for my amazing fiancée who had given me the space to learn about myself without any expectation when we first met. I felt gratitude for a very good friend and his wife who had helped me out when I needed a space to mentally recover when I first left my ex-wife. I also felt thankful for a colleague in another office who had sent me the data I had requested, in the format I wanted, earlier in the day.

By stepping back, observing and then focusing on gratitude I succeeded in stopping the negative circle dead in its tracks and replaced it with positive thoughts and emotions. Rather than dwelling on them and becoming attached to the good times, I stepped back in the same way I did with the negative emotions. I observed my renewed positivity without attachment. But why did I do that? Because positive emotions are also governed by the rule of impermanence that directs everything in life. If I had become too fixated on them, claiming them as my own, when they passed, as they surely would, I would have found myself suffering again. So my response was to accept the good times, to enjoy them but not to involve myself in them too much and this brought an acceptance and a deep peace.

I know some people find it quite odd to not react to the positive as well as the negative emotions. Surely, we all want the good in life and just don't want the bad? By all means, be grateful for the good times, soak them up. However, it's really important, for me at least, to respond rather than react to any emotion, good or bad. When I start grasping after a nice experience I'm having and don't want to end or wishing away a bad experience, it always takes me out of the moment and causes suffering in some way. Usually I feel less balanced if I grasp or have aversion. If I do stop grasping after what is happening and just observe the event, it becomes very noticeable that I maintain a more even keel and life is actually more enjoyable, whatever the mental weather.

I know I'm lucky in so many ways. Yes, I've had my struggles but I've always had a roof over my head, food in the fridge and have always had work. I'm fortunate because I've had the time and space to work out so much stuff about myself, for which I'm very grateful, but

Mindfully Saving Myself – One Moment at a Time

that doesn't stop life trying to see if it can get me to react to negative situations. Life will always do that. Even the richest person in the world can slip into negativity and a lack of gratitude no matter how good life may seem.

My ex-wife and I alternate who has the kids on Christmas day morning and who has them for the rest of the day and overnight onto Boxing Day. Christmas 2019 it was my turn to have them in the morning and then drop them off at their mum's just after noon. It's not the first time I've done this and it certainly won't be the last but it always brings up difficult emotions because like any parent, who loves their kids, I don't want to spend just part of that day with them, I want to spend all of it with them. I still feel that way even though two of them are now teenagers!!!

After dropping the kids off, I usually give them a hug, say goodbye and drive away. As soon as I'm out of sight of the house I'll then pull over just to give myself a minute or two to work through some quite upsetting thoughts about not being there for them, feeling as if I were letting them down each time I said goodbye. I acknowledge them, accept them and then stepped away from them before driving off for the rest of Christmas. Last time I did that I also practiced gratitude and wrote the following once I got home.

"Today I'm grateful for the breakdown I had in 2013 and all those breakdowns afterwards. Without them I would never have found myself on a path to being awake in life, actually being in this moment, and accepting it for what it is right now. Whilst I certainly wasn't grateful for those moments of extreme distress at the time, I am so thankful for them now. Without them I would not have the peace I have. Between then and now there were a few Christmases in which I felt out of control of my mental health and I was extremely lonely. It's been a battle but

Stephen McCoull

now I'm on the right path and have been for well over three years. This Christmas I feel peace. So if you're feeling bad right now on the festive day, then don't beat yourself up for it, it is as it is. However, let me tell you this, the fact you can feel shows you are human. It may be a hard day today, a hard day amongst other hard days, but I promise you this: even if you can't see it right now there is a light at the end of the tunnel. Even if you feel like this is the worst moment you have ever experienced there is light on your path. There is light. You just need to get through this one moment, each moment, accepting each one as it is. The pain and anxiety will pass, it might not be immediate but it will and one day you may even be grateful you had all those bad times. You will find a place where you're at peace even when times are hard. Just keep up your practice, have confidence in the process, of course faith in yourself, because you are good enough and one day you too will be able to have limitless gratitude for all the bad times as well as the good". Then I shared it in the Calm online community in the hope that it would help give at least one person some hope and reason to explore themselves further even if that person were just me.

I spent so much of my life in emotional pain, which I now recognise was often of my own making. It could be argued that it was all of my making. Either way, I never found much to be grateful for and I certainly didn't feel any gratitude. That is quite the understatement because I'd often find the opposite was true. I would be ungrateful even when there was reason to celebrate. I used to be angry about past events and would blame them and people for what had happened to me. I would be unhappy about almost everything that had happened in my life and I was not thankful.

That all slowly changed when I took my first steps on this mindfulness path. Gratitude gave me another way out of the darkness

Mindfully Saving Myself – One Moment at a Time

that was my life. Step by step, I slowly got out of the abyss and started to see life for what it really was. I became thankful for it, all of it. I'm human, so I don't always openly express gratitude for absolutely everything that happens but I do often express and acknowledge it internally. Gratitude is such a powerful string to your mindfulness bow. It can help you advance towards that point of being in the present and accepting everything as is, without judgement. Gratitude has helped me look at life with wonder and I often have a smile on my face.

Stephen McCoull

Fixing your Spiritual Roof whilst the Sun is Shining

I've come to realise that Meditative practice is the spiritual equivalent of fixing the roof when the sun is shining. There's probably a few of you who may be scratching your heads at that sentence so let me clarify what I mean.

When we say the word "spiritual" or "spirituality", some people can think this is all getting a bit "woo woo" and that can turn people off, I know it's made me do that in the past. Rightly or wrongly, the word "spirituality" also had, in my mind, a connection with organised religion and I've never been a fan of religious dogmas. Dogma, for me, is being told what to think, accepting it all without question or without direct experience but with unquestioning faith and never really exploring anything or learning anything for yourself. Whilst many religions have texts that can point to a better way of living, and that is far from being a bad thing, the driver is always about the next life to come rather than learning to live in this very moment we find ourselves in. It's about getting to heavenly afterlife instead of finding you can have a deep peace on earth, whatever your life looks like.

Since I've been meditating spirituality has come to mean something far different to me than it used to. When I Googled the meaning of spirituality it told me that it is "the quality of being

122

Mindfully Saving Myself – One Moment at a Time

concerned with the human spirit or soul as opposed to material or physical things". What that sentence really means is being in touch with yourself. Understanding who you are, what you are made of and what subconscious processes drive you. Spirituality is about being alright with whatever you find. Being spiritual is not only about understanding yourself, it's also about that you are then able to see that others are also driven by internal processes. Even when, they themselves do not see what drives their behaviours and actions. Spirituality means realising that other people are much like you, with a good heart, no matter what they externally do. In short, being spiritual is having an understanding of others and yourself no matter how difficult that may be, and being empathetic and kind. Spirituality is now disconnected from religion in my mind.

That doesn't mean a religious person can't be spiritual, many are. It means that many non-religious people can be spiritual. The opposite is also true, a religious or a non-religious person may not be spiritual or have any empathy for others.

That is what spirituality means to me but how on earth do you fix that whilst the sun is shining? Many of you will be interested in meditation because you want to work out why you behave a certain way. It's possible that you've accepted poor treatment at work, you put up with someone who isn't really present in your relationship with them or perhaps you feel depressed and anxious and you don't know why and you want to explore all of that. These are big things, large chunky bits of ourselves to work with. Working with them can be difficult without practicing first because these are certainly not sunny thoughts to deal with.

What can we do on a day when we're feeling at peace with ourselves and the world? You are just in the flow of life, you can't

123

explain it any more than you can explain why you were feeling bad the day before, but right now there is harmony inside you. Days like those are sunny days. Even when you've suffered from depression and anxiety for years you still have sunny moments and days amongst all the gloom. On a day like that we note that we've got nothing particularly bad within us to work on, it's easy to practice acceptance of what is when the present moment feels pretty damn good. Yet we need to go and fix that spiritual roof for when the next storm hits.

Just like an athlete, who needs to train for an event, we still need to practice non-judgemental acceptance when life is good. That way we prepare ourselves for when that sunny day passes and clouds begin to appear again or, worse still, if a full blown tornado pops up out of nowhere.

Here's an instance of practicing when the sun is shining. A few months back I wasn't able to meditate first thing in the morning and I knew I wouldn't be able to easily meditate after work, as I would be getting my children as soon as my work day was over. If I haven't had a chance to meditate in the morning, I will go into our first aid room at work in my break and do a brief ten minute practice. The first aid room is used not just for first aid but as a prayer room by Christian and Muslim colleagues (and me - the meditator). There is a sign on the door to say whether the room is in use or not so that no one will accidently walk in on someone ill or someone praying.

On that day I was in a pretty good mood, it was going to be a peaceful practice because I felt great and my mind was quiet. As I went into the first aid room I set the sign to say the room was in use, then I got myself settled on the seat, set a ten minute timer and closed my eyes. Suddenly, about halfway through my meditation, someone ignored the sign on the door and loudly walked into the room and then noisily

Mindfully Saving Myself – One Moment at a Time

walked out again when they saw me. As you can imagine, this caused irritation to arise but, whilst this might be quite a strong trigger for some people, I had been practicing for some time at that stage and for me it was a minor event. Someone walking into the room when I am meditating and causing annoyance when I'm feeling good, is a chance to fix your spiritual roof whilst the sun is shining.

There's my peaceful meditation and now there's a condition of the mind, irritation which has arisen, that I can observe. I looked at all its facets without judging whether it was good or bad, it was just there, and I accepted it. I kept up my focus on the thoughts, emotions and my body and then I just slowly watched as the entire experience morph and change until the power of the feelings subsided and finally I shifted my focus back on to the breath and continued my meditation. That's practice for you. It's working with something minor, remembering that what is an insignificant event for me might not be so trivial for others and vice versa, and practicing on whatever mental conditions arise. This is just one example but it can be absolutely anything that triggers a minor reaction in you. It could be your noisy fridge, or a neighbour's dog that barks when you're meditating or even the fact that the question of what you're going to cook for dinner keeps appearing in your mind whilst you're trying to focus on your breath.

It's not just minor irritations that you can use to practice with, you can even use physical sensations too. Such as, something for me is just a minor difficulty, itches! It's certainly not the end of the world, but it's a great physical condition to practice on. Who doesn't itch at some point during the day and who doesn't have an itch when they sit for meditation? Itches appear nearly every time I sit. Use itches and other mild physical sensations in the same way as you would inconsequential mental events. Put all your attention into the itch, observe how the itch

125

changes with time, how there's a temptation to scratch it and how that temptation also ebbs and flows over time. Nothing is permanent and if we face that itch with non-judgemental acceptance, then slowly we find that the physical sensation loses its power with time. This is great practice that strengthens your spiritual roof.

If you're anything like me then you'll have both physical and mental events that you can work with nearly all the time. I'd be surprised if you didn't have them at least once an hour if not much more. Each minor difficulty is a chance to practice non-judgemental acceptance of what is right now, this very second. The incredible thing is that this is something you can do not only when you're meditating, when you're having a good day, but even as you go about your day away from the cushion. That person who annoyingly jumps into the queue in the shop has just given you the opportunity to fix that spiritual roof some more.

And that is what fixing the spiritual the roof when the sun is shining is. We use difficulties, that aren't too great, to help us increase our abilities to find acceptance in the present moment. Just like a footballer who uses repeated training sessions to prepare for the big match, if we can gain equanimity during these occasions day after day, month after month, when, as invariably will happen, a major life event occurs we can deploy what we have learnt to help us through whatever horrible situation has happened to us as mindfully as possible. The practice won't stop sad events being unhappy. Meditating can't reverse what has happened in life or stop very strong emotions from arising, but it can help you come to accept what is and be at peace with those events far quicker than if you'd never practiced at all.

That's why I practice every day even when life feels like the sun is shining - I am always fixing my spiritual roof.

Converting Loneliness Into Alone Time

When I left my ex-wife a lot of friends distanced themselves from me. With hindsight, it made sense. I was the person who'd done "wrong" and they had no idea how my ex-wife was within our relationship so they supported her and not me. They knew I was in a bad way, some of them knew I'd been close to taking my own life, but what could they do when my ex-wife's emotional state was their priority?

Whilst I understand it now, at the time I didn't understand it at all. I had just escaped what I felt was a toxic relationship and I had traumatised myself by how close I'd come to taking my own life. Back then I was a person who needed my friends. I needed someone I could talk to at any time so that I didn't go completely into my own mental abyss or worse, find myself seriously considering taking my life once more.

Some of my friends came out a couple of times for drinks but slowly they stopped responding to my requests to meet up. The rest of my friends either didn't speak to me from the moment I left or told me that they couldn't be there for me because they had to support my ex-wife. The circle of what I considered to be my friends went down from about twenty people or more to only a couple over a period of three or four months, the majority being lost almost instantly.

Stephen McCoull

Whilst I immediately accepted the responsibility for what I had done, I hadn't really learnt anything in depth about myself at that point and I became very needy, even more than before. Rather than ease my own suffering, I was about to make it much worse.

As my ex-wife started to use things against me, either through the children or just a continuation of the emotional blackmail I had been subjected to for years, I started to get angry. I was angry that I was still being manipulated. Angry I was still out of control of my life and now I was furious that I had lost the vast majority of my friends. If only they knew what she was like they would understand. But they didn't.

With one exception, not a single one of my friends from those times asked me what had really happened. Not one had asked me if I was ok. So I started posting on social media about things that were being said or done by my ex. Just the act of posting about whatever had happened was a lack of acceptance of reality as I hoped the post would mean people finally understood the pain I was in and how I was being treated by my friends would stop. They'd be there to support me again. But all it did was escalate the anger inside.

The fury drove me to yet more dark places. It was from these places, close to the edge, that I stupidly thought that if people saw the posts that they would feel sorry for me and they'd reach out to see if I was alright. I still hoped that they'd return to my life and things would be as before but without my ex in my life. Thinking in this way propelled me to post more. Yet, the less I accepted the situation the worse I felt and the more I posted. If only people knew they would see that I was close to the edge. They'd see that my thoughts were so dark that I was likely to do something stupid, and they'd be there for me. Right?

Occasionally Facebook would ping with a message from a friend from that era. I had hoped for redemption of some sort but instead what

128

Mindfully Saving Myself – One Moment at a Time

I read was never positive. It was usually someone telling me how awful I was for posting what I had. Sometimes what they said was even worse than that, deriding me for what I was doing to my ex. I just wanted someone from that group of friends to reach out and have some kind of empathy with the situation I found myself in. Instead, with the odd exception, if they did contact me, they just passed judgement, often with hostility.

When posting on Facebook didn't work, I would message people directly, usually when I had been drinking. I would beg for their time or be the opposite and berate them for abandoning me. Mainly, though, it was pleading for someone to listen to what was going on. I would do anything to win favour with these people but my neediness and lack of acceptance of the current situation was pushing them away. I was the antithesis of mindfulness.

This behaviour went on throughout 2015. I went from one bout of suicidal thoughts to another as I was rejected time and time again by people I thought were good friends. I didn't understand it and felt extremely lonely most of the time even when I was with other people. I just wanted my friends back. It was a very painful time.

Something changed in me, though, in early 2016. I had got myself into another toxic relationship. She was broken and I was broken but her issues had hardened her and mine had done the opposite to me. The relationship fell apart and I was bumping along the bottom seemingly moving from one breakdown to another. I had gone out to a pub with the house mates I had lived with for a year. As we were chatting, almost the entire group of my old friends came into the pub and walked past me. Some said hello whilst others just looked awkwardly away, not wanting to meet my eyes, and escaping deep into the large pub.

129

People I had spent so much time with over the years just walked past as if they didn't care.

It all happened pretty quickly but I crashed into my final breakdown. I experienced the start of it right there in the middle of the pub. It had been building for a while but seeing everyone troop past was the final straw. I collapsed on a mental level and at first I wasn't even able to get out of the pub.

You may think my former friends were heartless but they weren't. A couple of them must have seen I was in a bad way and they took me outside and spoke to me. I can't remember what was said but they showed me kindness and looked after me until I finally had the energy to get into a taxi.

The following day the same two people checked up on me over text and then that was it. No one else contacted me and the loneliness I felt that day was overwhelming. I knew in that moment that I had to move on from these people, my former friends, if I ever wanted to be happy again.

Acceptance, of sorts, at last! As I came to accept that my friends were no longer my friends, the pain that I had created around the whole situation began to subside. It was 2016 and I had started my mindfulness practice. Whilst I wasn't particularly good at doing this at the time, when I did start to ruminate about my lost friends I could use those thoughts as a point of meditation. I would accept that I had the feelings but that I would do nothing about them. I wouldn't judge them and say "I wish I didn't feel this way about my friends" or dive into some fantasy about us becoming friends again, I would just watch the emotions and eventually they would disappear.

With this change I slowly stopped the Facebook posts that were made with hope that someone would finally wake up to what had

Mindfully Saving Myself – One Moment at a Time

happened. At the same time I stopped feeling bad for myself. I stopped pestering people over text, WhatsApp or other messaging services and I stopped feeling beleaguered in my own mind.

I can't say I found peace often but I did find it on occasions and that gave me hope. At the time this was happening some of those former friend, started softening towards me. A lady, who had been like a sister to me, asked me out for a drink. I went because my diary was empty, not because I was desperate for her friendship. Desperation had been replaced with curiosity. Maybe we could clear things up after all and I wanted to see what would happen.

When she arrived at the pub we'd arranged to meet in, she made it clear that she didn't want to talk about anything in the past and not about our friendship. She wanted to act like nothing had happened and it was just a normal night out with the two of us having a laugh. I had changed a lot in a short time, so I accepted that was what she wanted and we had a fun couple of hours chatting to each other. I didn't mention how dark life had been or how much I'd missed her. I didn't ask her why she sent nasty texts in reply to mine when I was at some of my lowest points. Instead we just enjoyed each other's company and then parted ways.

The evening made me remember why I had liked her in the first place. I'd had fun, but I wasn't the same person any more. I contemplated the evening in my head. What good friend wouldn't want to discuss what had happened? What valued mate wouldn't want to try to at least understand how their friendship had become so distant, even if it couldn't be fixed long term? The answer was not someone I wanted to waste my time on any more. Upon realising that, I let that friendship leave my heart without too much struggle.

I started questioning the way everyone who I had considered a friend behaved towards me because of the new way I was looking at the world. I realised many of these people were no longer positive forces in my life and in some respects they had been very negative. As I contemplated my friendships, the need to prove to people that I was good enough for them disappeared. I stopped feeling that the issues between us were my doing. I was good enough for me, so I stopped trying to get any of them back in my life. I didn't need them as friends any more. I didn't hold them any ill will and still don't. They weren't, and aren't, bad people. They were just trying to get through life and I was no longer something that helped them do that. How could anyone begrudge them just trying to get through the difficulties of their life? I couldn't.

Accepting that I'd lost friends was one part of the process of stopping being lonely. Another part was working out whether or not my remaining relationships were good for me. Even though I had few people in my life then, if someone wasn't positive for me then I had to consider if I wanted to keep that friendship alive. If it was not a good relationship for me, I had to work out if it could ever become a positive thing in future, something worth fighting for or not.

The most difficult friend to lose was not a person who abandoned me but the person I chose to part company with. He was my best friend. Someone I'd known since I was twelve or maybe thirteen. Someone who I had believed had always been there for me. Someone I'd always been there for.

When I first left my ex-wife my friend had had his 40th birthday party a couple of weeks later. I went and my ex also chose to go. It was awkward. A couple of people had a go at me, and I expected it wasn't quite the great party my best mate had wanted because of this underlying tension.

Mindfully Saving Myself – One Moment at a Time

A year later at the end of 2015 my ex started harassing me over text asking if I was going to my best mate's birthday drinks, because she wasn't going to go if I was. I didn't know what she was on about. He wasn't having birthday drinks as I'd only just spoken to him and he had not invited me or mentioned it. I asked my friend if he knew anything about what my ex was saying. He denied any knowledge but she was incessant that entire day, as if she knew I hadn't been invited. I asked my best friend several times if he understood why she was continuously messaging me, sharing the messages I'd been sent, and in the end he admitted he had invited her to his house for birthday drinks and made some excuse about having invited another former friend of mine and he accidentally invited my ex as well.

I was really hurt. Firstly, he'd not invited me, his best friend. Secondly he had lied to me repeatedly, over several hours, until he had no choice but to tell the truth. That fact alone completely unhinged me because I just couldn't understand how, when he knew I didn't have many people in my life, he could do that to me. I would never have done that to him. Rather than being apologetic or just shrugging it off he went on the attack, blaming me for ruining his 40th birthday party, telling me that was why he'd not invited me and that it was my fault.

I was still grasping for friendships, though, and after a period of distance when I broke down again in 2016 I rang him up and actually apologised for questioning him over his inviting my ex to his party. I was low and I couldn't stand to lose my best friend so I accepted fault and we started to occasionally see each other again.

The trouble is I noticed that he'd sometimes exclude me and include my ex, which would happen every now and then. I understood he did it, because our old circle of friends included my ex, but he knew it hurt me if he invited her specifically, because I told him how much it did.

133

Other times, especially after the divorce when money was really tight, I sometimes asked him to come around to my flat rather than me travel to see him. Usually I had to go to his house to see him, but sometimes I simply couldn't afford the petrol or train fare. But rather than come to mine he'd just cancel and say "some other time". Another time I'd bought him a ticket for a gig and asked him when we should meet up and he suddenly wasn't available because he had to save his money for another gig he was going to with other friends. I started to realise I was the one making the effort for him.

As I progressed on my meditation journey and became comfortable with myself, I learnt, through the lens of mindfulness, that what he did appeared to be for his own self-interest, not through loving kindness, and often without consideration for me. Keeping in contact with my ex and the people who surrounded her was more important to him than loyalty to his best mate. It was more important than empathy for a human being who he'd known for decades, one whose stories, from my marriage, he knew very well.

I was slowly accepting that our friendship wasn't solid when I saw on Facebook that he and his partner had run a charity quiz night. By this stage I wasn't using Facebook as a tool of escape and it was purely by accident I discovered it. It was immediately obvious that my ex and her partner were there as I could see who had been invited. I had spoken to my best mate the day before and even asked what he was doing that weekend and there was no mention of any quiz at all. Unmindful me would have had another breakdown but mindful me knew this relationship wasn't no longer a good one for me. His actions were not the actions of a best friend, not those of someone I could trust.

I recognised that the relationship was no longer a positive thing in my life. I broke off our friendship and told him why. As much I was at peace with the fact the friendship needed to end, ending it was still difficult. And when I did, he was very verbally aggressive towards me, telling me that I was an angry and controlling person, trying to mentally hit me as much as possible, knowing that I'd been in an emotionally manipulative relationship with my ex. No matter how much he told me I was an angry person, over email, I continued to feel peace. In fact, it was almost humorous seeing that he kept telling me how irate I was as I read his emails with equanimity. I know ending the friendship was the right thing for me to do. Whilst he spilled anger at me over email I wished him luck in life and secretly offered him loving kindness in my heart. I meant it too. To this very day I still hope that he's as happy as life can allow him to be, because I know deep down he's a good person who is just following his own unhelpful behaviours.

Mindfulness exposed to me what was always there with him and with the others. It allowed me to acknowledge my emotions about certain people and to move away from them and accept it all. Mindfulness showed me the reality of these friendships, so letting the ones that weren't productive go was relatively easy.

When I think back to 2015 nothing was different with those friends to how they were once I found mindfulness but my earlier reaction to those people caused me intense suffering, a terrible sense of loneliness that was sometimes dangerous to me. It's almost impossible to imagine I was like that, so needy. Remembering it makes me grateful for everything I've learnt since and the peace it's brought. This peace I've obtained not only meant I was able to remove negative relationships from my life, it meant my view of loneliness changed too.

We hear all the time about people being lonely and isolated, often in plain sight. I know how much that can affect a person because during 2015 and 2016 I went through bouts of intense loneliness as well.

Stephen McCoull

You feel like you will never have friends that mean something to you and who are on the same wavelength ever again. You feel worthless. You need companionship. The feeling of isolation was so intense, at times, during those two years that it felt like a physical pain.

However, as I practiced mindfulness and slowly accepted the friendships I'd lost, I started to really see what my drive to be with people as often as I could was actually about. I wasn't an outgoing extrovert, as I had led myself to believe. Instead, this necessity to be constantly surrounded by others was another one of my behaviours that was about me not being in the moment. It was about not being alive in life. Counterintuitively, it was the need to be surrounded by people, no matter how good or bad they were for me, that was causing the loneliness in me, not the fact I was on my own a lot. Wanting to be around people was about not wanting to be with myself.

Needing to be with people all the time had another dimension as well. When I was with someone, whether that was in a pub drinking beer, sitting around a table discussing politics, chatting as we walked or just talking amusing rubbish at someone else's dining room table, I was not being present because I put all my focus outside of myself. Being with people was a distraction from who I was and it helped me to not deal with anything I had done, experienced and felt. This was a revelation to me. I wasn't a people person at all, I was a distraction seeking person. Once I understood that, my desire to be with people all the time changed to an aspiration to just be in the moment, whether that moment was with people or on my own.

I tried doing something different. When that pain of loneliness struck, I started to observe it rather than getting overwhelmed by it. I stopped being attached to the idea that I was lonely. I no longer saw myself as an isolated man without friends but instead that although there was loneliness, I didn't need to identify with it. As I detached from the emotions and physical pain isolation generated, the loneliness stopped and over time it became alone time. Time I could enjoy doing anything I wanted. Sometimes it was playing a computer game or watching a decent programme without worrying what someone else wanted to watch. Often the alone time meant more time to meditate and read about meditation, mindfulness and Buddhism. When I finished work and would be heading back to my flat I started to get excited for my alone time because, rather than something to dread, it was now a positive experience.

You may be thinking that might work for me but not for you. Because the behaviour is too well ingrained into your mind so there's no point fighting it. I understand. I never thought I could change before I did. Transformation had seemed impossible. The problem with behaviours, especially ones that have developed over decades, is that those mental pathways will still exist even after having been mindfully identified by you. Yet that's no reason not to apply the practice of mindfulness to them. The more we practice the weaker these pathways become until they become so faded that they are hardly noticeable. You find you can easily separate yourself from them.

The greatest bonus is that this transformation of loneliness to alone time has given me the space to start having a better relationship with myself. When I have a better connection with myself, it's easier to have nourishing friendships with others.

Unless you're an introvert, you might think that all this talk about alone time sounds horrible. You don't want a life without people. I'd agree that a life without people would be a little dull (although of course you could observe that feeling as well). ut life changes if you stop being attached to the need for people. That is because it is the

Stephen McCoull

requirement or the need for people that disappears but that the enjoyment of the company of others doesn't. So you start to find the people you want to be with and they find you too. It means that you can still have wonderful relationships, healthier than those you'd had before.

I confess that very occasionally the feeling will enter my head that I want to be with people and that familiar sensation of loneliness will appear. It's usually when Marta is away with work or visiting Poland, so yes there is loneliness at those times. But now when that happens I don't identify with it and instead it becomes a meditation in itself. I accept that loneliness is there and I just observe it, until it passes, and the lonely time becomes alone time. Even though occasionally there is loneliness, I have stopped being attached to it. My bond to that emotion is broken and I am no longer the lonely person. I'm just me and I feel at peace when I am on my own and I have become peaceful within the new relationships I do have. Those friendships are deeper, more meaningful than any friendship I had before. I even have positive, supportive friendships with a few fellow meditators who live on other continents, who I have never met in person.

Mindfully Saving Myself – One Moment at a Time

Death or Forgiveness?

Years ago, I would use social media to brain dump almost everything that was going on in my head. I wasn't mindful at the time, quite the opposite, and I started to live for social media. Everything that happened was immediately converted into a post for Facebook through an almost unconscious process. When I say everything, I really do mean everything. Nothing was off limits for my social media posts. I would post anything from how crazy the last night out was, to pictures of my kids, amusing things I'd observed and sometimes negative stuff too. Over a period of time the more I used social media, negativity became the predominant theme of what I posted.

At one point in my life I would post complaints or whinge about something that had happened to me. Maybe my favourite packet of sweets wasn't available at the shops, or someone in the gym was not being considerate to other people. Sometimes it would be complaints about companies or products. It could really be anything. I would post about whatever was annoying me at the time, in as an amusing a way as I could. Then I would ask the question "Death or Forgiveness?" The packet of crisps is now 47.5g instead of 50g and are the same price, death or forgiveness? A person pushed in front of four of us at a supermarket queue and then swore at the man in front of me, death or forgiveness?

Asking whether someone should be put to death or forgiven for sometimes minor misdemeanour upped the stakes somewhat. Death for mowing your lawn at 8am on a Sunday morning? Those people who didn't completely ignore my posts would often reply "DEATH" and add their own rage about similar situations that they had dealt with. It was a good old rant session for everyone involved.

It certainly raised the odd smile at the time. Clearly no one took the posts seriously. No one expected me to actually put someone to death. Also, I thought I was kind of clever coming up with the "Death or Forgiveness?" angle. Yet, there's the question as to whether any of this helped. Did I feel any less reactive about the situation that had occurred after I had posted? No. When people reacted with their own tales of annoyance was the boil lanced then? No, I was still pissed off. In fact, I was probably more irate than before I posted because I'd given it so much thought. Why did I do that? I look back from my new perspective and I think deep down I wanted the person who'd slighted me in some way to know that they had offended me, to make them feel shame and change their behaviour. Did that happen? Of course not. There was no way the bloke in the BMW who cut me up nine hours ago in the morning rush hour traffic would read my post. And if he did happen upon it he would probably laugh, enjoying having wound someone up.

Did it help the people who read it? Those who saw it and scrolled past probably just shook their head sadly wondering why I was so negative on Facebook. Those that did engage got as wound up as I was. Despite getting a brief dopamine hit as people liked the post and commented on it, it was negatives all around for everyone involved, even if none of us recognised that at the time. It definitely didn't give me a peaceful heart or a feeling of loving kindness towards myself and the world.

Mindfully Saving Myself – One Moment at a Time

Despite the negativity it brought to my, and probably others' life, none of us ever chose forgiveness. It was always death. I can't recall anyone ever saying forgiveness, not even once. No one really thought they were choosing someone's actual death but still no one thought it was better to have empathy. Nobody said that we don't know why the person jumped the queue and was aggressive but perhaps they had low blood sugar and were diabetic and had become hypoglycaemic? We didn't know their lives so why couldn't we forgive and forget instead? No one said anything like that, least of all me.

Since I've come to a mindful way of living, I've started to contemplate that fact. Whilst it might not be all the time, why do many people choose the negative and sometimes aggressive reaction to life's little hiccups? Why don't many people respond with forgiveness and understanding? For me, I just didn't know any other way. As a child and a teenager, I learnt that you had to stand up for yourself, that you needed to protect your own interests. I didn't stick up for myself that often and I was bullied a lot for it which made life very miserable. As I grew up, I started to go the other way. Not violent, but willing to be more verbally aggressive than I had been because I felt I had to so that I could feel safe. It was easier to do if people didn't think you were weak. Forgiveness wasn't something that looked strong. Tolerance of others appeared to be feeble and I couldn't show too much weakness. Forgiving someone, I believed, gave the impression that you were letting someone get away with something and we can't let others get one over us. I learnt that we react with anger to guard ourselves from others.

You see it every day with people shouting abuse at other people as they drive, screaming in rage at the minimum wage shop assistant who has no power. This behaviour is especially prevalent online. On the internet people have taken what I used to do one step further and cause

Twitter storms of negativity about people whose only crime, in some cases, is purely to think differently to them.

So, what would happen if we chose forgiveness instead? Are we letting that person off the hook for what they did? No. In a way that could seem counterintuitive. Surely if you forgive someone they win? But the person actually who benefits from forgiveness is essentially the person doing the forgiving, not the person being forgiven.

If you don't forgive and don't let things go or offer understanding for someone else, even If they have done something wrong, it doesn't really wound them at all, instead it hurts you. You are angry, you are affected physically as your blood pressure rises and you're tense. If you've held onto the resentment for some time just thinking about the person who you believe has done you some harm can instantly cause negative and damaging emotions.

If it happens rarely not forgiving someone, might not affect your mental health too much but if you often don't forgive then you are starting to develop a habit. The habit of not forgiving means that you become ever more sensitive to others' behaviours. You start judging people negatively because no one is really doing what you want, and pressure starts building up over time. There are always other issues to be annoyed with and feel let down about. The more you think that way, the more adept you become at finding yet more drama to get upset about. It starts to affect your sleep as you question why people act the way they do, and you begin suffering mentally. When you become tired it becomes even easier to find fault with almost anything everyone does. You sleepwalk into the habit of not forgiving and begin to really hurt yourself emotionally.

Not forgiving is very harmful. It not only does nothing to change the past and the feelings around it but it affects you in the here

Mindfully Saving Myself – One Moment at a Time

and now. It takes you out of the present moment and you stop experiencing your life directly. Worse still you can see other people, who you hold negative feelings about, at peace with their lives and that can also seem unforgivable. It's the story of many a bitter person.

When you are finally able to become aware of the weight of hatred and anger in your life, and what it is doing to you, then you are able to disconnect from negativity and towards forgiveness. You see that forgiveness helps you. To unconditionally forgive someone, no matter what they have done to you, and to truly mean it is a huge release from the pain that has been generated. It's an escape from the past that you've held on to for so long. Forgiveness can lead to that incredible weight that hanging on to anger generates, slowly evaporating. If you've carried that anger for years, that change can be stark. Your brow unfurrows, the tension that knots your body and mind is eased and you feel a lightness in yourself for the first time in a long time. Finally, you can stop having to think about that terrible wrong that you've held close and have allowed to define you, because it's accepted and forgiven. Suddenly you can turn your attention to the present moment. Forgiveness allows you to live your life.

The person you are forgiving doesn't even need to ask for forgiveness for you to benefit from forgiving. You can just forgive them for yourself, as long as it's genuine. So, that old school mate who turned into a bully and made your life hell twenty years ago doesn't ever have to hear that you have forgiven them, but then you are free from that torment.

It's worth remembering, when trying to embrace forgiveness, that whilst there are some exceptionally bad people in the world, the vast majority of people are good. It's extremely likely that the people who treated you badly are good people who just did a horrible thing. Could they have a good reason for their behaviour? The person who cut you up on the motorway may have just had a call that their mother had been taken sick. The girl in the gym who sat on the same machine for twenty minutes staring at her phone could have social anxiety and she was using her phone to distract herself. The friend turned tormenter may have been a victim of bullying themselves and became a bully as a form of emotional protection. The angry person in the office, who verbally attacks and belittles everyone, may have been abused as a child. The point is we just don't know what has driven anyone to act the way they have. Look inwards at yourself. Is there anyone reading this that can truly say that they have never done a single negative thing to another person at any point in their life? We all have done something to someone else that wasn't nice, that we later regret. Contemplating a person's misdeed towards you, with all that in mind, may further assist to help you forgive the individual.

With forgiveness comes understanding and empathy for others even if they are in the wrong. It doesn't always mean people should not be punished for what they've done. For instance if the person who cut across lanes, caused an accident, they should still be dealt with by the authorities. Yet, despite the necessity of their punishment, you can still offer them forgiveness. You stop carrying any of it as a burden because it was never your weight to lug around in the first place.

I'll admit it's quite difficult to forgive at first, especially after years of learning not to, so start slowly. Begin with the small slights that affect you, such as a person pushing into a queue in front of you. Watch as the feelings of irritation or even anger appear then let the feelings go, as you offer them forgiveness. Keep practicing on the small stuff until the time when you realise that you can do more. Maybe now you have the strength to forgive a friend who only thought about themselves and

Mindfully Saving Myself – One Moment at a Time

offered you no empathy at a difficult point in your life? As you keep practicing forgiveness you will find that, slowly, the serious things that others may have done to you can be forgiven. When you get into those deep hurts that have held you back for years, you can finally say goodbye to the pain you've been holding on to.

But it doesn't end there. Because we're only human and something that someone does is bound to wind us up or hurt us in some way and we may initially react. But if you have been practicing forgiveness, it will become an almost instantaneous process to not attach to the feelings, to watch the internal events unfold and pass and then to forgive the person who did not do right by you. Even when somebody does something that upsets you, the forgiveness kicks in and in the end you may find that things upset you less in the first place.

Forgiveness is a powerful tool for ensuring that you can learn to have a peaceful heart even when the world around you is not. Finally, the emotional impact of the things that people do to you is less and doesn't last as long. We may have been taught, through our life experiences, that forgiveness is weak and standing up for yourself is strong but through our practice we can discover the opposite is true and that it will also help us to be happier with our lives. By forgiving, we are going against the grain and for me, that makes a person who learns to forgive readily, a bit of a warrior.

Stephen McCoull

Why Trying to be a Good Meditator can be Counter Productive

The change in my life that mindfulness caused became very noticeable after a short time of practicing. I'd been lost in anxious and depressive thoughts for so long that I'd forgotten what it was like to think any other way. Then I slowly started to let the negativity go, it was both markedly different from what I was used to and at the same time amazing. I wanted more.

When you start meditating regularly it's quite possible that, like me, you will become aware of some positive effects within the first few weeks. And you may, notice a slight change almost straight away. You may feel calmer or find that you don't follow negative thoughts so easily Perhaps you're slower to react to uncomfortable situations, or maybe you just love that twenty minutes of silence you give yourself each morning and the way they set you up for the day. If you observe any positive changes, it's very likely you'll have the thought that this practice is working.

When something we are doing in life is working and improving things our natural reaction is to do more of it. Put additional effort in. The more you try, the better the outcome. It makes sense in many situations. If increasing your professional skills means you get a

Mindfully Saving Myself – One Moment at a Time

promotion, you consider doing more training so you can expand your current role or take another step up the ladder. You reinforce that strength in your life by putting more effort in and making sure you get better at it.

Then one day you may discover that the calm you've gained from the practice is gone. You can't sit still when you do your morning meditation or you find yourself reacting to what your boss said to you in a meeting. You get upset and question your abilities or your worth, and you can't shake it. If this is the first time this has happened, it's not unusual to wonder what happened to the calm you'd been feeling for the last few weeks, since you started down the mindfulness path. Meditation and mindful living has worked for you until now and now it's not.

Some beginners realise that their lives have been better because of meditation. They know that striving to do better works in other areas of their lives, so by the same logic, meditating more often and for longer should help them gain peace once more. They begin to try harder to be a good meditator because that's the intuitive thing to do. They want to put more energy and focus into mindfulness and meditating and, that way, they think they'll be able to ride out these waves that have put them off balance. Unfortunately, it doesn't quite work like that with meditation. Trying to be better at the practice can be counterproductive.

If you start thinking in that manner, meditation and any positive changes you may have experienced transform from being a practice you undertake into a task you must do to help change your life, which is very different. You stop just sitting and experiencing whatever you find, without judgement and an open awareness. Instead you start expecting a variation, an improvement in life. I know that's what I did when I hit my first meditation bump in the road.

147

Stephen McCoull

If unrecognised, the desire to become a great meditator may become a problem. You want to use the practice to achieve something for yourself, so you put everything into it but now you are grasping for the outcome of inner peace. By increasing your practice with that thought in mind, that grasping for improvement, counterintuitively means that you can become less mindful because that leads to a lack of acceptance of what is. You have a restless sit on the cushion and suddenly you want the meditation to be like it was yesterday. When you react to your boss, you stop accepting what is happening, and instead you want to be calm. You feel you've lost and become frustrated. Wanting your experience to be different to what it is means you've stopped being aware and mindful and have become judgemental. That is the opposite of mindfulness. Mindfulness is about accepting what is, not about longing for something that isn't. f you're currently reactive to the fact that you can't sit still or to what your boss said to you, then that is something you note and observe, rather than pushing it away and creating mindfulness goals you need to achieve.

If you've noticed this happening, the best thing to do is not worry. It's a problem that I've faced and others meditators I've spoken with have had the same experience at some point during their journey too. The way to counter this tendency is to relax, give yourself some space then recognise and let go of any preconceived ideas of what meditation should be and expectations of what you will get out of it. If you think meditation will help you be calmer, then accept that the thought arose but then let it go. If you think meditation will help with your mental health then observe that belief and then release it. Being mindful is simply a case of being aware of what is right now, it's accepting what is happening in your mind when you meditate and also in

148

life away from the cushion. Mindfulness is all about that awareness of what is. It is not about wanting it another way.

If you've been less calm recently to the extent that your sleep has gotten worse or you can't focus so well when you meditate, note that. Note the feelings that it generates in you but without any judgement. There may be a tendency to think "Argh I can't concentrate on the breath for longer than 5 seconds this week" or "Even when I meditate I'm still anxious. I'm never going to get better at this, I'm just useless." Those are just thoughts, conditions of the mind. You can think to yourself "judgement" or another label that makes sense and then let those thoughts go and return to the breath.

The important thing is not to follow the thoughts, and just return to the breath, or whatever anchor you are using, each time you become lost in your mind. If you have to return back to the breath every five seconds then that is fine. If you get lost in thought for a minute or more before realising it and returning to the breath, well that is also fine. The important thing is that you notice you've become lost from the present moment, you bring yourself back and you do it with kindness and acceptance. Each time you come back to this moment, your mental muscles become stronger.

When meditating don't try and push the negative thoughts about how mindfulness may or may not be working away, but don't try to follow them either. Just accept that they are there and don't fight any of it. Completely surrender to your experience. It is what it is.

If you are still under the impression that meditation absolutely quietens your mind, know that it doesn't. Our brains have developed in such a way that they are designed to think. Even if you've been meditating every day for fifty years, thoughts will still occur, that's just how the mind is. This is the reality we need to accept. There will never be a completely quiet day, there will still be occasional mental storms. Yet, through meditation we learn to respond rather than react. If you don't grasp after a calmer mind then you will very likely find your mind will get calmer. Try and remember this if you are struggling with self-doubt.

I've been meditating daily for well over three years now and fairly regularly for more than 18 months before that. I'm still very early in my lifelong mindfulness journey and I have meditations when I can't focus on my breath for long at all, and I find myself having to repeatedly return to the breath every few seconds. Other times I'm really peaceful and any thoughts that do arise I immediately become aware of. Whether the mind is busy or calm, it is what it is and I accept that. Acceptance of how it is right now on the cushion really is crucial.

One problem you may come across is that you have an expectation of what this practice should look like. In my practice I tend to do unguided meditations but one morning I listened to a guided meditation by meditation instructor Jeff Warren. It was a session in a series he named "How to Meditate". I was struck by the thought that, whilst he's saying a lot of things that appear to be very different from what other instructors I've listened to or read say, he was really talking about the same practice with all its different facets.

It made me think back over the history of my own practice over the last few years. I realise that this is what has helped me develop this practice in a way that I have no expectations and do not try to meditate the 'right way' or meditate well or whatever. I just sit and accept the experience. What has helped me to practice in that way is discovering all these different viewpoints, or methods, of the same thing. I've listened to and read about so many different ways of viewing and carrying out this practice. From the highly spiritual Theravada Buddhist monk, Ajahn

Mindfully Saving Myself – One Moment at a Time

Sumedho, all the way through to the non-spiritual and very scientific, Mark Williams and many more in-between. Whilst they are all talking about practicing meditation, at first glance you could be mistaken to think that they are talking about something very different, because they each practice in their own styles. What you need to keep in mind is that no matter how they word it, or how I explain it, they are still all talking about mindfulness. They are all speaking about being present for your life. This one right now. That understanding can help you to not fixate on goals or outcomes and trying harder to be better.

This is a journey of a lifetime so having goals, trying to be better than you were before actually boxes you in and limits your ability to discover more. It ultimately stops you being mindful. There's so many teachers out there, whether in online videos, books, or on meditation apps. My advice is to get as many different perspectives to the practice as you can. You could then find, that you will take out what works for you and the practice will become your own. Your practice may look slightly different to how I practice mindfulness or how a Buddhist in Sri Lanka or Japan practices mindfulness, but it's still the practice and you're doing the practice without expectations. Once you find yourself in that space, keep searching, keep learning, but keep any anticipation for results out of it.

I think the fact there's so many ways of practicing being present is what makes this practice such a good fit for many people. There's no dogma to it. It is what it is for the person doing it. There's no right or wrong way to do it and the practice will almost certainly develop and change with time as you gain experience. What works for one person doesn't always work for someone else. One person might meditate on their breath, another person may meditate on the noise around them and a third person may meditate on a different point of concentration every

151

Stephen McCoull

day. One person may gain insights into their past behaviours, another may learn to be present in their work and learn to enjoy it, whilst other people may develop tranquillity when there was none before. There is no right or wrong way of practicing, there's no right or wrong outcome, so trying to be the best meditator with the finest technique, to iron out that bad day you had, will take you away from true awareness and learning to live our lives as they are right now.

Mindfully Saving Myself – One Moment at a Time

Not Self

In my quest to learn more about mindfulness I started Googling the word "Buddhism" a lot. I found Wikipedia and other similar pages gave me basic information about Buddhism and aspects of it but I didn't really get a feel for the spiritual side of what appeared to be a very spiritual religion (or philosophy, as many people consider Buddhism).

Desperate for more, I changed my search to "Buddhist locations UK" and that is how I found the Amaravati monastery I mentioned earlier. That's where I first heard about the monk, Ajahn Sumedho.

It turns out that Ajahn Sumedho is an American who had gone to Thailand in the sixties and had become a monk under Ajahn Chah, a well-known Theravada Buddhist teacher in the Thai Forest tradition. Years later, in the 1980s, Ajahn Chah had asked him to relocate to the UK to help spread their tradition of Buddhism here and that's exactly what Ajahn Sumedho did. After some time in the UK he helped open the Amaravati Monastery, became its abbot and remained so until 2010, when he returned to Thailand. The monastery's website was full of his teachings, both recordings of dhamma talks and the written word.

As well as the "Four Noble Truths" mentioned earlier, I also read "The Way It Is" and then I listened to as many of his dhamma talk podcasts that life would allow me to.

Stephen McCoull

I was confronted by various ideas that I'd never come across before. Sometimes what he taught made sense, as if he told me something that I've always known but never acknowledged in my life. Some of them, however, I didn't really understand at all. Fortunately, Ajahn Sumedho has this amazingly mellow yet deep voice, with a soft American accent, that is almost hiding from the listener. His voice just drew me in. It made listening to him very easy. So even when I was initially confused I continued to listen anyway.

The first concept I had to get my head around was that attachment leads to suffering, covered earlier in the book. The next idea that initially confounded me was the Theravada Buddhist notion that there is no self: that what happens within and directly to you is Not Self, that the thoughts in your head are Not Self, our body is Not Self, your feelings, your passions, your likes, your dislikes and anything else associated with you is Not Self, the fact you are a millionaire is Not Self, the fact you are poor and have to work three jobs, is Not Self, the pain you feel if you break your leg is Not Self, even being a monk or not being a monk is Not Self. There is no self.

Unlike other religions, which have strict dogmas and explanations, Ajahn Sumedho didn't provide any detailed dogmatic descriptions about Buddhism. He just advised the listeners to explore what he was explaining for themselves, so that the realisation could be discovered and understood first hand. Even though I was drawn to the idea of no dogma, of discovering Buddhism for myself, as a person who likes facts, the lack of specifics was somewhat disconcerting. I Googled online and no matter how much I looked I didn't have any more luck getting a more detailed explanation from other sources. It turns out that the Buddha wasn't too descriptive about dogma either.

Mindfully Saving Myself – One Moment at a Time

Not Self? What on earth did Not Self mean? I wondered if there not being a self meant I didn't exist at all. If somehow all this experience was a kind of make believe, almost as if I were a dream within the consciousness of some other being from a spiritual realm I was unaware of. As nice an idea as that sounds, especially to someone who still had very vivid memories of what depression and anxiety was like, I didn't believe any of that for a minute. If I bang my arm on a door frame by accident, it hurts and I yell out in pain. If I don't eat, I get hungry. When I finally do eat I feel physically satisfied. If I didn't exist I wouldn't feel pain or hunger, or anything else for that matter.

So, whilst I was confused with ever expanding questions generating in my mind, I knew that mindfulness was a positive thing in my life. I'd witnessed it first-hand so I kept exploring because I understood that mindfulness came from Buddhism. A religion which had survived for centuries just through being passed on orally after the Buddha's death, before it was ever put to paper. The philosophies had crossed over 2,500 years to reach me. There had to be something to this Not Self malarkey that I was missing.

I had always said I was not a man of faith. Incredibly, at this point I finally became a man of faith. Not a blind faith in that everything is "Not Self", whatever that meant, but a faith that exploring Not Self, as Ajahn Sumedho suggested I did, wouldn't be anything other than a positive thing to do, whatever I found out through my investigation. Therefore, I kept reading and listening and whenever I came across a mention of Not Self I gave it some more thought. I contemplated it. Sometimes, many in fact, I didn't even contemplate it, I just sat with the thought of Not Self as a point of meditation.

Slowly, over a period of many months, an idea of what Not Self is started to develop in my mind, almost as an understanding that was beyond communication. That said, I will try my best to explain what I discovered. This is purely how I understand it. It is how I've applied it to my life in a way that has led to me having greater peace with how things are.

How many of us have looked at another person and thought "that person is such an angry person" or "that man is one chilled out bloke" or "that lady is so giving" or "that person is just stupid" and "how incredibly clever that professor is" and sometimes not as pleasant things? I know I have thought all sorts about people. What I am equally sure about is that both positive and negative views I have held about others similar thoughts and opinions are held by other people about me. I have been told by people that I am always chilled out, always angry, always over emotional, always lacking in emotion, smart, stupid, confident, shy, scared, brave and many other things.

How can I be all of those things? How can one person be so sure that I am always an angry man when another can be so sure I am always a happy person?

I always saw myself as a happy, positive person. I had had years of depression and anxiety, which sometimes brought out very negative behaviours in me, but deep down my natural state was one of positivity, despite any mental torment I may have felt. I put the fact some people thought very badly about me down as a result of me being a Marmite person, someone people either really liked or detested. However, through my contemplation of Not Self I've come to realise that is a wrong view of how things are.

People have so many different views of me because I have been all of those people. I have been angry, I have been happy, I have been caring, I have been callous and I've been everything else people have labelled me as being. In fact, there have been times when I've made the

Mindfully Saving Myself – One Moment at a Time

same judgements about myself because all those negative and positive thoughts and emotions have all gone through my head. Being a man who has worn his heart on his sleeve, means that I have expressed all those emotions to the world around me with very little filter.

It's important to remember that the vast majority of people have biases, as we all do.Some people prefer to focus on the negative things that they experience. Those individuals spotted my negative traits and then applied those prejudices to their overall view of me as a person. Other people, with a positive outlook, did the same.

That got me thinking whether that means we are all of these things, because we've all been those types of people at one point or another. If that were true then how could Not Self make any sense? Doesn't this prove the opposite of Not Self, that instead we are everything? All things are self?

I don't believe any person is capable of being everything, that's not my experience. What it does show is that nothing within us is permanent. If you get angry, at a person or event, we are not angry forever, eventually the rage will pass and will be replaced by another emotion. Maybe you'll be happy next, or excited. Or perhaps there will be a period of time when you don't feel anything at all. Are any of these emotions or feelings "you"? Or are you the awareness behind these mental events? Are you the observer of everything that occurs within you rather than what happens itself?

I've come to realise that I am not the anger that fills my mind on occasions, but I am what experiences it. The anger is not me, the anger is Not Self. It will arise at some point, it may change in intensity, either strengthening or weakening, and then, after a period of time, it will disappear altogether. And yet the awareness that witnessed the anger still exists. Emotions are Not Self because they never stay the same. Yes, we can get drawn into them, becoming reactive and following them into thought cycles, but if we don't identify with them, as we're learning to do, we can come to the realisation, through direct experience, that they are not us. We can just watch them play out without getting too involved.

When I started looking at Not Self like this, through the lens of impermanence, it suddenly made perfect sense. Like many things I've learnt on this mindfulness journey, it was knowledge that I had always known deep down but I had never unlocked that understanding until I started my practice. I am not the negative things in me, such as being sad, angry, or being less than clever. But equally I am not the positive things in me either, so happiness, excitement, those rare moments of intelligence, none of them are a self. I can experience those emotions, but they don't make up who I am, if I choose not to associate myself with them.

Some of you, as I did when I first thought about Not Self like this, will not like that second to last sentence. You will want to be the positive emotions, you want the happiness and you want everything good to be you, so this idea of Not Self doesn't fill you with any joy. At this point I'll remind you that attachment can lead to suffering. Wanting to be defined by the positive mental states we experience, the happy person or the clever person, is attaching to the idea of positivity. It will lead to suffering because it's impossible to only experience positive emotions. At some point there will be negative emotions and all those mental conditions will cease and be replaced with something else in the end. Think back over your mood over the last day, week or month. You will see, from your experiences, that you do not have the same emotions every day. One day there will be sadness, or you'll just be completely off

Mindfully Saving Myself – One Moment at a Time

your game at work, you will not be that happy, bright person you were last week or visa versa.

How does this view of Not Self help anyone? If you've ever suffered from a mental illness, or just lean towards certain emotions, such as anger or sadness, because they've become patterns of thought, then you will know that thoughts generate further similar feelings.

Someone who is angry more often than not may be in the car when someone cuts them up, and anger appears. Then they get home musing over the incident on the road half an hour before but someone has blocked the driveway so they have to park on the street. Anger builds again. They go to the local shop but the shop doesn't have what they wanted, more rage and memories about that shop not stocking what they needed last week arise feeding their fury. Maybe they shout at the owner in frustration as they leave the store. Anger, anger, and more anger. It gets to the point when even mildly inconvenient events will automatically generate extreme wrath. If this becomes a regular feature of a person's thought process, that can lead to their experience of life being mainly negative. In the worst cases, following the same emotions regularly, can take them down the route that has depression and anxiety at the end. This could be thoughts about everyone and everything getting in their way and making their life difficult or thinking this is their lot and that this always happens to them. Imagine, if each time anger arose in them, instead of feeding it they just let the rage go? Would their life, that day, be better for it? The shop keeper's day certainly would be.

Scientists have started to show, through incredible brain scanning, that thinking a certain way sets specific mental pathways in your brain, which makes it easier for your brain to think those thoughts again. When we were all hunter-gatherers, who needed to react quickly to a sabre tooth tiger deciding to attack, this would have been a great

Stephen McCoull

evolutionary leap for humankind. It's not so good when our greatest threat is whether the local shop has stocked our favourite packet of wine gums.

So, we can use this idea of Not Self as a tool to help us detach ourselves from those thoughts and feelings. When our boss unfairly attributes one of our successes to a colleague, we can't stop the frustration appearing, but we can observe it and realise it's Not Self, it's just a temporary happening in the mind. Instead of reacting to the anger, we can recognise that it is just a passing emotion, and not increase it by thinking about what happened more. Understanding that the emotion isn't us gives us the ability to choose not react to it. That recognition and just standing back from it is like meditating but in real life, away from the cushion. The moment you can do that, rather than following the anger and exploding in a rage, is extraordinary and you feel a peace inside.

Not reacting to the emotions that arise within you can make some people question whether you become passive, but it doesn't mean that at all. Sometimes, conditions appear in our mind for a reason and some kind of response is required. If your boss has mistakenly attributed one of your successes to someone else, then it might require you to say something. Now, imagine saying something to your boss if you're reacting to the anger in your mind? Then think how different that conversation with your boss will be, if you've stopped for a moment, observed the anger, watched it wax and wane before disappearing, and then speak to your boss? Which scenario is going to have the most positive outcome for you?

If you use the understanding that the anger is Not Self to not attach to the emotion, even if your boss still doesn't recognise their mistake, anger hasn't grown within you and taken you over. When you start to be the awareness behind thoughts and emotions, it is a real step in the direction of finding inner peace, even when things externally aren't great. The same is true with positive events to. Either way it helps you to directly experience every moment.

Remember what I mentioned earlier about scientists discovering that our mental pathways become ingrained? Well, we can change those pathways. When we start recognising anger and not reacting to it, that anger pathway weakens and the one that allows us to become the observer strengthens. At first this will be a difficult practice. I don't pretend it's an easy one for me, but it is definitely much easier than it used to be due to negative pathways fading and the pathways that lead to being the observer are strengthening. My experience of life becomes more positive, more peaceful with each passing week, no matter what is going on.

I mentioned earlier that Not Self can equate to other things too. I would be surprised if you didn't have thoughts and opinions about how you look, how healthy you are, your wealth or worth, what your job says about you among other things. These too are just mental conditions that are Not Self. The thought that you are ugly doesn't mean that you are ugly, it's no surprise that people who do not attach to such thoughts can come across as beautiful, no matter their physical appearance. Their peace with how things are just shines through in undefined ways that people can detect yet cannot really put a finger on. They just know there's something ineffable about that person.

Lots of people do attach to the thought that their bodies define them. The body is Self. I've been pretty fortunate with my body so far, I'm very fit for my age because I have exercised a lot over the years, so it would be very easy for me to identify with my body. But our bodies are Not Self, our bodies will age and decline as the years pass. The awareness, however, that experiences my body through all its stages of life, hasn't changed. It doesn't matter whether I can run ten miles a day or whether I'm in a wheelchair, I can still note how things are right now and not attach to my body. I don't have to make it who I am. It is Not Self. Whatever we think defines us, no matter how real it may feel, are all just views that will change. The thing that doesn't change is the observer of all that is being experienced. I have come to the conclusion that whilst everything is Not Self, the self is really the consciousness behind everything. So, we do exist, life is not some strange dream.

This discovery is how I use the idea of Not Self to jump out of the thoughts in my mind and become the spectator and not be driven into reactivity. I just tell myself that I am not defined by anything, but that I am alive in this moment. Understanding Not Self is another tool which has completely changed my life for the better by helping me become more aware of what is going on. Greater awareness, in turn, had led to a lessening of judgement, both of myself and everyone around me. It leads to a far more peaceful heart.

I understand it may still be a concept that is confusing, so I will give the advice that Ajahn Sumedho gives to his readers and listeners. What I have explained is just what I have come to understand about Not Self. Not Self is something for you to take away and consider, to contemplate and, just sit with. You need to come to understand Not Self from your perspective, equate it to your experience, and know it for yourself.

Accepting the Rain

I woke up one morning to extremely hard rain. Despite a deluge having been predicted for the entire day in Southern England, a little "Urgh, I hate the rain, I really hate the rain" thought popped into my head. I felt sullen knowing that my drive to work would involve so much water and it occurred to me that for a person who hates rain I live in the wrong country. The glumness almost turned into sadness at that thought but I suddenly realised I was suffering and it wasn't the rain that was making me feel bad but my mind. That recognition was enough to help me detach myself from the mental swirl of rain based negativity and be aware that this was the part of me that grasps for something that isn't here. It was the lack of acceptance voice that has dominated a lot of my life.

Now that I was aware of how I was thinking instead of following that negative line of thought I did the opposite of running from the present moment, I embraced the rain. I got in my car and started my journey, as I often do with a gratitude practice "I am grateful for this rain. I'm grateful for the water it provides. I'm grateful that it sustains us. I'm grateful that it contrasts the sun". Once my gratitude practice was over I would have normally turned on the radio or Spotify but that day I left the music off and just listened to the rain on the car. I needed to be mindful of driving, so I couldn't meditate formally, but I kept the sound in focus. I observed as the sound increased or decreased as my speed changed, I noticed how the rain danced on the windows after the wipers had passed by. I was as mindful as I could be. A few times during that 30 minute drive thoughts stole in but when that happened I put my attention into my body and noticed the feeling in my belly associated with the thoughts, letting whatever was there go without judgement and returned to the rain and the road. I felt alive and part of something bigger as I drove. It was a wonderful experience.

In my office there were loads of frazzled people, having had a tough drive into work, hating every minute of it but my experience was different. I neither liked or disliked the rain, it just was. I accepted it without judgement. Strangely, I felt rested after a drive that may have left me feeling as drained as everyone else, if I'd not accepted the situation.

It's so obvious now that I've been on a mindful path for a while, but for the majority of my life I had no idea that I didn't have to follow my thoughts, that I could be separate from them and that my thoughts were often so negative whether about the rain or more serious matters.

Mindfulness can't bring you happiness. It can't stop external things, good or bad, from happening. There will still be upset, still be happiness, anger or whatever. Mindfulness can't change any of those things but it can change whether you cling to the good parts of life or have aversion to the bad. It is within our power to live in peace, with an experience of being connected, even with the rain, if only we allow ourselves to untangle our being from our thoughts and reactions to the world around us.

Turning Nostalgia into a Useful Tool

Earlier in the book I talked about how my depression affected me at every level. A lot of my issues stemmed from the past affecting the present moment. There are many ways in which the past can. One of them is nostalgia. Nostalgia is defined on Wikipedia as "a sentimentality for the past, typically for a period or place with happy personal associations".

Nostalgia has the ability to strike a person at pretty much any time. I've spent a lot of time being nostalgic for times that no longer exist. Absolutely anything can set it off but for me two things are more likely to trigger it than anything else and are most easily generated by my sense of smell and hearing.

The sense of smell is a ruthless covert operator for nostalgia. You're walking along the street when someone wearing the perfume or aftershave of a former lover passes you and just a tiny whiff of it enters your nostrils. Suddenly, wham, you're back there with that person even if it's been twenty years since you've set eyes on each other. The memories of meals you've had, intimate times you've shared, journeys you've taken together, arguments, conversations, their laugh, all come rushing in. As

Stephen McCoull

the smell fades and the memories start to dissipate, you try to grab onto them in your mind, almost desperate not to lose those precious memories but they become hazy and it all disappears in a fog. Now there's this weight in your chest that stays beyond the life of those memories. Strong emotions fill you, not positive but you can't say they're negative either. All you know is that you feel something strong that you are drawn to. The experience has elicited a reaction that life right now doesn't give you and you develop a strong hankering for a time that has long since passed. Things were better back then and you feel sad that they aren't like that now-a-days. Maybe you felt more alive at that time, more exciting, more sensual, more vibrant, more everything. Nostalgia tells you it was so much better back then, it really was.

The same is true with music. I hadn't heard Ride's song "Leave Them All Behind" for at least fifteen years when it came on the radio a few years back. There's a thick bass line that starts the song, drawing you in, expectantly waiting for the guitars to kick in and when there's a slight mellowing of the song and you start to wonder where the guitar is, suddenly a heavy guitar riff almost overwhelms you. The hairs on the back of your neck stand up and your senses are assaulted by that dense "shoe gaze" song that you once loved. I was only 18 when the song came out at the end of winter in early 1992, and all memories from those times came flooding back. The sixth form parties I'd been to and friends I'd not seen since. The girls I kissed and even other people who had kissed each other. How I hated school in a way I thought was quite cool at the time. The sense of freedom that was developing in me and my then still joyful use of alcohol to enjoy everything. Wow, those were good times. I had so much freedom, and no responsibilities. I partied all the time without any consequences.

That familiar feeling appeared in my chest, a feeling of longing for that moment, regret it was gone and a real desire to experience it just one more time, because life isn't like that now, and somehow it's just not as vivid as it was back then. Then the song changed, and the memories faded, and I was just left with a sense of loss, wanting to experience the memories and feelings for just a little longer. I believed the present moment was nothing compared to those times, although, the melancholy I felt was better than feeling nothing at all.

Nostalgia had been a regular companion, going through bouts so many times in my life and always with the same result: unhappiness combined with the knowledge that life now is different and wishing life were how it used to be.

Although, until I started to meditate and practice mindfulness, I never properly explored nostalgia, I had been very aware of how powerful an emotion it was. Everyone appears to experience nostalgia. No matter who people are, they all have a time from their life, especially their youth, which brought back memories of what they felt were better times and that they really missed. I remember my mum driving me when I was a kid, also hearing a song on the radio and exclaiming how much it reminded her of her youth and then driving quietly with a wistful look on her face as it played. There are old men who wistfully talk about how it was all fields or woods around here and how they climbed trees where now there's a supermarket. Middle aged people are known to do something very similar as time gives their past a rosy hue.

The other thing I noted was that, no matter what made you nostalgic, it was very unlikely to make anyone else nostalgic and vice versa. When my mum said that song reminded her of her youth it did nothing for me other than make me think that the music that I was listening to at the time was much better than what she had listened to as a kid. If I found the perfumes that provoke a nostalgic reaction in me and got someone else to smell it, it was unlikely that smell would do anything for them.

As I've got older, with more years to look back on than I used to, I've began to notice something else about nostalgia. Nostalgia doesn't show us the truth about our past. In fact, nostalgia is a big fat liar. I would hear a song from a time that I knew was bad, maybe a time of a break up, when I knew I was devastated, inconsolable and just wanting the pain to end, there was nostalgia trying to convince me that those times past were great. Or I'd smell a distinctive perfume of a former colleague and I'd get nostalgic for a job I knew utterly bored me to the point where I had to leave it. Nostalgia was making me feel that that those times were somehow something to be missed and longed for. I'd feel sad because I was missing a time in my life that I hated at the time. It's important to recognise that nostalgia twists memories.

The more I understood that, the easier it was to see that nostalgia was deceiving me nearly every time. Even the strong pull of those school days that I ached for when I heard that Ride song were a lie. Yes, there were good times, parties, dancing and meeting all sorts of people but it was also when depression, which would blight my life for decades started setting in, unbeknownst at the time. I'd endured years of bullying and, even though by the time I turned 18 it had ended, I had zero confidence. My school hadn't supported me. I drank and took drugs to counteract the feelings of worthlessness I had and would end up feeling even worse the next day. I'd end up kissing loads of girls at various parties because I wanted connection with people. But these drunken brief get-togethers left me feeling more disconnected than ever. Even when surrounded by people, I would often feel overwhelmingly lonely and isolated. I was lost. I didn't go to university because I did not

Mindfully Saving Myself – One Moment at a Time

value myself at all, had zero idea of what I wanted to do, and was incapable of making a decision about my life. I ended up working in a restaurant for a while, which I hated, until I finally took a business and finance course which I wasn't thrilled with either. Yet, when nostalgia arrives, it tells me that these were the best days of my life.

It didn't matter that these times were, at best, not quite as shiny as I remembered them, and at worst were downright awful, because nostalgia made me want them anyway. Even once I realised what nostalgia did, how it twisted the truth and served it up as a terrible narcotic, it didn't stop me feeling it.

When I started meditating it helped me be able to see things for what they are. But I already knew nostalgia was a great deceiver so I had a head start on it. As I used my developing mindfulness skills, suddenly nostalgia became like anything else that happened in my brain, an impermanent mental condition. As surely as it starts, it will fade away and you can move on. So I started to notice nostalgia and observe it for what it was without getting involved with it, just like anything else that disrupts my peace. As I did this, nostalgia began to lose its power on me.

Quite early in my journey into mindfulness and my recovery from depression and anxiety, I started to use nostalgia for my own aims, using it against itself and turning it into a tool for improving my mental health. There were times in my life that I had never processed and had run and hidden from, which ultimately led me deeper into depression and anxiety. So I put specific records on that were thoroughly tied up with those times.

Almost everything I had done since the summer of 2005 was an unconscious attempt to escape the pain of a failed relationship. I had avoided it for almost ten years but at the beginning of 2015 I faced it head on. Yet, when I slowly came to mindfulness in early 2016, I still had

Stephen McCoull

more of the grief to process, so I decided to use nostalgia as a device to help me finally accept everything that had happened.

Moby's album "Play" became huge in 2000, after one of its tracks, "Porcelain", featured in the 1999 film, "The Beach". After the success of that record, the rest of the album was played in bars, in clubs, on TV adverts. It was impossible to escape. It was being played in Malaysia when I met my ex-fiancée. We both ended up buying the album and when we moved in together it was regularly played on car journeys and in the house. In my mind all the music from that album is completely entwined with both when we met and our entire relationship. For years I couldn't listen to the music because of the depth of nostalgia and emotions I felt. Just hearing a brief fragment of any of the songs by accident on the radio in the car could lead me to crying as I drove, hoping it would pass by the time I got home.

Knowing things had been changing, one day in 2016 I decided to put the album on. I just sat and listened to it without any other distractions. As the music played, I focused on it intently as nostalgia did its job. The excitement, the happiness, the pain of loss I had felt, the utter sorrow that had enveloped me for weeks after our breakup, all the emotions presented themselves. Despite everything I had come to understand about nostalgia, about its pure deception, through the music, it gave me the yearning for those times. Rather than react to it by following that thirst for that failed relationship, I was able to observe it all without getting drawn in. Everything I had felt, the good and the bad, was laid before me to pick apart and look at without any judgement. The worst part of that experience was the pain I had felt. But I faced it. I looked it square in the eye and, as tears flowed down my face I found a peace and acceptance with what happened, that I had never had up until that point. As I've found with everything that I have mindfully faced, I

Mindfully Saving Myself – One Moment at a Time

realised that everything I had run from for so many years had no power over me when I didn't turn away and try to escape. Making many mistakes that were damaging not only to me but others, and had ultimately led to a period of time in which I'd had several breakdowns, none of these events had any sway. The trauma I had caused by running from that sad time in 2005 ran deep, so on three separate occasions I sat and listened to "Play". I know it was three times because the third time I listened, no strong emotions came up at all. It became clear I had finally released the pain that had infected my life for too long. I had accepted the trauma was there and that I didn't need to get away from it anymore. Mindfully using nostalgia to stir up all my emotions had completed the work that I had started more than a year before in therapy. The decision to use nostalgia was actually the greatest leap forward I had during this mindful journey. With it I had accepted and therefore negated a major root cause for all my misery. As the summer of 2016 approached, I moved away from depression and was finally entering recovery.

The thing is that I still feel nostalgia now. It hasn't gone away. It appears hardwired into our heads. Yet, when I hear music, nostalgia no longer lies to me like it did before. I can still see the memories it brings, I can reminisce about what took place but I don't view these times as better and want to experience them again. I can see the past fully, the good and the bad. That terrible feeling in my chest is no longer there, more just a love of great music that no longer gets made. I even saw Ride play live in May 2018. I went with a friend from my teenage years. We had a couple of beers, listened to great music but I had no desire to go back in time because nostalgia is no longer a cheat that offers up falsehoods to me. It's a friend that helps me process and be present when memories do come up.

Stephen McCoull

Mindfully Breaking my Attachment to Alcohol

In the UK we have a thing called Stoptober where people are encouraged to give up something that harms them for the entire month of October. It could be smoking, it could be overeating, anything you consider bad for you. There's a similar message for January aimed specifically at alcohol consumption, with calls to do a Dry January for charity or just yourself.

This means that there are two months of the year when people in the UK are encouraged to look after themselves better. Even smokers and heavy drinkers like a challenge so as you can imagine all over social media people are extolling the joys of giving this or that up and how they are getting on throughout the challenge. You have the people who can do it easily, but are asking for donations to specific charities for their efforts, and there's others bemoaning how hard it is, but saying how they will stick it out to the end, even if it feels like they're dying inside. In some cases it can come across as virtue signalling but for many it's a real attempt to improve their health and their lives.

I used to laugh at this concept and in fact, I felt great disdain towards it. People going on about Stoptober or Dry January on

Mindfully Saving Myself – One Moment at a Time

Facebook annoyed the hell out of me. Life is hard enough already, why give up things that make life more bearable? Why try to make other people who haven't done it feel bad about not doing it? I used to make social media posts in January about "retoxing the detox" as I hit the beers and laughed at those clean-living people who tried to look after themselves. Back then, whilst understanding that too much alcohol was very bad, I didn't realise the harm I had been doing to myself for years. I was adamant I was never going to ever give up these vices because I liked them and they made me who I was.

That was before I realised how messed up I was. Before I started to recognise the correlation between my drinking and my poor moods. Mindful living helped me wake up to lots of truths about my life and my dysfunctional relationship with alcohol was one of them. By October 2016, the realisation that booze wasn't the greatest thing given to man was taking hold, so I decided that I would take part in Stoptober and abstain from booze for the entire month. I didn't really think I could do it. Even though my drinking had decreased a lot, it was still very much part of my life. I didn't mention it online in some big announcement and would only talk about it if I were out with people and they were wondering why I wasn't having a drink.

In 2016 I'd only just started my mindfulness practice a few months before and I didn't meditate daily at that point. I knew my drinking was bad for both my physical and mental health. It's one of many reasons why I left my ex-wife. I knew I couldn't cut down whilst in that relationship. I wish I could say that the decision not to drink in October 2016 was due to my mindfulness practice but I would be lying. Despite knowing how my mental health suffered due to alcohol, my immediate concern was about the physical damage I had been doing to myself. That's why I wanted a break.

Stephen McCoull

The 1st October hit and I stopped drinking. I would like to say it was easy and everyone should try it because it's not as daunting as you may imagine, but that would be another lie. It was anything but easy. In fact, it was downright difficult and the calendar appeared to hang on each day of that month for an entire week. If I was being honest, during October 2016 I felt as if I was missing out. The days and weeks dragged on as I was unable to indulge in my vice of choice.

I got through October 2016 by pure willpower and willpower can never last. I eagerly waited for November, without considering that that desire demonstrated how much of a hold drink had on me. The strange thing is I really can't remember my first drink on 1st November. But I did settle back into drinking again with some ease, albeit I drank slightly less than before October. I do remember thinking, as I crossed the finishing line, that it felt like I'd gone through a marathon of sorts and that I'd never do it again because it was just too challenging to accomplish. At some deep unconscious level I still tried to convince myself that drink was not a problem.

But as I found out, you should never say never. It was about this time I started to realise that mindfulness was a massively positive thing for me. I had begun to meditate more and more often. My awareness of what was going on within me and had always been going on was expanding. Slowly, I started to see that everything that was happening inside my mind was including the need to drink, a mental construct. I started to be able to observe the thoughts about alcohol without making them me.

I began to see that I would want to drink when I was bored. I learnt that alcohol helped me put up with situations that I found dull, whether that was being on my own at home or at a party where I had the same conversations with the same people over the years. T The alcohol

Mindfully Saving Myself – One Moment at a Time

didn't really liven things up, the boredom was still there. I just stopped caring about it once I had a few drinks. I could see that I would drink when I felt awkward in social situations and when I felt that I wasn't good enough, or that the people I was with were better than me in some way. I thought that it made me feel a little more relaxed in the company of others but, like the boredom, the awkwardness was still there, just dulled.

Drinking helped me when I wanted to dance. It didn't help me dance *well*, but at least I thought I *could* dance once I'd drank. I drank when I wanted to be emotionally close to people. I drank when I thought about the past. I drank when I thought about the things I could have done better, the things I could have done. I drank when I was worried about the future. I suppose the real reason I drank was because I was very unhappy. As I observed my inner workings, I saw that I had thought drink had been helping me in a variety of ways, but all it did was make me live some kind of fake existence with fake emotions.

I was starting to see that I drank to deal with many issues, and no matter how I might have convinced myself that drink helped, none of these issues were ever fixed. In fact, many of them were made worse. I'd say or do the wrong thing. I'd treat people badly or I'd get treated badly. I'd get confused about my emotions. Life was ultimately just a big blur of blocked emotions and false promises. I often couldn't recall what had happened the night before, wondering what I'd done, often feeling great shame, even though the events from the previous night were at best a blur. Drinking the way I had been gave me nothing and took away what little peace of mind I had.

My new awareness made me attuned to my thoughts about booze and with practice and time I was able to see them for what they were, just thoughts. If I was bored and the idea of a drink came up I watched it with interest and then I decided not to drink. When I say that I decided that gives the impression that there was more thought into it than there was. Just the act of recognising I wanted a drink because I was bored was enough to stop the thought. As my awareness and understanding of myself increased, drinking less became easier.

Whilst my increased awareness of what had been driving me to drink had a huge impact on my alcohol consumption, two other things happened around this time as well that helped. The first one was meeting my partner, Marta. Marta has been a positive influence in my life in many ways but there were two particular things about her that had a beneficial impact on my drinking. The first was that, whilst she liked to have a drink, it wasn't a necessary thing for her. She could take it or leave it. This made not drinking much easier when I was around her. Secondly, Marta accepted me exactly as I was. She made no demands of me, other than to be open and honest with her and be myself. With some former partners, even if I had said I didn't want to drink, they would insist I drink. In my marriage there were actually demands that I drink and my attempts at abstinence would lead to arguments and insults. Marta did no such thing. If she wanted a drink and I didn't it wasn't a problem. There was never a request that I join her with an alcoholic drink. In fact, if I didn't want a drink then she tended to decide not to either, even though I equally had made no demands on her to drink or not.

In late 2016 was the first time in more than a decade when I felt that it was completely up to me whether I drank or not. I found that I often chose not to. It helped me recognise that I was in control of alcohol.

The second important thing that happened was that I purchased a flat. My divorce had been finalised in March 2016 and I had been looking for a property to buy since then, so I could have my children stay

Mindfully Saving Myself – One Moment at a Time

over in my own place (until then I'd had them at my parents' house). Unfortunately, I hadn't come out of the divorce with much of anything, but after my solicitor's fees were paid off I had a very small deposit for a flat. In December that year I managed to secure the right mortgage and the right priced property and I became a flat owner.

At the time I really disliked the fact I had almost zero money each month after my all my expenses, but that actually helped me in so many ways. Immediately after buying the flat I was so cash strapped that I often had to eat dinner with my parents because I just couldn't afford to feed myself every day. The times I didn't see my parents I would sometimes skip meals or eat tiny portions just to stop the hunger. Even if I had money for food, I would sometimes skip a meal so I had chance to socialise once in the month. With the money I did have for food I'd buy the cheapest food I could find and cook huge curries and put them in the freezer to last me until the next pay day. It was a tough time but many people have it much tougher and I'm so grateful that it gave me an opportunity to really face myself because I didn't have enough money for alcohol anyway. It could have been a stressful time and in some ways it was, but I made the best of it. When I was bored in my flat, I couldn't afford to drink, even if I wanted to. I'd watch that little thought that a drink would ease the boredom and instead I would meditate. When I fancied a drink because I felt sad, I would meditate. Even when I was hungry and had nothing else to eat that day, I would meditate on it. I had so many points of focus to meditate on, so my practice blossomed, maybe because of those hard times. My meditation practice helped me recognise what alcohol was to me, a method for escaping the now and blocking my awareness of life, the booze lost its power. During 2017, without any effort, my drinking slowly reduced as I just didn't fancy it anymore even when I could afford it. Living in the moment and having awareness means that when you have the desire to do things like drink, or anything else that takes you out of the moment, you don't have to follow those thoughts.

When October 2017 came around I had a completely different Stoptober experience from the willpower trial of the previous year. I had had an occasional glass of wine the previous month, so I was still giving something up, but I just stopped drinking for October without any effort. I had spent so much of the year examining my thoughts and drivers around drink, that the idea to drink rarely even popped into my head. October came and went and I still didn't drink. I went through nearly all of November without a drink as well and made it all the way to my work's Christmas party, which was held on the last weekend of November, without a drink.

I didn't really want a drink then either but alcohol is such a big part of British social life I felt that I should have one , just to be social and not make other people feel awkward. It wouldn't matter because I no longer wanted to drink to escape the present moment but I failed to spot that these thoughts were also just mental constructs of my own making and I didn't need to follow them. I drank at that party. My tolerance for alcohol had completely disappeared, so I actually got quite drunk on a lot less alcohol than I used to. I was doing better as I was no longer drinking to escape myself, but it still wasn't great. I felt awful the next day so I decided that drinking like that was no longer for me. It was not something I could return to.

December 2017 began. I was back to not drinking again and the yearning to do it just wasn't there. Over Christmas there was a time when I met up with old school friends I've kept in touch with. Whilst as a group we've never gone crazy, getting so drunk we don't know what we were doing, we've always had a drink. The thought that it might be social

Mindfully Saving Myself – One Moment at a Time

to have a drink appeared again but I just let it go. I went on an eight hour
pub crawl with them, and didn't drink a drop of alcohol. One friend
acknowledged that it was amazing that I was not drinking and asked how
difficult it was. I told him it wasn't difficult at all. No willpower was
necessary since I'd started down the mindful path. I don't think he
believed me.

2018 began and I still was not drinking. I even went through my
birthday in early January without a drink. I was loving it. However, at
that point, I realised I'd become quite attached to the idea of not
drinking. In my head I had started to strongly identify with the thought
"I'm not a drinker" and my ego had taken over. I'd even started to have
fantasies about being able to say that I'd not drank for a year, then two
years, then five and so on. I became mindful of that and realised that
these thoughts were also able to take me out of the present moment, as
much as anything else. When I let that thought go as well it lost its
power. I accepted that if I never drank again, it was fine but that if ever I
wanted to drink in moderation it was still ok, provided I did so
mindfully.

Occasionally I found I wanted a glass of wine with a meal out.
So I had that glass. I didn't follow the thoughts that admonished me for
breaking my alcohol fast and I didn't heed the thoughts that maybe I
should drink a bottle, instead of just a glass. I enjoyed the wine in that
moment and that was it.

That is really how it has stayed and my drinking is very minor in
comparison to the years gone by. I rarely fancy a drink and sometimes I
will go weeks, even months, without booze, without even thinking about
it. Other times I might have two or three beers or a couple of glasses of
wine, in a social setting, but that's it. I don't go on to have more, or get
home and crack open the whiskey, as many years ago I would have done.

There's no will power involved, I just don't want it most of the time and those times that I do, I often just observe the thought and it slowly disappears before any alcohol ever passes my lips.

Since 2018 there have been rare occasions, I can count on one hand, when I've had a few more than a couple of drinks. I've had a maybe four or five drinks with mates and there was also Marta's sister's wedding. But the way I drink, when I do drink, is very different from before. I'm not doing it to escape or block something out. I'm as in the moment as you can be with drink. Sure, it may be better to not drink at all but in the morning, whilst I won't feel completely healthy, I don't feel terrible either because I've not drunk 6 bottles of beer, a bottle of wine, followed by some whiskey or tequila or whatever else I used to get my hands onto. Mentally I'm fine as well. I know it's something I do incredibly rarely so I just think to myself, it is what it is and get on with my day without giving it another thought. I have no attachment or aversion.

So this is how it is now. I may drink but I most probably won't because there's no need.. Maybe I'll go another month without a drink or maybe I'll have a glass of wine tonight at dinner. What I do know is that I don't fancy one at the moment and that I feel healthier in body and mind because of how little alcohol I now put into my body.

I'm not doing this to say "look at me, how good I am with (or without) booze!". It's not really about booze. Or my ego. . It's about the fact that, with mindful reflection and living, these behaviours that can be so damaging can lose their power over our lives. Reaching for booze was one of many things I did to take myself out of the moment. It was one of the most powerful tools that I had used to help me escape the present moment.

Mindfully Saving Myself – One Moment at a Time

I say this not to virtue signal but to be an encouragement to anyone reading this. I imagine all of you have your own things you do, maybe for you it's drink as well, but perhaps it's obsessively watching TV, or judging other people's behaviours, gossiping or eating junk. Ask yourself, what do you do that takes you out of the moment in your life right now? Sit down and really contemplate the question. You might not get the answer straight away but because you've started your mind going it may pop up unexpectedly during meditation, or when you are walking the dog or another random time. Whatever it is, you may be able to recognise what that behaviour has done to your life: the enjoyment of life that it has taken away, why you've done it, what you used it to run from. Then, living mindfully, you can take away its power through awareness of what it is.

I would like to say one other thing about alcohol, seeing that is the crutch I've highlighted. I was very lucky that while drinking was a big part of my life from my teens I was never physically addicted to alcohol. I may have drunk four or five times a week towards the end of my love affair with it but not once did my body demand I drink to make myself feel physically normal. I had a psychological dependency on drink but never a physical one. That is why, now I've broken that psychological dependency loop, I can have one drink and then not another. If you have been addicted to alcohol, in the physical sense, you can never just have one drink. One drink will always lead to another. So please, don't think mindfulness will help you go back to taking the occasional alcoholic drink without losing control again because mindfulness can't reverse your physical addiction. What mindfulness can do is become an additional tool for dealing with the desire to drink or take drugs. You've remained sober for so long because you have used willpower to resist the urge to drink or take drugs but now you can also mindfully not become

Stephen McCoull

involved with those cravings. Mindfully you can remind yourself that you are a better person for not drinking or taking drugs and that your life is better without these substances.

What Other Addictions Can You Observe and then Escape?

The previous chapter covered my attachment to alcohol, a psychological addiction that I had lived with for a long time, but it's not the only thing I have been psychologically addicted to. Whilst the symptoms of my psychological addiction to alcohol can easily be recognised, once you start paying attention, because they are well reported and known about in society. Other addictions in your life can be more difficult to identify. Some of the other pastimes that I unconsciously used to escape my reality and had power over me are often thought as normal or not harmful.

When I was 8 years old my Dad bought me a ZX Spectrum 48K home computer. It was the 80s computer with rubber keys and I guess that my Dad thought it would be my first step into computing. Instead it was my gateway into the world of gaming. Back then the games were basic, although my favourite, Elite, was an in-depth space simulator in which you'd trade goods so that you could upgrade your spaceship and have battles with other spacecraft. I bought versions of that game for every new computer I got as I grew up. As a child, every spare minute I had at home would be spent playing games in my room. Gaming hadn't completely overtaken my early life though. I still went outside and ran around in the street, playing games and sport, or going on childhood adventures over the fields and woods close to my house, but when I was home I didn't sit and do nothing, or read, or even watch a lot of TV. What I did was game.

I continued to game into adulthood, buying various PlayStations and getting online to game with other people, as soon as the console and internet technology allowed me to. My space simulator passion was replaced with first person shooters such as Call of Duty and Battlefield. Much like when I was a child, I played games when there was nothing to do, yet slowly, as I got older, and less comfortable with myself, I also gamed when I probably should have been doing something more constructive with my time. If I was bored, I gamed. If I felt ill I gamed. If I was massively hungover and I wished I had never heard of the word "beer" before, I would game. I'd miss sunny days in summer because I was gaming. I gamed as often as I could, to the detriment of other activities. Even once I had kids I would game once they had gone to bed. Maybe only once a week, as my ex and I would want to do other things, but always the first opportunity I got I would game and regularly at the expense of sleep. I didn't want to stop despite the fact I could have been involved with something else more positive for myself and those around me. Because I had other ways of distracting myself, I wasn't completely out of control with gaming, but I wasn't in control of it either. But I didn't think it was a problem, even when I realised I had wasted so much of my time getting nowhere and that it had tempered my overall enjoyment of life. Gaming was damaging to me, it was an addiction because I couldn't stop.

Mindfully Saving Myself – One Moment at a Time

Another addiction was people. I've already discussed loneliness in some depth but as I slowly started to recognise that my desire to always be with people might not be healthy, I still thought that I felt lonely because I had no one that I could interact with on a certain emotional level. I needed emotional contact. I wanted to be around people and I would do anything to get that. Even when I wanted to stop drinking, in 2015, I would go out drinking if it allowed me to be with people. If needed to get to bed early I would stay up if I could be with people. If I had work to do, I would waste more time than I needed to in the tearoom, to get those extra minutes experiencing human interaction. When I was with people I would enjoy in-depth conversations about subjects I was interested about, or talking amusing gibberish. But I would also speak to them about anything, whatever they were willing to talk about, even if the subject matter wasn't anything I was interested in. I did it because I needed company.

At first, once I finally realised that my behaviours were a major problem, I thought the addictions to gaming and to people were problems that needed to be resolved. However, they were just the symptoms and there was something much deeper to it.

The reason I wanted to be with people, to be surrounded with my former friends, was because I did not want to have time with myself. If I was alone, I had to face me, I had to face my pain, my issues, my depression, my anxiety, my unresolved emotional upsets accumulated over an entire lifetime of evasion. I had avoided that in so many ways my whole life and many of my friendships were all about me escaping the present moment, getting away from myself. When I studied what had been driving my behaviour with people I also discovered that my desire to game, whenever I had time alone, had exactly the same source. I did not want to be with myself in my head and face everything.

Stephen McCoull

As I became mindful and began to understand this I started to do the opposite to what I'd done before., When I was at home alone, I stopped filling my time with non-friends and I started to face myself and everything that I had run from. My intention became to meditate and to do anything else that assisted with my practice, and just accept whatever happened in my life. So every day, without exception, I faced myself. It was incredibly hard. It certainly did not bring about calm at first. It was the opposite of calm. How can it be peaceful to face everything in you that you have avoided for decades? It can't. But you have to face all of what you've been running from if you want to find peace in the end.

In time I gained acceptance for who I am, for the fears I'd avoided, for everything negative in my mind that I had run from all those years. I accepted me in the moment and didn't want anything to be any other way. And you know what? Suddenly, for the first time in my entire life, I was comfortable with myself, truly comfortable. I was at peace.

Without conscious effort, my desire to fill my time, to stop being in the present moment, dropped away much like my need for alcohol did. My pathological need to be surrounded by other people slowly disappeared. When I found myself alone I was no longer lonely. I no longer wanted to fill that time with games. I approached everything that was going on as something to enjoy and to investigate.

Does this mean I have become all anti-social? Not at all. If I am alone, I have a great relationship with myself but that makes me more comfortable with other people. So I still enjoy the company of others, but I don't need it or grasp for it. Therefore my relationships are more nurturing for both myself and the other person. How my life collapsed in on itself does mean that I have fewer friends now than I did previously, but my friendship circle has begun to expand again. On the whole, I recognise now that I never had nourishing relationships before. I used to

Mindfully Saving Myself – One Moment at a Time

live for those friendships. I imagined those relationships to be the most important part of my life, yet they were the opposite of healthy in many cases. Now I don't need people every minute of the day to make me feel comfortable, and even if I only see my current friends once every three months, they are wholesome relationships that truly enrich my life.

In this chapter I've discussed two types of addictions and why I used them but this theme is explored further in the chapter "Distraction is not mindfulness" where I discuss how distractions can take you out of the moment if you allow them to.

Stephen McCoull

Exercising Smart

As a society we understand more about the importance of exercise than ever before. We know that being active improves our brain function, including concentration and memory and it actually increases our energy levels throughout the day. As well as strengthening our muscles, it also strengthens our bones. It helps people maintain a healthy weight, it can aid in better sleep and most importantly it can make you feel happier. It certainly helped me be happier throughout my life. Without exercise being a big part of my lifestyle, my refuge in difficult times, I would have succumbed to depression and anxiety, and reached a crisis point, years if not decades before I actually did. I would say that exercise saved my life.

We know how good it is for us and yet so many of us struggle to get in the right amount or intensity of exercise. I'm a keen exerciser, I run and lift weights, and can sometimes exercise six or seven times in a week. I could mistakenly give the impression that a drive to exercise isn't a problem for me but like everyone else on this planet, I can have struggles with motivation.

A problem with motivation can result in some days when you wake up and you just can't be bothered to do any exercise. Other days, instead of that lunch time work out you go out with colleagues and eat a ginormous curry, even though you'll be having dinner when you get home that evening. Another classic reason for not exercising is the thought that you've already missed three days, so what's the problem with missing the fourth day? Or fifth? Or waiting until after Christmas in a month's time?

Lack of motivation, however, can present itself in other ways than just not doing the work. The issue doesn't have to be not exercising at all but not getting the most out of exercise when we are at the gym, out running or whatever our go-to fitness activity is.

That has been an occasional problem for me. I will train but I just don't push myself as much as I could. I can be running and only ten minutes into an hour long run, in my head I'm imagining how much of a run I've still got left to do, and the thought *there's no way I can run for another 50 minutes* arises and refuses to leave. Before I know it, I'm cutting my route in half because a thought has told me it's a no go today. During exercise other similar thoughts, such as "I've not eaten enough this morning to work out too hard", "I just can't run fast today", "what's the point as I'll never be fast enough for the half marathon next month", "I don't think I can lift anything heavier than I did last year so I'm obviously doing something wrong", "that person over there is way better than me so I just look stupid"

. These types of thoughts can lead to me cutting out part of the training or in some cases deciding to stop outright right then.

Yet, we're starting to understand, through our mindfulness practice, that our thoughts may not be true, and we don't have to follow them. When I do unconsciously trail those thoughts about exercise, *yes, I am really rubbish at running today, I'm way too slow* then it affects my

189

motivation and I'm not going to get the most out of an activity that I really enjoy and which helps me maintain a positive mood.

If you want to exercise more but are struggling, then start to apply mindfulness principles to how you deal with your thoughts about the dreaded workout. One way would be to recognise any negative connotations the language you use has, such as the word "dreaded", and mindfully detach those semantics from any thoughts or conversations about exercise. Furthermore you might have the thought that you don't want to exercise today, as you can't muster the will to move, but rather than let it demotivate instead observe it without attachment. The thought might be genuine, perhaps you have not slept well the night before or you've already worked out really hard the last two days, your body is tired and needs a proper rest. In that case you mindfully observe the lack of motivation, then listen to what your body needs, do the right thing for it and give it the day off it requires. You haven't worked out but you'll feel a peace knowing that you're nourishing your body.

If, however, you see the thought that you can't be bothered has no basis in reality, that it's just the lazy part of you not wanting to put the effort in, the fact you've not attached to the thoughts and seen what is happening in your mind means that you can respond positively. *Hey this is just a thought about being lazy, let's put those running shoes on and I'll feel great afterwards!* Off you go running and before you know it it's over. Not only have you just done a great run but because you figured out that the thought in your mind was trying to take something great away from you and you spotted it and called it out, you might feel like you've developed as a person

You can do the same if you are experiencing self-sabotaging thoughts as you exercise. Those types of thoughts mainly affect me outside of the gym when I'm running. The classic *there's no way I can run that many miles* early in the run can be seen for what it is, a mental obstacle that can be ignored. Instead of attaching to the thought and feeling the energy drain out of me, I move my attention to my legs and check in with them by doing a quick body scan. My legs feel fine, so I move my attention to my heart and lungs and simply observe them. Yes, both are under some strain but that's because I'm running, and both are well within their limits. In fact I could possibly push myself a little bit more. Before I know it, the original thought that it was all too much for little old me has vanished and I'm back to pounding the streets fully aware of my body and being in that moment. How does it feel to exercise and actually listen to your body as you do so? For me, I feel alive! The same is also true when my body really has had enough and I should rest. Using the same mindful method, I may recognise that now is maybe the time to ease off a little as I've run faster than planned for the distance. Alternatively, if necessary, I pay attention to a pain in my legs or something else that is a warning sign. I recognise I need to look after my body and can return home and let my body recover. Yes, I still returned home, not because my mind just kept churning out "not good enough" propaganda, but because it was what my body needed right then. The funny thing is, the more you are willing to go home when your body really needs you to, the less often you go home because previously it had been your own head talking you out of a good thing.

If you hadn't realised it yet, mindfulness isn't just about sitting on a cushion and being quiet. Mindfulness can help you in every aspect of your life. Even the sweaty ones.

Stephen McCoull

What is this? A tool to bring you into the present moment

I'm quite active on the Calm app's online Facebook community. I've been one of the moderators on the forum for nearly three years. I found it really useful and motivating to share my mindfulness journey with other people who are also on the same journey but who have different histories, backgrounds and reasons for coming to mindfulness. Through interacting with people at different points of their journey, I've noticed that people can struggle with the concept of remaining mindful at all times. Every now and then one of the community members will ask a question along the lines of *"How can I stay mindful throughout the day and never get lost in thought? How can it be done?"*

If you've started to try and be mindful and meditate recently, it's very likely you've had the same question. In fact, it's a question that even the seasoned meditator will occasionally ask themselves if they're going through a period of unusually high mental activity. Like many of you, I also struggle to remain present at times, and occasionally those spells are prolonged and frequent, filled with such highly useful thoughts as to whether I should have dinner in the work cafeteria or wait until I get home that can pull our attention away from the moment with no obvious benefit.

A popular misconception is that meditation is about shutting your mind down and being in some kind of blissful mental silence. Because of that, many people think that meditation sounds like an impossible dream and don't even try. Yet meditation is quite different to that. Your brain is built to think. Meditation is about learning to not react to your thoughts and not getting dragged along with swirls of (often negative) mental activity. It's not about switching your mind off altogether. Meditation teaches you to be the aware of the thoughts rather than associate with them and make them your own identity. I It teaches you that you can find peace even in the middle of a storm.

The mistake that some people can make is that they grasp onto the idea that living mindfully means that the person will be present at *all* times, without exception. It's almost impossible to be mindful every waking second of the day. Having that expectation is a sure fire way of leading yourself into self-imposed suffering because it's just not going to happen. Without fail your brain will drag you away from the activity you are doing right now, this second. You can be in the middle of a fun activity, something you hate, something boring, something mega exciting or even an activity that scares the hell out of you. Yet whatever you are doing right now, your brain, even if briefly, will definitely ensure you end up thinking about something else not at all connected with this present moment you are currently in.

It's not a failure if that happens because it gives you a chance to notice that your mind has drifted from the present moment. That is when you develop the most, by practicing returning to your awareness and stopping being too involved in your thoughts. It is a practice after

Stephen McCoull

all. The difficulty can be noticing you have drifted in the first place. There could be times when you stay lost in thought continuously for many minutes or even hours before you become aware of what you have been doing. Or you notice you've lost yourself in your own mind but as soon as you've realised that, and have become the awareness behind the thoughts, you almost immediately fall back into the same mental thought pattern. This can generate frustration, so being able to take advantage of any tool that helps us get back to the present moment and our life as it really is, is a good thing.

Two or three years back I read that in some Zen schools monks are taught to ask the question *"What is this?"* about everything. And I mean everything. If they wanted to go to the toilet they asked *"what is this?"* If they missed their family they asked *"what is this?"* If they were enjoying their food they asked *"what is this?"* If they hated their food they ask *"what is this?"* If they wanted to leave the monastery and become a rock star they asked "what is this?" If they thought they were asking *"what is this?"* too much they ask *"what is this?"* If a fear about leaving the monastery struck them they asked *"what is this?"* They asked *"what is this?"* about everything within their experience. The idea of the practice isn't to ask the question and then seek an answer, as that will draw you into more thought. The question is purely there to help you separate yourself from all parts of your experience, so you can really observe what is going on.

When I first read about it, the practice didn't seem like something that would work for me because I wasn't going to ask myself that question repeatedly throughout every day. That said, the practice definitely struck a chord, because the question remained very fresh in my mind, waiting for me to put it to good use.

Mindfully Saving Myself – One Moment at a Time

One day I found myself lost in a thought and even when I noticed myself out of the moment I allowed my attention to be dragged back into thinking. Thoughts about past friendships, that were no more just wouldn't leave me alone. More precisely, I wouldn't leave them alone. I played with them like you will tongue a cut in your mouth. Rather than getting frustrated with myself for my inability to let go of what was happening, the question *"what is this?"* suddenly appeared in my mind. What I think initially put me off the practice, beyond the repetition, was that I didn't like the idea of a question. I felt it would give me answers, whether I wanted them or not. Finding answers would mean I'm attaching to other thoughts, which would cause yet more mental activity, so that I would still not be the awareness of my thoughts.

But on that day when I asked the question, I wasn't actually after an answer to the question at all. Instead, it was natural just to use the question as a tool to separate from all the mental activity. *"What is this?"* I asked again and finally I could put all my attention into the mental happenings and physical sensations that had affected me, without becoming them. I asked the question and the question helped me separate from the thoughts. As I observed, the thoughts stopped being fed by my mind and without that fuel they weakened and disappeared.

"What is this?" This is another instrument that can be used at any time to help you be the consciousness that is fully aware rather than the person controlled by thoughts. You can use the question anywhere any time. If you're walking down the street, in the car, having a conversation with a friend or standing in a supermarket queue. You can use it if you've become taken over by fear, excitement, sadness or any other emotion. It doesn't take long to simply silently ask yourself the question and use it to focus on what is. Although you can be, you don't need to be meditating

195

at the time you ask the question. In fact, my experience is that it's a better tool to use when you're not meditating.

It's not just thoughts and emotions that it can work on either. You can use it on physical symptoms too. There was one time when I had my kids on the weekend. The three of them were all being noisy and playing around, but their ages span six years and they can have quite different needs and requirements. At the time I'd been a little ill and I'd not slept well for a couple of night. There I was in this lovely, if chaotic, moment, with my kids all demanding my attention when all of a sudden, I had a bout of tiredness that swept in out of nowhere. I just wanted to sleep. I mean, I really wanted to sleep immediately. I could have just got on the sofa and closed my eyes and I would have been asleep within seconds. Yet, I don't see my kids every day, and I really didn't want to waste my time with them sleeping. Instead of giving in I asked myself *"what is this?"* The question helped me become separate from the physical sensations of exhaustion so that I could observe the tiredness without judgement. It also helped me really focus in on the sensations I was feeling. However, as I tried to really watch everything that the tiredness was made of, my whole experience of fatigue simply disappeared. Almost instantly, I felt awake again. As it was the first time I'd ever tried to observe this type of tiredness I was quite struck by the result. This is why the *"What is this?"* practice is something I still use today if I have extreme physical sensations that are likely of a temporary nature.

I appreciate that asking yourself a question to assist you in becoming more conscious can seem a little peculiar. I didn't think it could work for me and initially it did seem like a strange concept. It may not be something that immediately works for you or even makes sense right now. Like almost everything with mindfulness, it's a personal experience. The way I use the question may be different from how the

Mindfully Saving Myself – One Moment at a Time

Zen monks I read about use it, which in turn may contrast from the way you will use it. The important thing is to give it a try without any kind of expectation or judgement. It may work for you straight away or it may never work for you. If it doesn't, just use other methods for brining your attention into the present moment that do help you, but if it does work then you've got another mindfulness skill that can assist you in your search for peace.

Stephen McCoull

An Inferiority Complex is just a Collection of Thoughts

I would be very surprised if there was a human being who, at least once in their life, haven't thought that they weren't good enough and felt inferior. In fact, I'm sure that a large chunk of the world's population will have occasional thoughts about not being good enough. Whilst at first glance it may appear to be something you wouldn't want to feel, thinking you are not good enough in itself isn't actually a bad thing because it can become a driver for positive change.

If you think you're not a good enough friend, you may reach out to the friend you've neglected in recent months. If you feel inferior around people who are better read than you, then you may choose to put away the fiction and invest your time in reading more non-fiction. Or, you may decide that actually they're not the people for you, as your interests differ, so you try and find other friends who are more on your wavelength. Like any difficulty, the feeling of inferiority can lead us through to personal growth if we allow it to.

The problem with feelings of inferiority is not when we occasionally experience them, but when we begin to attach to those views. Rather than having moments of doubt about ourselves when we need to re-evaluate and respond by making some changes, we can start to question ourselves more deeply rather than questioning the ideas themselves. That is when we can unconsciously allow ourselves to start to define who we are by them. If that happens, we can experience quite strong feelings of inadequacy, which start to last for days and then months. The feelings can become beliefs. We convince ourselves that we are not good enough and that inadequacy is a fundamental element of our personalities. We can soon find that we are no longer able to escape this belief because we don't even recognise that a way out from these thoughts is even a possibility. If we really can't disconnect, then the belief that we are not good enough and that we are lacking in some way, can span years and even decades.

We allow this to define who we are as human beings. Everything negative that happens in our lives is because people are better than us or we're in some way lesser than everyone we come into contact with and ultimately we feel we are not good enough, never good enough.

The thought that you need to improve in some way, which could have been used for growth if it hadn't become the belief that you are not good enough, becomes something much more frightening and can inhibit our ability to live life and to feel joy. If left unchecked, these thought processes can ruin whole lifetimes.

The feeling of not being good enough, of being worthless, was a key aspect of my own depression and anxiety. It had been something that had affected my life, with slowly worsening symptoms, ever since I was a teenager all the way through until 2015, when I gradually started my journey away from it. The whole "I'm not good enough" thought process was insidious.

One of my escapes from the pain of myself, as mentioned, was being with people and socialising. In the 1990s and early 2000s I was blessed with some friends who were musically very talented whereas I, despite my love of music, don't have a musical bone in my body. There would be nights when, after going to the pub or a club and having a load of drinks, we would end up in one of their houses. Before long there were guitars out, or some electronic music app on someone's laptop, with people singing along having a great time. I'd be there singing along with them (and what amazing people they were that they didn't say anything about my complete lack of vocal skills) and it would be a fun time. The thing was, I wasn't really having a good time. I wasn't having an enjoyable time at all. I already had the general view that I was not good enough, and my lack of musical skills just fed my internal thoughts that I was somehow less of a person than my friends because I wasn't musical like they were. I would chat, smile and laugh with them and would seem great. Yet I often thought "look what a loser I am compared to my mates" one that was fully attached to and followed down the dark plug hole of despair whilst I smiled along with everyone else.

When my hangover was fully kicking in the next morning, trying to teach me a lesson I refused to absorb for many years, the thoughts of being inferior to my friends continued. I always felt like the junior friend, that they were my friends because they felt sorry for me. Because who would really want to be friends with me?

It wasn't just when I was out drinking with friends that I felt inferior. I would feel inferior at work as well. I had started working for an IT company as a trainee in 1999 and I was given all sorts of praise

Mindfully Saving Myself – One Moment at a Time

very early in my career by the people I worked with as well as higher management. I was learning what I needed to learn, fast, and within a very short time I lost the "trainee" tag. Yet when my parents asked me how the job was going, I can vividly remember telling them that it was only a matter of time before they work out I'm no good at it and I'm found out. Despite all the external evidence to the contrary, I felt like an imposter, someone who was inferior to the job I held. When I was looked over for a promotion to a senior operator, a couple of people around me were enraged by the decision. Yet, whilst I was upset, I didn't do anything about it because deep down, despite knowing the job inside out at that point, I didn't think I was good enough. It made sense that I didn't get the job. When I finally got promoted I went back to feeling like an imposter.

The feeling that I was not good enough has hindered me throughout large chunks as my career in IT. The thought that I was inferior and didn't belong stopped me from taking some risks in my career that would have been extremely advantageous in the long run. However, despite that, and under an excellent manager, my company's division's director, who saw the potential in me I couldn't see myself, I became Operations Manager and for a while life looked good. I was constantly given the pep talks and advice I needed by my manager and I did what I look back on as an amazing job in some challenging circumstances. Yet all the time, deep down within me, I had thoughts that I was not good enough and I believed them no matter what evidence to the contrary presented itself.

A company restructure changed the director above me and made me one of only two managers in the division, when there had been five before the re-shuffle. Both the new director and the other manager had strong opinions and weren't easily swayed from their positions. At the time I thought they were really combative people, although looking back I can see that they were really just being forthright with their views. Faced with a wall of opinions, I couldn't make a dent in the feelings that I was not good enough, that had moved to a lesser role in my mind for a couple of years. Suddenly my belief that I was simply no good was centre stage again and led me to not value myself or my own opinions. Instead of being plain spoken with them, I doubted I was the right person for the job and became unassertive. Whilst I was dismayed by their behaviour, when compared to my old director, my main feeling was that I deserved what was happening as, despite my earlier successes in the role, I knew I was useless. I wasn't of the required standard to do the job.

The feeling of others being superior to me was something that accompanied me throughout my life but towards the end of the 2000s and into the 2010s it began to increase. In the run up to and during my several breakdowns these were the thoughts that filled my mind nearly every second of the day. I latched onto them without ever questioning whether I had a choice to do so, a key symptom of my depression. I remember going out for drinks with friends, as the advice I was given by a therapist was to try and keep up social occasions despite my mental health difficulties. I heard about their days, their jobs, their hobbies, whatever was going on in their lives and was constantly thinking I was beneath them. Whatever they were doing was superior to what I was. That I was nothing compared to them. Of course, we smiled and laughed and they probably didn't know anything was too seriously was wrong with me. But my mind wouldn't turn off the thought that they shouldn't be my friends. I was simply not good enough.

When all your mind sees is that you are inferior to everyone and everything, when you allow it to become a belief, it doesn't lead to

Mindfully Saving Myself – One Moment at a Time

growth and becomes a severe obstacle to you having even a second of peace in your own mind.

Look back over the last few paragraphs. Can you spot the trend? I was not paying attention to reality. I did my job really well. As a human I am worth as much as anyone. We all have different skills and experience. Yet I didn't see any of that. It was my mind, and not reality, that was driving everything I felt and those feelings of inadequacy were driving me further into the rabbit hole of the inferiority complex. Such a complex can be a vicious cycle that is very difficult to escape from. But remember, what is happening in your mind, even something so deeply entrenched, is purely made up of a group of thoughts.

Are thoughts real? No, they are mental conditions that occur in the mind. They can be useful tools but if we attach to them without critically reviewing them, they can also drive our behaviours in some extremely unhelpful ways. If we don't learn to escape them they can lead to mental distress that can greatly affect our lives for decades in some cases.

As I carried out my mindfulness practice, I began to notice what I was doing. I realised that the thoughts I had hadn't questioned, since a teenager were the real problem in my life. It wasn't friends or colleagues who were better than me that was the issue. It was the thoughts about friends and colleagues being better than me that was causing me pain.

It's not easy to unpick what may be a lifelong habit of thinking but mindfully recognising what you have been doing is a powerful first step towards liberation from your inferiority complex. Once you see the mental conditions for what they are, their power starts to be diminished. You can then decide to not react and act upon them. Mindfulness always sounds so easy: "Hey, notice your thoughts, don't attach to them, let them float away as if they were a cloud and respond to them as and when

203

you need to". On a practical level, that is really all there is to it, but the mind is not a simple system, it's extremely complicated in ways that even the great neurological scientists of our age are yet to fully discover. So, escaping these thoughts, through mindfully paying attention, may sound easy but it is anything but.

When you first note that your mind is telling you that you are inferior, even though you've had that insight, you'll likely still follow the thought. You still end up feeling like crap but each time you notice that there is this heinous voice in your head screaming "I'm not good enough!" it becomes just that little bit easier to disengage from. If you keep practicing then you will reach a point when most of the time, if the thought appears in your head, you will be able to recognise and greet it "Hey, here you are again my inferiority complex" and then wave it goodbye as it disappears. I can't say the thoughts will stop coming. They still visit me on special occasions. But if you keep practicing mindfulness you will gradually develop the skills that will allow you to disengage from your negative self-talk and then you'll be able to make new decisions.

An important point to note is that inferiority tells you, in very strong terms, that you are not like other people. It isolates you from whatever this world has to offer as you retreat within and are confined to your own mind. Attaching to the feeling of being superior to others has exactly the same effect on the person who suffers it. The way they present themselves may be very different from a person attached to an inferiority complex but the sufferers of feelings of grandeur are still isolated because their thoughts are also driving their behaviour and keep them separated from reality.

When you can let go of feelings of inferiority or superiority you may find something quite magical happens. When you stop seeing

Mindfully Saving Myself – One Moment at a Time

inferiority as defining who you are, you start to find that you are connected to others. You are no longer isolated from the people in your life. You suddenly see that their worth is equal to yours, no matter who they are, what their job, or their history is.

I no longer define myself by the thought that I am below, or above, anyone else. The amazing thing I have learnt is that we are all one, even if the other person has come to the same realisation.

Seeing that we are all one becomes a beautiful thing as you realise a homeless person on the street and the world's richest person are both human beings, both are equally as worthy of respect as the other, just as you are. When you appreciate that, it opens up a whole new level of loving kindness for both yourself and others. No longer do you step around the homeless person as if they are nothing, instead you engage with them and talk to them on your level and bring a small fraction of light to both of your lives. If you can help them, then you do, and if you can't then the fact you've seen that they are no different from you is enough because they can feel a connection too if you've been fully open to them. It may seem like a harder thing to do with the mega wealthy, especially if you're not particularly well off. Yet if you accept that they are neither more or less worthy of life than you, they may notice that you have come together as equals, even if they want to ignore that right now. If they do then you can just offer them loving kindness.

Mindfulness can help us see that our own thinking doesn't define us and isn't necessarily true and if we are able to disengage from our internal stories in that way, then not only does it improve our own lives but also the lives of everyone we interact with.

Stephen McCoull

Every day is a New Day

Have you really given the saying "Every day is a new day" consideration to understand what that really means? Before I started to change my life I had negative labels for myself and whilst I knew every day was a new day I would also think that the things I knew about myself couldn't change. I thought *I* couldn't change, no matter what day it was. That meant that when the sun went down and then re-appeared a few hours later I didn't see it as another day in which to live my life. It was just another day of the same old, same old. Whilst the specific events may have been different with each particular day, really each one merged into the next. I didn't see the new in each day. I couldn't comprehend the possibilities that each passing moment could bring. The question you have to ask yourself is, do you?

When you are living mindfully, feeling that you are living the same day, being stuck, or whatever thoughts and emotions fill your mind that day, does not have to dictate what you actually experience. If you are

Mindfully Saving Myself – One Moment at a Time

mindful most of the time, you are living not only in each new day but also in each new moment. You can be present for everything as an observer who is not driven by thoughts, When that happens, the peace, the connectedness, and the possibilities in just being the awareness of your life is really something special.

Like you, I am a human being, and even if we get this practice right most of the time there will be days when your practice slips or you may even fall back into reactivity for a period of time, an hour, a day, a week, a month or even longer then it's quite possible to think that you might as well give up on the practice. You thought you were being mindful but you've forgotten about it for so long there's no point going back and trying to live mindfully again. Through the online communities I'm a part of it's not unusual to meet people who used to be very mindful and felt a great peace with things as they are, yet they're not sure why but they have stopped living in a way that was so positive for their life.

There will be a time when this happens to you. You forget to or can't meditate for a week or you meditate but pay no attention for the rest of the day. Suddenly, you've been like that for a week, a month or longer. One day you'll wake up and realise what has been happening and see that you have strayed from your path. That is the time when you have a choice. You can do what some people do and wonder what happened but shrug and carry on living mindlessly. Or you can snap back into the practice because you realise each moment is new and you are not bound by what has come before.

Back in the summer of 2019, I had not been feeling physically that well for much of an entire week. Whilst I had meditated each day, at other times I wasn't being mindful at all and I was starting to overuse social media as a distraction from feeling physically under the weather. I

Stephen McCoull

found myself in a weird, not particularly positive mood but one that was non-specific. I suppose I could describe that mood as being "meh".

For much of the week I had gone against what I knew works. I hadn't accepted my sickness, I had a bad cold, as it was. Instead, like many men, I was trying to get myself out of the moment as I don't do colds at all well and I completely rejected feeling ill. Acceptance is key to mindful living and I had done the opposite of accepting how I physically felt. I was starting to pay for it mentally.

Earlier I talked about how lack of acceptance can cause more suffering than the thing we refuse to accept, and this is a great example. I was creating mental suffering on top of my already existing physical problems because I hadn't accepted reality. I wanted it to be another way than what it was.

Yet, here was an opportunity for me. I realised that I was no longer fully following the practice that had taken me from the brink of taking my own life to a feeling of peace. I could have shrugged and wondered what the point was, seeing I was ill, then continued to be mindless for days but I knew I had a choice in that new moment. I made a decision and I snapped out of my mindless thought patterns and from the reactivity of continuously checking social media. "*What should I do?*" I'd had the cold for days and the symptoms weren't as bad as they had been earlier that week so I decided to go for a gentle meditative walk.

I got up, dressed and I walked to the River Thames which was near my house in Reading, and walked along its banks. I felt my feet touch the ground and how each step felt slightly different from the last as the surface of the path changed as I progressed along the riverbank. I never judged whether this step was better than the last and I didn't anticipate the next step and how that one would be. I felt the wind blowing around me, sometimes quite fast and other times hardly at all. I experienced the sun on my face and then shadows of great trees dancing over me. Neither was good, neither was bad. Whatever the view was in front of me I accepted it as I continued my walk along the river bank. This part of the river is quite close to the centre of town and there are areas, both built up and full of nature, that can be beautiful whilst other parts not so much. Whatever the view that presented itself, I made no judgement. I did not think *"urgh this is the horrible part of the river"* or *"look at the way the light and shadows waltz beautifully between the willows and the water"*, I just accepted what I saw. I continued to be the awareness behind thought. I accepted the joggers who ran too close to me, or the cyclists who shot around me, the workers heading back to the office, some with quite heavy perfume or aftershave on that invaded my nostrils. Any thoughts that briefly appeared because of all these stimuli, I just accepted and let go. It is what it is.

I can't say it was an easy walk as this was done after a week of not being that mindful other than short sits. My thoughts stole into my consciousness but any meditation, even walking meditation, requires effort. The effort of recognising that you are thinking, the effort of acceptance, and then the effort of letting it all go. I walked for 45 minutes and as I did I put the effort in and it paid off. I finally arrived at a lovely park in the centre of town. I found a nice bench, closed my eyes and did a 15 minute body scan. My mind had quietened down and I felt back to how I generally feel now-a-days, quite calm.

When I opened my eyes, I watched the park for a short while before finding my earphones in my pocket. As mindfully as I could I listened to music as I headed home. My mind was tranquil and when I arrived back home I felt a peace with everything, including my cold. I didn't want it to be any other way than the way it was right then and the mental suffering I had started to generate before the walk had left. None

Stephen McCoull

of that would have happened if I didn't understand that each new second, new minute, new hour or new day really are new and exciting moments in which you can handle life in a different way to the moment before. All you have to do is make the choice.

Mindfulness is not always easy but persisting with it is definitely worth it. It's easy to forget how much being present can give us and to cease our practice, to let life get in the way, whether that's because of a cold or a work deadline. When we live mindfully, all these things that affect us take on a different shape and have a different impact on us, an influence that is neither positive nor negative. Because we don't hold them close to us but become the awareness of what is happening, it means that we can live in peace with ourselves.

So, when I say every day is a new day, what I mean is we have the chance to go into each new day or moment with an open mind and acceptance. We can then live with whatever that day brings us, good and bad, with a peaceful heart. That is what mindfulness is, coming into each moment with acceptance.

Recognising Judgement

The word "judgement" is used throughout this book and many other writings about mindfulness. Mindfulness isn't all that complicated. A large part of it is accepting whatever is right now without judgement. Ultimately, being judgemental of what is, of our reality, ends up hurting us even if that judgement appears righteous or positive. This is because, whatever the object of our judgement, the act of passing it leads to a reaction rather than a response. Reactions stop us being in the moment, whereas responses, made without reactivity or judgement, lead to being present.

Being non-judgemental when you're carrying out a body scan, and your leg has gone to sleep, isn't too difficult. You recognise the leg is asleep and, if it's not a real physical problem that needs you to do something about you let it be and accept it. If it is an actual physical problem then, rather than jump up suddenly and possibly fall over because your leg is asleep, you just gently respond by stretching out the leg and allowing it to wake up slowly. It's not too challenging to not have any judgement when you notice that thoughts about what you're having for dinner tonight are stealing into your focus as you are meditating. A

Stephen McCoull

negative thought about how you're always thinking about food when you're meditating may appear in your mind but you spot that and then let it go.

The problem you may find is that judgement isn't always so easy to identify. It can be disguised to the point where we are completely unaware that we're being judgemental at all. So how can you let go of an attachment to a judgemental thought process if you can't even see it?

Well, like everything with mindfulness, it takes practice and, most importantly, you've guessed it, a non-judgemental heart directed towards yourself. If you finally notice that, you'd been judgemental about a certain person and things have been that way for a while, recognise that, become the observer and be kind to yourself. You don't think *"That's just stupid that I've been thinking that way for so long. How couldn't I see how judgement was damaging me?"* because that type of thinking brings yet more judgement which can hurt you and take away your peace.

I had a judgement that started long before I started practicing mindfulness, which I hadn't recognized for a long time, but mindfulness helped me spot it.

When I left my ex-wife, as mentioned, I lost most of my friends. Some I didn't lose immediately. Some I still consider extremely good people but it just didn't work out. Some of those friendships ended because I decided it was better to go our separate ways and for me to start a new. The ones I lost almost immediately were different. Some of them refused to talk to me or would send me messages saying they were still my friends but behaved in ways that showed they were clearly not. I was incredibly frustrated by the fact that these people would not discuss what had happened with me and ask about my side of things or even just try and find out if I was safe when they knew how sick I had been. For some time the way I saw it was that they had behaved in this way because

212

Mindfully Saving Myself – One Moment at a Time

they had judged me regarding what had happened and thought a lot of things about me and the situation, that weren't at all true.

I couldn't understand how these people that I had spent so much time with over the years never made any attempt to find out my side of the story, to see who I truly was. On some occasions I had a hard time not getting caught up in anger. I would sometimes get hurtful or contradictory texts that didn't help. I got a couple of texts after months of no contact at all from some, saying that they were still my friend, but making sure I knew I wasn't welcome in their lives. I'd wonder how on earth they could pass judgement like that and I'd sometimes react sending back a reply via text. Of course it never worked out positively for me. It just made things worse. On one occasion I was told a couple were still my friends, but that I wasn't invited to a joint christening and wedding vow renewal celebration. I waited several weeks to reply, so that I could let the event pass. When I finally did reply saying how much they had hurt me, unbeknownst to me I ended up doing it the day before the ceremony. They had no idea that I had waited to avoid such a clash and they didn't try to find out. It gave them yet another reason to judge me and another reason for me to question the fairness of life.

I felt that all these people were thinking ill of me despite not knowing the facts. They didn't know how long I had waited to reply to their text message and they had no idea how hard my marriage was and what my experience had been like and had no idea that my mental health was used to emotionally belittle me within that relationship. They didn't know anything, yet they judged me. Peaceful was certainly not how my heart was back then.

When I started my practice and my experience with non-judgement grew. Whether it was my body or my mind, I started to know

213

deep within me that non-judgemental acceptance of what is was key to finding peace.

I had a thought one day about my former friends who hadn't wanted to talk to me. The anger and frustration with their behaviour and perceived judgement started to bubble up. Unlike shortly after I had left my ex-wife, this time I managed avoid the familiar thoughts that were brewing in my mind. I had a really good look at what was going in my mind and let the thoughts go.

Then something extraordinary happened. I had an awakening. Rather than all these people being judgemental towards me it, maybe it was me who was the judgemental one. Everything about them, whether in my head or my brief electronic interactions I had with them was pure judgement. I didn't know their story. Whilst I knew we had parted ways, I didn't know why. I didn't know what inner battles they were having, either at that point in time or when we were friends. I didn't know if my failed marriage, and the depressive anxious person that I had been for several years, was just too much for them to think about and cope with.

I understood in that moment that whilst they may not know what goes on in my life behind closed doors, their lives had also been going on behind doors which were closed to me. I only saw the outside of their worlds and I had been judging them based on that limited knowledge. I understood that I really didn't know anything about them, other than what they had chosen to present to me when we were friends. A couple of years later I knew even less about them. I wasn't living their lives and I had not walked in their shoes, so who was I to judge their behaviour?

To presume they were judging me was judgement itself. That judgement had led to anger and frustration of the sort that almost physically hurt. Yet, all of that wasn't their doing. It was a result of my actions because I judged them and had allowed reactivity to damage my life by following those thoughts without question.

Once I recognised my own judgement about those people, I was able remove myself from it almost instantly. For a brief moment I judged myself for not realising that I was judging them. Then I saw that judgement too, so I just watched those thoughts and let them go. I had disassociated from the internal pain of my own creation that by that point had existed for almost two years. I felt light. A huge burden was lifted from me that day - the weight of my own presumptuous thoughts.

I won't lie and say the judgement about those people didn't return. It did, but the great thing about having insights into your behaviour is that, once you've understood yourself on a deep level, you can bring the lesson back into play whenever those thoughts, in this case judgement, arise.

Seeing that I was the one actually judging people was quite a major revelation for me but hidden judgement of all sorts of things can exist in our minds. It can be quite difficult to distinguish judgement at times. It could be the person who jumps in front of people in the queue, who you judge as selfish, when actually they're late home where they look after their elderly mother, who they have selflessly given their life to take care of. It could be a piece of new software on your laptop for work that you curse and get stressed about but you don't realise will save you hours of work each week once you learn how to master it. It might be the fact you got an Indian curry take away, rather than the Thai curry you thought you were ordering, and you feel fed up with the fact it's not what or as good as what you were expecting. It's all judgement and can lead you away from having a peaceful heart and towards suffering, of one sort of another, when you attach judgement to anything and everything.

Stephen McCoull

If you can recognise the judgement that resides at the heart of many thoughts, then your relationship with others, most importantly, your relationship with yourself, will all improve. You'll gradually stop reacting and slowly you'll realise you're no longer causing yourself additional pain. The more you think this way, the more you will start to appreciate the joy in those parts of your life that before may have caused you discomfort.

Mindfully approaching Grief

Grief is an emotion that everyone will experience at some point in their lives. It is often associated with the passing of a loved one. For many people the passing of a loved one can be an intense time in their lives. Grief can be a very powerful emotion that accompanies them over a prolonged period of time.

However, it isn't just limited to losing loved ones. You may feel it when thinking of a beloved family pet that died when you were ten, or the fact your childhood best friend moved to another country with their family during your teens. You may grieve losing a job that you loved or being cheated on by someone you trusted and had opened your heart to. There can be grief from being excluded by others or even grief that you have not achieved what you thought you would have at this point in your life.

One of my sources of grief was not beating my 90 minute half marathon target. In 2011, when I had a shoulder operation, that meant I wasn't able to do anything but run for three months, I decided to give myself a running target. My target was to run a half marathon in 90 minutes.

Stephen McCoull

In April 2012 I had run my first Reading half marathon in just under 93 minutes. I was happy with my time, but I worked out where my training needed improvement and trained for another half marathon, in Maidenhead, in September of the same year. I was very serious about the 90 minute target. Not only that I was extremely confident that I could beat 90 minutes. On the day of the half marathon, with about 12 miles of the course completed, my running watch was telling me I was on for just over an 85-minute half marathon. I thought that I just have to keep running and smashing 90 minutes will be mine . . . then my leg twinged. I ignored it. Then the leg hurt a little more and within about 200 metres I was hardly able to run. I hobbled the remaining mile or so of the race and crossed the line with over 95 minutes on the clock. People were congratulating each other at their fabulous time. Someone even applauded me. But I was in denial. I'd done all the work and I got so close to making it. But I didn't. I immediately felt a huge sense of loss and that grief actually took me several years to get over. Initially there was denial, then I got really angry that my leg didn't just wait another couple of miles before injury reared its ugly head. I became depressed that despite everything I had done in training I had still missed my target. Unfortunately several years later, I came to accept that it just wasn't to be and that, as I approach my 50s, that target will never be beaten.

There are over a seven billion people in this world. Each of us can have different things that may cause us to feel grief in one form or another and no grief is wrong.

Like many people I've also suffered the grief of losing someone. For me it was my grandmother, who I called "Nan" and who I was extremely close to. As I grew up I would see her at least three times a week and even into adulthood I would see her fairly regularly and when I couldn't see her I would call her and talk.

Mindfully Saving Myself – One Moment at a Time

I could tell her pretty much anything. I didn't always tell her the full details, I'd soften my explanation of what was going on because I didn't want to upset her or make her worry too much, but I felt like I could tell her things that I couldn't tell anyone else in my family. Whilst I'm sure there's lots of people out there who had similar relationships with their grandparents, ours was a pretty unique in the context of my other relationships. She was a rock for me. I relied on her and I would also be there for her too.

For as long as I remember my Nan had been diagnosed with a non-progressive form of Multiple Sclerosis and that was something that was in the background throughout my early years. As she aged, she needed a pacemaker after having developed problems with her heart, and then was diagnosed with Parkinson's. There's probably other things I've forgotten, lost in the noise of my other memories of her. Along with other family members, I would help my Nan as often as I could, taking her to the hospital for appointments and other errands.

What I didn't realise was that I was handling all these problems my Nan had in a mindful way. I accepted them fully. I never once thought *"damn you, life, can't you give my Nan a break for a change"*. It just was the way it was. Maybe because for as long as I could remember my Nan's health was always considered bad it just made it easier for me to accept.

My Nan was a proud woman and proud women of her generation had a thing about cleaning the door step every day. Despite her whole family telling her not to do that anymore as she was getting unsteady on her feet, she insisted and one day as she was cleaning her door step, she slipped and broke her hip. In the hospital she looked like death. I held her hand and wondered what was going to happen.

Her hip was fixed by the fantastic National Health Service, and she went into a ward for recovery. The problem was the Parkinson's.

Stephen McCoull

Whilst she had been able to walk before the fall, the Parkinson's was making it difficult for her to do the physio exercises required to strengthen her hip so she could start walking again and unfortunately, she could never walk properly after that.

For the following two years we all watched as my Nan got weaker and weaker. She was house bound and needed helpers, in addition to family, to help her continue to live in her home. She just kept going downhill and then one day she started experiencing pains in her abdomen. It was summer 2011.My mum got her checked out and the doctors thought it was cervical cancer. More tests were needed to find out precisely what it was, but that initial diagnosis was enough to make my Nan finally give up on her battle with her aliments. It all happened so quickly that the NHS never even had chance to carry out those additional tests.

Maybe two weeks, possibly three, after that initial discovery I found myself by her bedside in her private hospital room with her lying on her bed and her vicar standing on the other side. The rest of my family had left the room for a break and the vicar began to read something from the Bible, but I put my hand up to stop him. Then I told my Nan exactly what I thought about her, the things she'd done for me, how grateful I was for her support and love, how she didn't need to worry about me (a bit of a lie as life didn't feel good in so many ways) and how much I loved her. She could no longer speak but she made a noise and gripped my hand tighter. That night I slept in her room with her so that she wasn't alone. For some strange reason the way the light from the street lamps outside the room danced across the room reminded me of lying between my Nan and grandad in bed as a child, when I had stayed at their house but couldn't sleep. So I told her the memories that had arisen, told her I loved her again and tried to sleep.

Mindfully Saving Myself – One Moment at a Time

Her condition hadn't changed by the following morning and I decided to go for coffees with my ex-wife. As we were half way to the hospital coffee shop my mum or dad, I can't remember which called saying her breathing had suddenly changed and it was about to happen. We ran back, as quickly as we could, but didn't manage to reach her side before she passed away. I missed her leaving us by mere seconds. I was not there for her at that time.

I was devastated that my lovely Nan was no longer with us and I remember thinking that the person who understood me more than anyone else in the world was no longer there to support me. I wondered what I would do.

I cried a lot about my Nan after she died. I missed her greatly but looking back I realise how mindful I was at that time. Like her illnesses, I accepted her passing fully. She was dead. I didn't pray to God, pleading to see her one time or wish things were different. I accepted that she had died because she was old, she had a myriad of physical problems, her body could no longer cope with it all and she allowed herself to shut down. I was even able to come to terms with the fact I wasn't with her when she died. Thoughts that I'd let her down as I'd not been there did come up, but I saw them for what they were. Wrong. I had been there when she was ill and throughout my life as an adult. I had been able to tell her how I felt about her and offer her gratitude for all she'd done for me as she lay dying. I'd even slept in her room on her last night on Earth so that she wasn't alone. Yes, I wasn't there when she died which was unfortunate and it would have been better if I was, but I was there for her in life right up until the end. So I let the thought that I'd let her down go. It appeared occasionally for a year or two but each time I accepted it. Over time I stopped crying about my Nan, except for rare occasions that still occur. The emotional pain subsided, more something in the background. Mindfulness in action before I even knew what mindfulness was.

Whilst I handled my grief mindfully, I had no awareness of that. I took no lessons away that I could apply to the rest of my life and my extremely depressed and anxious mind. What was that lesson that I couldn't see back then? It's the same lesson that can be applied to any pain or hurt in the human experience. If you run from pain, hide from it, or block it out, rather than getting better, the suffering only gets worse with time. Not looking your grief in the eye will definitely make it stronger. In the end it becomes harder and harder to run from our distress, or block out whatever you are hiding from, and it finally catches up with us. Facing the pain head on, accepting you feel the way you feel, not judging yourself for your feelings, just letting it be in you, means that you process the pain naturally and you will come out the other side having learnt to live with whatever has happened. That's the mindful approach. It's not easy. If it was, most people wouldn't spend every waking minute trying not to be in the present moment. Whilst facing our grief with acceptance can't guarantee you happiness, in the end it will give you peace.

There may be some people who are now thinking they never handled their grief in a mindful way or think that it's an impossible feat, either now or in the future. That's OK, that is your experience and is completely valid.

There is no right or wrong way to grieve. Grief affects everyone is differently. Some people will be like me and will go through the grieving process with full acceptance. Others will try to deny the death and shut anything that could possible unsettle them away, acting almost as if nothing had happened.

Mindfully Saving Myself – One Moment at a Time

I once had an online conversation with a mother who had lost several of her children. It had happened months before but she told me how she'd only started crying five days before we spoke. I told her that there is no wrong way to grieve. I told her all I know is you need to accept it as it is and go through whatever is happening right now. If you realise you've been avoiding the pain, the sorrow, for months or years then that's is OK. It is how it is and you can accept that as well. You accept whatever has happened, whatever you feel, whatever you avoided, and   awaken to what is.

I avoided pain over the years, for decades in fact, and ultimately it led to numerous breakdowns that continued until I realised I had to face everything I had been running from. I told the grieving mother that if it took her until five days ago to start crying then that is how it is, it really isn't right or wrong. If you need to talk to people right now, then that is also how it is. If, you need to retreat from people for a while so you can reflect on all your emotions about your children and everything you feel about life, then that is OK too. Whatever you feel is needed, is the right thing to do. Nothing is wrong, nothing is right, it just is. Whilst this applies to life generally, it's doubly as important when you've suffered loss. Don't judge any of it, just let it be as it is whilst looking at what is happening in you and not running from it. You could be grieving right now and the pain is so raw you you'd do anything to block it out, but blocking it out will only lead to a much greater suffering further down your path. If you run from it you are not dealing with things, or processing them, and, like me, you'll end up emotionally twisted up until you break.

You might be considering mindfulness as a way of escape. Part of you might be thinking that it would be great if mindfulness could lead you to a future of blissed out existence. To be Zen with it all. After

223

Stephen McCoull

everything you've been through and everything you are dealing with right now that is understandable. But mindfulness can't do that. You will never find real peace through some kind of oblivion, be that from a drink, drugs, relationships or even meditating yourself into ecstasy.

You can achieve that peace if you face whatever feelings you have with acceptance. Maybe you don't want to be at peace. Maybe you believe that somehow being at peace invalidates the person who's passed away? You can be at peace and still grieve for whoever you lost. Your loved one will still be a part of you. Having acceptance doesn't make you forget them, it just helps you be at peace. It's possible that, in the future, remembering them will put a smile on your face. Peace is born of acceptance of this moment, the good and the bad, not wanting things different than reality. Accepting grief is no different than accepting any other moment in your experience.

It's worth remembering that grief isn't just an individual thing. Grief has a butterfly effect that spreads outwards from the person experiencing it and fans out from others who may be mourning towards you. There will be your other family members who are also grieving. They have lost the same person as you but their relationship with that person is not the same as yours. Your relative may grieve in a completely different way to you. Maybe you face your grief with acceptance and tears while they head to the pub to drink enough to momentarily block out their suffering. We are all different, which means there's over seven billion ways to grieve, no way being right or wrong. If you look at others and wonder why they are behaving differently than you, and possibly question whether they loved the person at all, recognise you're thinking that way. Thoughts in your mind are just opinions and nothing else. They have no weight if you don't engage with them.

Mindfully Saving Myself – One Moment at a Time

When you are deep in your own pain it can be difficult to think rationally. You're unable to understand why your sibling are losing themselves in their work and not saying anything about your loved one, who you both lost, so you react and say something horrible to them. If you react you will not only add to your sibling's own distress, but you will be adding a new layer of your own suffering at a time when you should be bravely allowing your own grief to take its course. As hard as it might be, when trying to process your own challenging emotions, you need to be mindful of everything else that will come up in your mind. If you're able to examine your whole experience as the observer.

It's not just your family that grief will affect but other people in your life too. It will disturb those who are really close to you, and those you deal with on a more superficial level. This in turn will generate further thoughts and feelings that will mix in with the swirl of emotions that you are trying to witness.

When a friend or colleague hears that someone they know is grieving due to a bereavement, they know that something is expected of them, that they need to take some kind of action. But many people really don't know how to behave at times like this. They might be worried they'll upset you if they mention your loss and end up not saying anything to you. Others will not want disturb you too soon after the loss, so they wait with every intention of calling you in a few days or next week, but time passes and maybe they feel because so much time has gone, they shouldn't say anything. As most people aren't mindful and in the present moment, it leads them to avoid the difficult moments. They either back off completely or act like nothing has happened. Some people may try and help without ever explaining themselves. A colleague might pile on more work onto you because they figure you might need a

Stephen McCoull

distraction, whereas if they'd spoken to you, you might have explained that is the last thing you want.

There are also many who will think that they should say something. Some of those people will speak about your loss just once, to show you that they care, but in an attempt to protect you they say nothing more beyond that single time they acknowledge what you've been through. Others will hear the news and immediately call you or come to your house with a dish of food so you don't have to worry about cooking. Friends may call every day to check up on you. You may find that some who broach the subject say the wrong thing, at the wrong time, and it causes you upset. They see you're emotional and they're scared to say anything more. Finally, there will be those people who do nothing other than offer themselves and their time to you, allowing you to experience whatever is happening to you, with a non-judgemental shoulder to cry on. I said there was seven billion ways for people to experience to grief but there's also seven billion ways to respond to someone else's grief too.

I mentioned the wider group of people affected by our grief could be friends and colleagues. Your relationship with those people will not always tally up with their response to your loss. Some of your closest friends will be the ones who say very little and others, often people you would never have expected to be of much support, will be there in just the way you need at the right time. Your friend who says very little does so not because they don't care, but because they just can't deal with things as they are. Remember, most people are running from the reality of life, so they hide from the situation and pretend it's not happening.

All these reactions of others will cause thoughts to occur and if you react to them, in often understandable ways, you will have more suffering to deal with. You could verbally attack your best friend who's

Mindfully Saving Myself – One Moment at a Time

said very little, and lose a good friendship, when really they were feeling the loss too but felt unable to process it. However, if you respond to extremely difficult events as mindfully as you are able to then there may still be that thought but it doesn't cause you further suffering. In the spirit of loving kindness, if you are feeling particularly strong, you could ask your friend what is going on and whether it would help if she talked about why she'd said nothing about your loss? You might then discover that her silence was brought on by her own pain and you can open up together. Of course, there is the small possibility that you may find that she doesn't really care but through mindfulness you can deal with that knowledge. This could be a friendship that has run its course, one to let go in a peaceful way.

Dealing with your grief mindfully, no matter how extreme, is no different than dealing with anything else in life. It's all about not having aversion for the grief, all the additional thoughts that grief, and other people's reactions can cause. Wanting it another way will never change what is but it will make you suffer more. Acceptance takes away that secondary layer of torment and allows you to stop reacting and start responding. Most importantly, it helps you be in that moment, no matter how hard that moment is, and be at peace. It allows you to go through all the sorrow that presents itself, so that you can come out the other side a stronger person who has looked the worst pain in its eye and not blinked. Grief is one of the toughest emotions that a person can experience, so remember, if you do blink and you stop being mindful, then don't be hard on yourself. At every point offer yourself loving kindness.

Stephen McCoull

Confrontation does not lead to Peace

In many of our societies we are taught, both implicitly and explicitly, that we have to stand up for ourselves and not let people walk all over us. Whilst, if someone physically attacks you, you must defend yourself in some way, or escape we are subtly encouraged to aggressively defend ourselves. If someone is verbally hostile to us, for example, then our reaction should be aggression to reassert our rights. We must not make way for any perceived slight and we must react.

Non-reaction is considered by some as a failure or a demonstration of weakness. If you let an insult go with a shrug and move on, many will ask "why on earth did you let them get away with that?" Yet what does forcefully reacting lead to? Does it make the person who we've shouted back at stop and question their actions, or does it lead to escalation and worsening hostility? In many cases it will be the latter. We can see this play out on our streets, in our towns, at sporting events between fans, and worse still between nations. Arguments, fights and even wars are all fed by escalating reactivity between two parties who do not want to be seen to be doing nothing.

If you are physically assaulted you have no choice but to try and defend yourself but in most cases we aren't physically threatened, so is reactivity helpful? Does your life fill with more peace if you swear back at

228

Mindfully Saving Myself – One Moment at a Time

that driver who just stuck two fingers up at you? Do you feel serene or more disturbed after your reaction? I can only speak for myself but even if I win an argument, whatever winning means, I lose because I don't feel peace. Instead I feel agitated. I will often regret my actions afterwards even if someone else started the exchange and my reaction seemed justified. This adds another layer of misery to life. I'm sure I am not the only person who feels like this when they have fed a conflict.

The problem with confrontations is that the person starting the interaction actually wants the other person to reply in the same manner. Something unconscious within them wants to argue. That is almost the whole point of whatever is going on. The event that causes their initial frustration is just an excuse that allows them to enter a phase of conflict. If you don't believe this, think back to the last time you had a go at someone and they simply said "sorry" and offered no other defence at all. How did you feel? Was there a feeling of anti-climax, of disappointment that the other person offered you no resistance? I know have felt that way in the past. It's almost as if something has been taken away from you. *Hang on, I was looking forward to that stand-off, why the hell did they not allow me that?* The problem is that you have not been aware of the thought processes around this and you've attached to the first thought that entered your mind when life didn't go as smoothly as you'd like. You never stopped to examine what was happening in you and whether it was advantageous to you to just react.

What might your life look like if you stop automatically joining every field of battle ever offered to you? It can be peaceful. It can mean you have harmonious relations with the people you interact with. Not only do you have a more peaceful existence but you show other people, once they've got over the disappointment of the lack of a confrontation, that they can have a peaceful existence too.

Stephen McCoull

Here's how non-reactivity, in a situation that would have formerly caused conflict, can make life just that little bit better for both you and the person who you were going to fight with.

Anyone who's lived in the centre of any UK town will know that parking is a nightmare. owns were built way before cars were even a distant dream. Depending on where you live, permits might be required to park on the roads in those areas. Even with residents getting permits to park on their own streets, parking can still be extremely difficult.

One of my neighbours likes to put wheelie bins in the road directly outside his house, when his car isn't there, to reserve the space. Even though we don't have specific spaces for each house, you can just park anywhere within your parking zone, I have no problem with them doing that. On rare occasions, when I must have the space directly outside my home, I will also save the space in front of my house using our wheelie bins.

One day I arrived home and due to how my neighbour had put the bins outside his house I couldn't manoeuvre to park in the space directly behind his. I got out of my car, moved the bin,then parked. There was still plenty of space for his car to park. I hadn't thought it would be an issue, but he appeared at the end of his garden and, although I was still in my car and I couldn't hear what he was saying, he was clearly very angry I'd moved his bin. I got out and asked him what was wrong and he angrily told me "those bins are there for a reason". I explained he still had enough space for his car and he replied with more anger "they're not there for my car, someone else is coming who needs more space than a normal car". His body language demonstrated that he wanted an argument and the way he was speaking underlined that.

I must confess that old me quite enjoyed an argument, especially if I thought I was clearly in the right. This was one of those times and a

Mindfully Saving Myself – One Moment at a Time

little twinge of old me appeared in my head. How dare he act like this when all I've done is park exactly where I'm allowed to park . . . But, instead of jumping on that feeling, running with it and verbally giving him what for, I realised what I was doing and let the thought go. It didn't take long, as by that time I'd been living mindfully for several years, so that process happened in milliseconds it just passed through and away without a reaction.

Instead of starting a quarrel with him I did something different. I made my body language really open and I said "Oh sorry mate, I thought you had them there for your car. I didn't realise it was for something else. Don't worry if it's a van or something I'll drive back around (it's a one way system) and I'll park further up the road, it's not a problem". With nothing for his anger to fight against, because I'd offered no resistance, there was a brief look of confusion and then he gave up his extremely irate posture. I was really surprised at how quickly he stood down and even more taken aback when he thanked me for offering to move but said actually my car was probably ok where it was.

Eckhart Tolle says that people have pain bodies that take them over, which they feed with negative behaviour that causes them yet more pain. I paraphrase, but Eckhart said that the way to counteract someone else's pain body is to simply not join the battle. That day in the middle of our street was a perfect example of that. I could have had an argument with a neighbour but what would have that achieved? Both he and I would have gone back into our houses in bad moods, probably berating each other under our breaths. When we would have next seen each other we may have ignored each other or shot each other evil looks and our relationship, well there wouldn't be one. We'd both have to live a couple of doors away from a neighbour we had negative feelings towards.

Stephen McCoull

Even as being mindful becomes more entrenched in my life I still find it extremely fascinating how most people react, or not react, to mindful behaviour. Because of my non-resistance an argument didn't happen. Rather than exasperated with one another, we parted company on really good terms, even having a bit of a laugh. Despite having lived close to each other for several months that exchange was the first time we had any direct interaction. After that we started nodding hello to each other, then occasionally stopped for brief chats and what I learnt that he's a really nice bloke. The sort that will fix small problems with your car's body work for nothing more than a grateful "thanks". The sort that along with his partner would organise a gofundme page to help out a family who had suffered a devastating house fire. Not joining that battle led to short, medium and long term harmony between two people, and I had a first-hand proof that non-reactivity, in the right situation, reaps great rewards. That is what non-reactivity and non-resistance can help you achieve.

Life Unmindfully Passing You By

How many times have you heard someone say: "Oh no it's Monday" or "I can't wait for it to be the weekend again"? And that same person complains on Sunday that they wished weekends last forever and then start to dread Monday even before Sunday lunch has been served? You've may have heard yourself say something similar. It's not at all unusual for people to think this way.

There's so many versions of this wishing things would change or wanting things never to transform in any way, that that way of thinking infects nearly all of our lives. From the early morning groan of "I don't want to get out of bed" or the late night "I don't want to go to bed". There are first year students who can't wait to finish their degree and get a job and there are third year students fearing the end of their studies. There are parents who look forward to the days when their baby can finally walk so they can have their hands to themselves more. Parents bemoaning the fact their child walking means they have to have eyes in the back of their head, praying that their child get through their terrible twos in double quick time. Parents of teenagers who miss the cuddly child they once had and additionally are scared that their child will leave to go to university to start their own lives without ever looking back. There's the worker who hates his job and wants a promotion and the manager who misses the freedom from responsibility before they had to lead people. There's the person who doesn't want to be in work and wants to be on holiday and another person who is on the plane home hating the fact that they have to work tomorrow. Wherever you look there are people wanting what they don't have or never wanting things to change.

People have that nagging feeling that the good times won't last forever. Rather than enjoying the good times, they spend that moment worrying about the future. Or they look forward to the future when things will be better than they are now, and they fail to be present for their lives and miss out on the gold that can exist even in the bad times. Either way, this type of thinking can lead to us ignoring the present moment and ultimately wishing our lives away because we aren't fully conscious for our lives right now. So often we are mentally elsewhere.

These are, all mental constructs. We don't have to follow them and miss our lives that are happening right before us, if only we could spot what we are allowing to happen to us. What is happening to us is that rather than choosing which thoughts we wish to pay attention and respond to, we allow our thoughts to control our lives.

Mindfully observing that Monday feeling we can choose not to engage with it. Instead, we can bring our full attention to whatever we are doing (even the horrible jobs!) and accept it fully. Remarkably, when we bring our attention to the now, engaging completely with whatever the activity is, then our experience improves, no matter how negatively we judged it before. When Sunday blues start to enter your mind you can acknowledge them and turn your attention to the people you are about to sit down and share a meal with. When your arms are about to drop off from holding your baby and the wish that this stage would be over quickly, so you can enjoy the next part of their development, you can

Mindfully Saving Myself – One Moment at a Time

choose not to react to that and instead be present for every part of your child's life.

Mindfulness isn't just about calming your mind or stopping your thoughts during your time on the cushion, it's actually about living every moment of your life, one second at a time. It's about soaking up your life. All of it.

Stephen McCoull

Being a Snob Harms You So Observe It

The more I read about mindfulness and Buddhism the more I hear about teachers appearing in any guise when we need them. It's something that has always struck me, and I've been contemplating it ever since first heard of it. Mindfulness, at its core, is being aware of every little part of your experience. Things do happen that can teach us but what do we learn from the most? I think we discover, if we're living in awareness of the present moment, that our teacher is ourselves and our own reactions to the world and the things that happen to us. If we observe ourselves, our automated reactions, we can learn so much, even if initially we don't expect much is going on.

I'll tell a story to illustrate this. I went to a holiday camp in the UK with my kids in the summer of 2018. I took the children there mainly because it was what I could afford and I knew the kids, even my eldest who was 13 at the time, would enjoy it. Now, I would like to think that at my core, I am pretty non-judgemental about people. I don't judge people based their gender or their ethnic background, their sexual orientation, or their careers.. I am accepting of most people if they have a good heart. Since discovering mindfulness I've also been working on being less judgemental of people who don't appear to have a good heart. I interact with all sorts of people every day, as positively and politely as I

Mindfully Saving Myself – One Moment at a Time

can, with a smile on my face. That gives me a sense of peace and hope that a tiny bit of positivity rubs off on those people as well. All that said, however, in that holiday camp I worked out that actually there is a snob residing within me.

My ex-wife and I went to the same holiday camp in 2008, before my daughter was born, with our two boys. Back then I thought it was a very low brow place - even those brief words expose the resident snob, and I looked down my nose at the people on that first trip. There were parents there who drank too much in front of their kids and relied on the holiday camp staff to keep an eye on their kids as they did. I remember thinking how appalling people who enjoyed holidaying like that must be. I failed to acknowledge that the majority of parents weren't there drinking too much but were fully engaged with their kids and giving them their time. I just saw the bad and judged the camp based on that.

My boys, who were very young at the time, enjoyed themselves as it's the perfect place for toddlers. There's just so much for them to do and see, with loads of onsite entertainment aimed at young kids. My boys had an amazing time and rather than recognising how much fun it was for them, and letting myself settle into those moments, I was too busy being judgemental about it all. I wished I wasn't there. I had a really bad time and I wasn't at peace .When we finally left for home I was glad but didn't realise at the time that heading home, that rush to get out, was not just a change of location. It was me escaping and avoiding my uncomfortable inner thoughts. I just thought it was a rubbish place to holiday. I didn't see those were just thoughts in my head that might not be true.

Fast forward 10 years to 2018 and the place hadn't changed at all. It had had a lick of paint here and there but essentially it was the same place my boys and I had visited ten years before. We turned up and

Stephen McCoull

I felt that inner snob resurface. I was there for my kids but not for me. The dread that this wasn't going to be a fun four nights for me descended upon me.

Despite my over two year mindfulness practice I really didn't enjoy those first few hours. The old resident snob reappeared and I internally agreed with all the judgement that he dished out and ended up having an internal dialogue about how unfair it was that things had turned out so badly that I could only afford to take the kids to that holiday camp. I bemoaned the fact I had to put up with this and like ten years before, I couldn't wait for the four days to be over despite knowing that the kids would enjoy the holiday., More importantly I was having more nights than I normally would have with my kids.

On that second trip in 2018, however, I now practiced mindfulness, so after a few hours of being stuck in my negative thoughts, and not being as present with my kids as I could be, I suddenly realised I wasn't in the moment. I was waiting by a fairground ride that the kids were on, so I took the opportunity to ask myself the Zen question of "what is this?" I stopped and noticed what was going on in my mind and how it made my body feel. Really focusing on the entire experience and seeing every part of it, The feeling of superiority that existed, I realised was a feeling that this is not me and then let it go. That the thoughts were just mental conditions that I had attached to. As I observed my mental activity as always happens when I stop being lost in reactions and instead become the observer, the feeling of superiority lost its power and slowly disappeared.

Once the kids were in bed, I had time to contemplate all this and I realised something very important. Whilst I did have acceptance of all people in general and wouldn't evaluate people for superficial reasons there was a judgement about what was "nice" in life. On top of that I

Mindfully Saving Myself – One Moment at a Time

did, in fact, judge people. Not based on their looks, their ethnicity, their gender or even their job but on whether they liked the same things as me. The closer their likes to mine the more favourably I thought about them and vice versa.

Whoa! For a person who used to say he only judged people by the content of their hearts, it was a bit of a wakeup call. I had failed to recognise all this judgement and allowed it to remain hidden with me.

I was worse when I was a teenager. If you take music taste, for example, we had ravers who liked electronic dance music, the alternatives who could be broken down into those who liked indie, Goth, metal and other subgenres and, finally, what we called casuals, who liked commercial chart music. I was an indie kid so I really liked people who liked indie music but I could also respect those who liked other genres of the alternative scene. I judged ravers and casuals poorly. When I got into rave music later in my teens I realised that actually we're all the same. Well, except the casuals, who I continued to judge.

Teenagers can be so silly and superficial and as people gain life experience their acceptance of others improves. I, however, carried this very specific judgement into adulthood. I was judgemental about all sorts of things even if not in a way that was as outwardly obvious as when I was a teen. Those unmindful thoughts streamed through my life and took away the enjoyment of a holiday camp experience in 2008 that my boys loved and despite everything I had learnt, also deprived me of enjoyment of the first few hours of the holiday camp in 2018.

As I contemplated these judgemental views in that holiday camp room, that wasn't all that I learnt. I came to realise, like of nearly everything else I had done in life until 2016, that the purpose of that judgement,, was to focus my mind on something other than the present moment. I did it to run from present moment, which for most of my life had been filled with some level of anxiety and depression. This snobby judgement was another device that helped me escape myself and get through the day, without having to dwell on the dark depths of my mind and face everything I was running from.

I found another teacher in that holiday camp who showed me another behaviour that I had developed along with all my others, that was designed to stop me being alive within my life as I find it right now. A behaviour that rather than give me peace, robbed me of it.

At that realisation I felt great harmony with everything. I remember sitting there with a big broad smile on my face. Nothing I ever did in my pre-mindfulness life would make me smile as I sat on my own but mindfulness has the ability of making me grin.

After this epiphany, the rest of the holiday was completely different. I enjoyed every single moment and didn't look down my nose at any of it. I soaked up every second, even the ones when the kids were whinging at me. Whatever we are experiencing it is all the present moment and it's all exactly as things should be, just as long as we can observe it all mindfully.

Sometimes it's the big life events can teach us about ourselves. Sometimes, if we really pay attention, we can learn something about ourselves and grow whilst stood next to a fairground ride in a holiday camp in the South West of England.

Distraction is not mindfulness

When people express that they are in pain, I've noticed they will often be given the advice that they should distract themselves with something so that they stop thinking about whatever is upsetting them or making them feel anxious.

Especially in western societies this advice isn't out of the ordinary. It's what we're taught from an early age we are taught that if we are bored we need to do something to divert our attention away from our boredom. If we get upset we'll be given food, a game, a toy, told to read a book, have the TV turned on, anything to take away the pain of the moment. On some level it makes perfect sense for parents to do so because we don't want to see our kids in pain. I've done similar things myself because I don't want to see my kids upset either., The downside is that we are teaching our children, much like we were taught, to escape the present moment, especially when things aren't pleasant.

Through my mindfulness practice and contemplation over the last four years I've come to realise is that I often used distraction as a way of avoiding my life. Usually the thing I tried to avoid was my poor mental state. That meant that life used to be me trying to get from this point in time to the next in as pain free a way as possible. Pain free meaning without noticing too much of my negative experience and using distraction as my method of escape.

There have been many activities, and I use the term "activities" loosely, over the years that I've used to that effect. There's running, reading, drink, drugs, films, pointless conversations about things I don't care about, conversations about things I'm really passionate about, watching sport, theatre, sex, music events, computer games, TV, weights in the gym, endless news and current affair programmes, documentaries, even work, to name but a few ways I used to escape the moment.

Whilst some of those aren't healthy activities, most of the things I used to distract myself are generally considered good for us. Reading anything can help you expand your horizons and start to think in new ways. Keeping fit is something that helps us all remain as healthy as our bodies allow and can have a very positive impact on our mental health. News and documentaries can keep us informed about current events so we can navigate the modern world with as much ease as we can. Even pointless conversations about things you don't care about can have their place in reinforcing our connections with people we like or love and help us build healthy relationships that nourish us and the people around us.

With the exception of the news, as mentioned in a previous chapter, I don't disagree with any of the above but I did all those things, often, without being in the moment and very often with the unconscious desire to avoid my own thoughts and emotional discomfort at all costs. As much as some of these activities are healthy, I was using them as distractions, which isis not a good thing to do. Take reading for example., I could be learning about some historic event which could give me a better understanding of the modern world, but no matter how beneficial an activity, I wasn't really there for these benefits. I did not get out of my pursuits all I would have done if I was there in that moment, if

Mindfully Saving Myself – One Moment at a Time

I was present and mindful and accepting of my entire life experience in that moment in time., Reading that really interesting book was just a distraction from the utter dislike I had of myself. It was all so that I didn't have to look myself in the eye and acknowledge what my life was.

The positive activities were actually harmful because I wasn't engaging in them for any other reason than to distract myself. Was I always like this? I'm not completely sure but I settled into that behaviour as I developed into an adult and I suspect I started down that path in my early teens if not before.

If my constructive activities ended up having a negative impact on my mental health, then imagine what happened with the not-so-healthy ones such as alcohol. From my late teens I'd taken to using alcohol to block out the fact that I was unsure of myself and lacked confidence. It helped me be social at sixth form parties and, crucially, it helped me talk to girls whom I would have been scared to approach otherwise. I was scared because I doubted myself. I couldn't see any value in myself so why would they value me? It was different when I'd been drinking. I was convinced I was having fun and making great friendships with my fellow drinkers. Yet, the next day, along with an awful hangover, my mental anguish would be worse than ever as a deep and dark anxiety would take over my mind. Any doubt I had about myself as a person would be twice as bad as it had been the day before. Added to that there was the torment of wondering what the hell I'd said or done the night before. Rather than question what I was doing with my life, I'd look to distractions to take me out of my renewed mental suffering. And to make matters worse, whenever I was hungover I also had a strong fear of dying, that I imagine was quite unusual for someone in their late teens and early 20s. I was fortunate that fitness was another one of my distractions, probably the most important one, so even when

Stephen McCoull

hungover I would head off to the gym or go out for a run as a way to forget. I'm grateful that exercise made it rare for me to use "hair of the dog", although I did use alcohol more frequently as my mental collapse approached in later years.

What did all this bring into my life? Fun? Yes, occasionally. Excitement? Yes, sometimes. Pleasure? At times. But it also led to me having meaningless relationships with people, even those I thought I had a real connection with. Distractions helped me create a directionless life, in which I never took any decisions. I just allowed life to take its course and if the course wasn't great there were just more ways of escaping the moment. Living with distractions finally led to me hating myself. My depression and anxiety, that had remained hidden by me not focusing on the present moment for many years, could no longer be concealed. Finally I got to the point where I couldn't cope and I ended up confronting the decision whether I should kill myself or not.

Fast forward to now, I still spend some of my time not being mindful. If I were judging myself, which I'm not, I could be present more than I am. The difference is now I often notice when I'm in a dream world, or when I'm on the edge of going down a worry black hole, or using a task not intending to be present for it, but as a distraction from life. Now rather than work myself further away from the present moment, in the mistaken belief it might make my life better, I bring myself back and focus on what the current experience is. I look the present and everything it entails in the eye, the good, the bad and the ugly and accept it as it is. That painful thought that appeared, that said I am unloved, is just a thought. Understanding it isn't real that means I don't need to resort to escapism to flee from the present moment.

When you live your life mindfully you can still do the activities you enjoy. I still do many of the positive things I did before to fill my

Mindfully Saving Myself – One Moment at a Time

time but now I do them mindfully and focus as deeply as I can on what I am doing. It's incredible how amazing mindfully engaging in the activities you undertake is. Even as your legs are starting to yell in agony when you're running, has a certain life to it that you can notice as you put all your focus into your screaming legs.

Beginning to enjoy positive pastimes in a more mindful way is not all that happens. Without any willpower most of the negative things I did to distract myself have dropped away. I still occasionally drink but do I drink to get drunk? No. I have a couple of drinks and don't feel the need to have more because I'm no longer drinking to forget. I'm drinking because a glass of wine goes really well with the special meal in front of me. Occasionally something will make me think that maybe it would be good to go out for a few beers and then a few more. But like with any other thought I don't attach to it. I look at the thought, I don't judge the idea or myself for having it, and as I acknowledge it and pay attention to it, it fades away.

Stephen McCoull

Triumphing over Fear

You've probably heard of people being described as fearless. To somebody like me for whom fear has been a constant companion, these people can seem almost superhuman, another species even.

We may think it would be wonderful to be fearless but the truth is that fear is an excellent evolutionary device that many animal species have developed. When people were living on the plains of Africa in hunter-gatherer tribes tens of thousands of years ago it was useful to be fearful of the wildlife. If you weren't scared of the big cats hunting in your territory, you would end up taking risks that would eventually lead you to being eaten by said big cats thereby depriving yourself of the opportunity to pass on your fearless DNA to the next generation. The same fearless hunter-gatherer, if they managed not to get eaten by the local sabre toothed tiger, may not have made the logical decisions to store food or to move to more fertile grounds if they weren't scared about dying from hunger in the dry season or during winter. Another dead end for fearless genes. Fear about how your life will progress can help you make sensible decisions about your future. Fear can also force you to take split second lifesaving decisions to act quickly when faced with a sabre toothed tiger without having to think about it.

We're now in a situation where humankind has taken control of a lot of the environments we inhabit. Tigers hiding in the bush ready to

Mindfully Saving Myself – One Moment at a Time

pounce is not something most people need to fear to get through the day safely. Unfortunately, whilst we now control our environment, we haven't yet managed to upgrade our natural reactions to what we deem to be threats. hese reactions, no matter how unhelpful now-a-days, don't negatively affect our ability to pass on our genes. Fear still has its uses in the modern world. Avoiding the group of drunk fighting young adults is something fear will skilfully help you avoid. Fear of remaining in a boring job for your entire life will help motivate you to learn new skills. But not all fear we feel is a useful response in the modern world. Sometimes fear paralyses us when we need to act or makes us want to remove ourselves from situations we may find uncomfortable, when persevering would be the best thing for us. Fear can also makes us behave in ways that do not nurture us.

There's the fear of failure, fear of making the wrong decision, fear of that kid down the street who's twice your size and punches people for fun, fear of intimacy, fear of emotional distance, fear of flying, fear of letting someone else drive you in their car, fear that your boss is secretly planning to fire you, fear that the work you did yesterday wasn't up to scratch, fear you're not living up to your full potential, fear you embarrassed yourself at the pub last night, fear that girl doesn't like you as much as she keeps telling you she does, fear you're selfish, fear that you don't put yourself first often enough, fear that career change you made twenty years ago has turned out to be the wrong choice/move, and many other fears that have no real benefit to our lives including the fear of fear itself.

How is it possible for someone to be fearless when there's just so much out there to fear? Most people cannot be fearless. We have not evolved that way as a species. Fear is a universal experience. It's what people do with the fear that arises that differs from person to person.

Stephen McCoull

We've all read stories about renowned actors or professional sports people who are sick with nerves and utterly terrified up until seconds before their performance begins. Some professionals are that way throughout their careers. Yet rather than run from their fear they embrace it. It doesn't make the feeling of fear any less, they still suffer with it like anyone else does, but they do not try to escape the dread, instead they turn its explosive power to their advantage. When they're on the stage or on a pitch, surrounded by crowds, their mental terror from seconds before allows them to focus on that moment. Their fear makes them alive and they find themselves deep within the natural flow of their chosen profession. No one watching would have any idea that only minutes before they were almost overcome with what many of us view as an extremely negative emotion. Yet, fear isn't a negative emotion or a positive one, it is simply an emotion. It's how we react or respond to that emotion that determines whether the outcome is a negative or a positive one.

It's only through mindfulness, from sitting on the cushion time and time again examining my own thoughts with awareness, that I've learnt how much fear has dominated my life ,or more crucially it wasn't fear itself that dominated my life but how I reacted to fear that impacted me throughout my life.

I had a hard time at school between the ages of 13 and 16. When I was 13 I had been moved from one tutor group I had been in for two years, where I felt quite comfortable with people and whom I either liked or wasn't scared of, to another tutor group with people I didn't know at all. I did not want to move and once I joined the class I found the new group were extremely boisterous, some were physically aggressive and at some level I felt quite a bit of fear.

Mindfully Saving Myself – One Moment at a Time

, My fear of their behaviour must have been clear to see because, like all bullies, once they recognised that I was scared, they unfortunately started picking on me. At certain points the bullying was relentless. I had gone from a fairly peaceful existence (for a school kid) to a constant barrage of negative remarks. You might think I should have just ignored them, and you'd be right, but back then, not unlike many teenagers, I just wanted to be liked, to have friends. I feared not having friends more than I feared these classroom bullies. So the more they picked on me the more I tried to become their mate so that they would stop, and I'd have friends again i but trying to be friends with them appeared to make things worse both psychologically and physically for several years.

The way the school dealt with the situation didn't help either. I had actually been tarred with the same brush as the very people who had been tormenting by the school authorities. The school system saw me as one of the bullies and I probably looked like one of them to a teacher, who may not have been paying too much attention due to the fact I kept trying to make the bullies like me. On top of being bullied by the kids of my class, it began to feel like the school was mistreating me too.

Whilst it's a bit different now, when I was 16, children in the UK had a big choice to make. After taking their GCSE exams kids could stay at school and take their A-levels for two years, go to college and do the same, take an industry specific course, or they could go to work. I made the decision to stay at the school and do A-Levels. Fortunately all the kids that bullied me choose the work route, so the bullying ended.

When I started to meditate every now and then I would start to get these flashes of understanding about my own behaviour and sometimes my school days would come into focus and I started to question my behaviour at school. Why did I do any of that at school? Why did my new form scare me so much before I'd even gotten to know anyone? Why did I try to be friends with people who were nothing like me and who took great pleasure in trying to hurt me in any way they could? Why did I remain at a school, an unhappy place for me that had affected my self-esteem, and ultimately stopped me from achieving everything I was intellectually capable of? These questions hovered within my awareness both on and off the cushion. When I meditated I never sought answers, I just sat with the questions, but slowly I started experiencing flashes of understanding away from the cushion.

I had been dismayed at being moved from one form to another, and extremely reluctant to move for one reason - Fear. I had a fear of change, a fear of the unknown. I had not wanted my life to change from my previous school year and that is why I had shrunk under the weight of my new circumstances, rather than accepting my fear of the new and embracing the new adventure before me. In fact, that same fear is also why I stayed at the school to do my A-levels, when going to college to study would have been a much better option for me. I didn't want to do that because going to college was a modification to the life I knew. I was scared of change, so I never even considered that as a possibility.

That's not all. I also realised that this fear of change had affected me my entire adult life before I found mindfulness. I would stay in relationships that weren't working because I was scared of change and I only changed jobs, when it was impossible not to, for exactly the same reason – fear of change.

But I can't blame the fear of change for affecting my life, the responsibility is mine. The cause of my problems had been my reaction to the fear of change. Instead of saying to myself "yes, I am scared but this relationship isn't working for me" or "maybe I need to get myself a promotion to a position in which I'm more intellectually stimulated by moving to a new organisation", I hid from the fear. What did hiding

Mindfully Saving Myself – One Moment at a Time

from that fear mean? It meant I stayed in situations that weren't as positive for me as changing my circumstances would have been. The roles I found myself in may not have been terrible, many were not bad jobs at all, but my running from my fear of change meant my life, on a mental and emotional level didn't improve, when it may have done so if only I had faced my fear and taken the risk of doing things differently.

There were several different fears that motivated me to try to be friends with my bullies, even as they hurt me, as my anxiety was building up to almost intolerable levels. I had the fear of being disliked. I wanted to be liked, I wanted to be loved and feared not being so. With hindsight, these bullies didn't like me at all, yet I clung to the hope that they would if only I got closer to them. My fear of being disliked meant that I ignored my own well-being and stayed in a mentally, and sometimes physically, dangerous situation. Instead of facing my fear and accepting that some people didn't like me, I put myself into mental and physical danger time and again as I ran from the fear of being disliked. If I had faced my fear I would have stopped trying to be friends with my tormentors, I would have left them alone and when I stopped reacting to their bullying with neediness, which is something many bullies get off on, it would have been likely that, with time, they would have got bored and would have finally left me alone.

The fear of not being liked can become insidious and can negatively impact your life in several ways. You detect someone doesn't like you and you want them to. You don't reflect on whether you actually like them, if they're your sort of person or someone who can add positivity to your life. All you know is that they don't like you. You try and turn them around, whether that's good for you or not. You do things that you probably wouldn't. You think that if you act in a certain way you will be liked. You trade off who you really are by doing things that aren't psychologically good for you in an attempt to be liked. It never works. Imagine if you acted in the same way towards a well-rounded individual? They may detect that you are needy and could feel sorry for you. They may keep you at arm's length, thus making you even needier. In the end they might remove you from their lives all together.

When running from the fear of being disliked can become most damaging, though, is when you are dealing with people with their own problems. Narcissists may spot your primal need to be liked a mile away. They may unconsciously use it to their advantage so that they can hide from their own hurt. They may use you as their supply of happiness because when it comes down to it they know you'll do almost anything for them to like you and will drain every bit of strength from you. To draw you in they begin with showering you with affection and making you feel safe and loved. Once you are hooked in, they will suddenly turn on you, tell you that you are terrible or just the worst person and that they'd be better off without you in their lives. This in turn triggers your fear of not being liked so that you will do everything within your power to win them back again. You feed their ego in the hope to return back to happier times and that is when they've got you. That is when you become trapped in their cycle of love and hate.

I have endured several people with narcissistic tendencies in my life. These people can cause great damage. If you face your fear and accept that you may not be liked, no matter how uncomfortable that may feel, narcissists will have difficulties finding any power over you. I am, therefore, responsible for running from my fear of being disliked and allowing these people to be close to me.

The fear of being alone was also a factor in my behaviour during my school years. If I had rejected the bullies, ignored them, accepted the fear of being alone and living with it, then it would have led to loneliness

Mindfully Saving Myself – One Moment at a Time

and I didn't want to experience that. Running from the fear of being alone is not dissimilar to the fear of being disliked. It has the same results. You will allow people into your life that are not good for you and who may use you.

The fear of being alone remained with me from my teenage years and affected me as an adult. It affected many of my decisions and I have suffered because of it. By facing those fears, not reacting to them, my life is so much better now because I make mindful decisions about the reality of my life, not reactions based on fear. If you face the fear of being alone and allow people who may not be a positive influence to leave your life, you will undoubtedly spend some time without the company of others. But if you practice mindfulness you will have some space to discover who you are and to learn to accept yourself. Once you have peace with yourself then you are more likely to meet people who fit into your life.

When I finally faced the fear of loneliness I created space in which gradually I came across people who were like me with similar ideas and interests and we could learn from each other. I started to be able to view the world differently. After a time you may find that you discover that the odd new person you've met may be similar to your old friends. When that happens you can let those friendships go too because you have faced the fear of being alone so you don't fill your life with people purely to avoid solitude.

My central fear, I've recently realised, is one I think many people can relate to and which played a significant part during my life from my school days until as late as 2016. The fear that I was not good enough. In school I had friends from my previous class who I could have continued to see at lunch times and after school rather than trying to connect closely with my new class. Moving groups I suddenly felt I wasn't good

253

enough for my old friends. As if the year head moving me to a new class had been an indicator of my worth as a person. I let friendships go. I didn't try to maintain them because I felt I was not worthy of those people. Believing I was not good enough not only led me to distance myself from my friends, but I also felt that when people were not nice to me I deserved it, another reason I to put up with bullying.

The fear of not being good enough has plagued me throughout my adult life. t has affected my decisions about work, relationships and even whether I drank or not. Otherwise would I have really drunk so much and so often? When I finally faced the fear of not being good enough I recognised the feeling for what it was - a condition of the mind, not me. It was not true and I did not have to act upon it. When it or any of my other fears come up, as they still do on occasion, I can just accept them and not react. When I do that it sometimes amuses me that I fell for those fears for so long.

The main point about any fear, like everything we experience internally is it is not self. Every single fear, no matter how strong it is, can be used as a point of meditation as it arises. If you can observe it, not trying to change it or push it away and without judging whether it is good or bad, you can bring yourself into the moment right now. The more you bring yourself into the moment, the more you realise that all these thoughts are not self and the only power they ever had was our refusal to face them. Running from fear can wreck your life. Facing your fears and using them proactively when it makes sense to can actually lead to great personal development. When you finally face fears, everything changes.

Benefits of Mindfulness – What you get out of it

So far I've discussed ways of calming yourself, being grateful, learning about your inner life and being present in the moment. I'm sure there's some of you that are wondering where this is all leading to. What will we get out of this in the long run?

Many people come to meditation and mindfulness with that in mind. They want something in return for all this sitting and paying attention to what is. They want to be happy, more focused, to have abundance, have better relationships and to just stop stressing about things so much. It's completely understandable. I am sure you have your own reasons. We wouldn't be practicing if we weren't motivated by our desire for things to be better.

The problem is that the desire for results and improving our lives, the thing that drew us towards the practice in the first place, is actually the opposite of mindfulness. It's a bit of a paradox because mindfulness is about accepting the here and the now rather than wanting it to be different. It's about responding to reality rather than following reactive thoughts, like "God, I wish it wasn't like this" or "If only I were different then things would be so much better".

You turn to mindfulness for a reason - you want change. My goal was for my overactive depressive and anxious mind to calm the hell down. To be told that the desire for change is the opposite of mindfulness, just as you're starting your mindfulness journey is, to be frank, quite annoying. Why else would I start this practice if I didn't have a desire for things to be better?

Yet if you grasp for some kind of outcome you will suffer because as we know no outcome is guaranteed. The more you desire a certain result the more you are focusing on the future and the less you're present in your life as it is happening. You have to let go of your desires for the practice. I don't mean just the big ones, like I want to be completely Zen in the middle of a pandemic. I mean you need to let go of every single expectation and desire you have as to where all this sitting and paying attention is leading. All of them. Even the one where you just want to be a teeny weeny bit calmer.

I could see early on from my experience that mindfulness was helping improve my life so I took the instruction to stop wanting anything from meditation literally. I stopped wanting to be calmer, or to be anything at all, and I just practiced as often as my life would allow it. Some days my practice was tough, with my head all over the place thinking about that time I threw up on someone's shoes on my birthday twenty odd years ago. Other days it was like a beautiful wakeful dream, as if I was completely at one with everything in the universe. Whatever my previous experience, I still sat down for my sit the following day never wanting a repeat of the previous day

Now, if you're like me you may have an initial, but brief, reactive thought that maybe none of this is worth the effort because if it's not going to give you anything then what's the point? Well, I never said it won't give you anything. I just said you can't want anything from it. The paradox is that it's the expectation of results that causes the problems - that will lead to no results. That's the difference. Mindfulness, especially daily practice, whether that's ten minutes a day or an hour, will benefit

Mindfully Saving Myself – One Moment at a Time

you in some way. You just need to understand that there is no instruction manual that guarantees a precise outcome if you follow all the steps provided. You just have to practice and be present for whatever happens even if nothing happens at all. That's really all it is.

This means that what I get out of mindfulness may not be what you get out of mindfulness. I accept all the rewards it's brought me without judgement or further expectations of additional benefits for continued practice. I never presume, because I've had a good month, that next month will be equally as good (it rarely is).

Early on I was curious to find out what other people achieved with their practice. The trouble was what I read was always quite vague. You could never quite put your finger on what other meditators truly accomplished by meditating. I'm going to help you by explaining how I've benefited from my practice. But the really important bit is this is what happened for me. , It does not mean this will happen for you. If you start grasping after the outcomes that I've had then be mindful of that and see if you can allow such desires to pass you by.

I'll start by telling you about a time almost two years ago. At the time people had been pointing out for a while, this is quite a personal thing, that I peed quite often, too often. When I still drank alcohol a lot I put it down to the beer but that was really before people started bringing it up. When people raised it with me I wasn't drinking anywhere near as much, yet I ignored these comments for years. I couldn't ignore them forever so I finally went to my doctors to get checked out. I stepped back from feelings of discomfort I experienced in the doctors, My heart didn't get raised or anything I just allowed the examination like millions of men before me have.

The doctor's first comment was that my prostate was extremely large for my age, at the time 44, which required me to be tested for prostate cancer. Two thoughts filled my head. One that my prostate was very large and two, this probably meant cancer rather than just an enlargement. The implications continued but I just watched the dance of the thought. I remember thinking that I should be a bit upset, but I was pleased that I didn't follow those thoughts any further.

I had to wait almost a week for the results of the PSA test which checks for prostate cancer, and had the occasional thoughts of *"extremely large prostate for my age"* and *"cancer"*. Each time I just watched them arise and then bid them farewell as they faded back to where they came from. My meditative training was cause for my ability to just watch these thoughts rather than getting dragged down into the "Bloody hell, it's going to be cancer and I'm going to die" thoughts which were surely lurking.

The test came back all clear. Good news, yet I didn't really feel relief because I'd not followed those scared thoughts and got lost in a bad mental place. I felt good. So good that I was absolutely unconcerned when the doctor referred me to a specialist for further tests.

A couple of weeks later, despite occasional dark thoughts about it appearing, often late at night when I was going to the toilet for the fourth time, I turned up for the appointment thinking that I was probably going to waste the specialist's time and that nothing was wrong with me at all.

He looked at the notes that my doctor had sent him. I had to take a urine flow test followed by an ultrasound of my bladder.

The consultant received the results. He spoke in a kind and friendly voice but the words weren't the type a 44-year-old wants to hear. "Mr. McCoull, I've seen 80-year-old men who urinate better than you do. Your flow is incredibly weak and you don't empty your bladder at all. It's nearly half full after you've been. We need to find out why." He then went on to explain that it was unlikely to be prostate cancer, but that bladder cancer could be a possibility and that I would need to have an internal examination of my bladder. There was that horrid C word again. I was immediately snapped out of the idea that the specialist would have been better seeing someone other than me. Suddenly, it was more real than before because he had graphs of my flow and scans from my bladder to prove that something was very wrong.

My thoughts got further than before. There was a thought about me lying on my death bed with my three children surrounding me, as I was about to say some prophetic final words. Rather than mentally play around with it I just let it be, which meant I didn't even think what those final words would be. Instead, I just watched the idea, as it briefly hung around, and as before it faded away and I felt completely at peace.

Another new thought paid me a visit - that all this may lead to me having a quite a fight on my hands. But I realised that it was just speculation, so I continued to watch this mental activity without getting too involved. Mindfulness in action.

It wasn't like I was naïve or in denial. I knew there was a risk of cancer and I understood what that may mean. But I didn't see the point in panic and fear mongering which wouldn't help me if I had cancer and it would most certainly be pointless if it turned out I didn't. Mindfulness gave me the skills so that I could stop myself getting involved in negativity about my situation. I certainly would never have been able to do that without my practice. Old me would have immediately been a mess. I would have mentally surrendered, at the first opportunity. I would have replayed that final death scene with my kids repeatedly for weeks. And there would be no way I could work until all the testing was all over.

Stephen McCoull

I don't want to give the impression that mindfully observing these thoughts meant I was running from them. I already knew that trying to escape negative emotions leads to more pain. What I did was face all this mental activity and accept whatever came up without pushing any of it away. That's what is really important to understand. I did not ignore the thoughts, I responded. That response was to continue down the medical investigative path in as calm a manner as possible.

When I went back for the second appointment I had a lot of fear about having a camera in the one place I really never wanted to have a camera inserted. Rather than succumb to my fear I knew what the response should be - which was to just get up on the bed and get ready without reacting but whilst being fully aware of that moment. During the procedure, which took about 15 minutes, I focused on my breath and after a while I even started to do a body scan of the lower part of my body. Making friends, in a way, with the unpleasant sensations the urologist was causing. It's funny how uncomfortable perceptions, or outright pain, loses some, if not all, of its power if you really focus on it. Right then I was really glad I had fixed my spiritual roof, with endless mindful observations of itches and other things.

Speaking to my doctor about my problems to that bladder examination took approximately three weeks. That was three weeks of one type of cancer or another being a possible reason for my symptoms. Fortunately it wasn't cancer and my peeing worse than 80 year old men could be addressed with medication.

I never thought mindfulness would give me the skills to navigate such circumstances without capitulating to negative thinking. But the skills I'd learnt on the meditation cushion were transferrable to real life complications. Compared to what some people have to live with or experience I know it was a very mild storm. There were a few gales yet it

Mindfully Saving Myself – One Moment at a Time

was certainly no hurricane, and my practice gave me peace at a time when it was I likely would have had none if I had never practiced.

It's not just dealing with health issues that mindfulness has helped with. It's improved my interactions with people on every level. Driving and reactivity is my mindfulness nemesis because, hey, I really like to whinge about other people on the road as I drive around. It used to be one constant grumble of dissatisfaction with everyone else on the road driving too slowly, lane hogging, signalling incorrectly and worse. If any of them dared to act aggressively to me then I'd up the ante and there would be angry hand gestures and shouting out of the window, with the use of the horn in return. *"Damn those other drivers on the road, if only the road was just for me"*.

Well, that is how I was before. Over a year ago I got involved in a road rage incident. It wasn't my rage, though, and I wasn't at fault. I was driving along minding my own business but the "incident", all in the other person's head, led to me being followed by the other driver with their horn on for a full minute or two, with them inches away from my backside, clearly angrily ranting to themselves. Old me would have shaken my fist at them or I would have given them a two fingered salute (the UK equivalent of the US flipping the bird) and had my own rant in my car about what an absolute lunatic they were. Instead, I observed the other driver's behaviour with acute interest. I used to be like that? Wow! After a few seconds I realised I recognised the person in my mirror. I worked with him! It was one of my colleagues acting like this towards me.

This happened as we came off the M4 motorway and it meant he had to drive behind me all the way to work, about another two miles. As we got into the work car park it must have dawned on him that actually his rage had been directed towards someone he knew.

Stephen McCoull

Now mindfulness isn't about being passive. It's about not reacting and instead responding to the real situation you find yourself in. If he hadn't ended up in our work car park my response would have been to do nothing. But I saw him park a few spaces away from me and his behaviour needed addressing. We got out of our cars and in a friendly, but firm, manner I asked him "What was all that about?" He was still wound up and he continued to rage in my direction, whilst explaining why he doesn't like that particular motorway junction because he feels it's a little confusing. I explained I understood the junction wasn't great but I asked him whether it was ok to act like he had done towards me. He continued to rage in my direction, still again more about the junction than me but he never backed down. Whist the odd aggressive thought entered my mind, I didn't follow them. I just calmly shrugged at him and let it go, understanding that really this was about him being angry at the junction or life or something and nothing to do with me.

Now, *that* is a demonstration of the power of mindfulness. If that had happened before 2016 I would have been gesturing back at him when we were still in our cars and then would have shouted back at him in the car park. If that had happened before 2015 I would have probably been compelled to square up to him in the car park and use my size to make him stop, without physically getting involved. Instead, my pulse was slightly raised, as it would be with someone extremely angry right in your face, but ultimately I just felt sorry for him. Sorry that he'd not found mindfulness like I had. I knew nothing he said was personal. Rather than joining the battle, I shared empathy with his situation. I even sent him a brief loving kindness meditation once I sat down at my desk. And you know what? There's no ill will between us. I could have held shouting in the car park and his lack of apology against him, but

262

Mindfully Saving Myself – One Moment at a Time

ultimately I'd be hurting myself more than him so why bother? I know I was clear that I thought he was wrong and I suspect, or hope, that was enough to make him think twice about acting that way again.

Did I ever want to be able to handle situations like that without getting wound up or upset? Of course, but I'd never expected mindfulness to give me those skills. I just sat each day and whatever happened, happened. Sometimes things happen in life that show you how much you have changed and that day, in my work car park, was one of those moments for me.

It doesn't stop with handling difficult situations in a way that is more positive. Mindfulness has helped me learn about myself. People don't call it Insight Meditation for no reason.

Since I've been meditating regularly I've been amazed at how, out of nowhere, often when just doing something mundane, I'll have a really important revelation about myself. I'd been thinking about why I'd previously got into unhealthy relationships. I hadn't come up with an answer so I tried out mindfulness for the first time. Rather than contemplating the thoughts and mulling them over in any intellectual way, I was being mindful, just watching them. I'd been doing that for a week or two when one day I was walking to the shop to buy some milk for my shared house. I hadn't been thinking about the subject of unhealthy relationships but suddenly, I realised that I got into bad relationships because of a cycle that had been happening throughout my life. In a flash I saw and understood the whole cycle of unhappiness which I had been going through. I would start to like someone and begin to focus on them and want a relationship with that person. It was exciting at times and gave me some hope for the future but ultimately going through this cycle was something I did subconsciously to escape the pain of the moment. It was grasping for relationships to make life all

263

better. If I could get with person X, then life would finally be great, and my future would be rosy. Sometimes I knew they were unrealistic fantasies but it gave me a focus and saved me having to face myself and the reality of my life. In that moment I saw I'd been following that sequence since the beginning of secondary school and with a couple of exceptions and it had affected every relationship I had at that point.

Sometimes I would end up having relationships with the people I fancied. Yet, being in a relationship didn't mean the cycle was paused. As soon as I was unhappy within those relationships, when reality was not great, I would find myself focusing on yet another person, to block out my current reality. This is what had happened before the end of my marriage, with my ex-wife's friend, which led to me making a huge mistake.

It was a revelation that meant I knew without a doubt, as I walked to the shops, that relationships would not fix me if I used them to run away from who I really was. I saw that I had to love myself before I could have a successful relationship with anyone else.

Recognising and understanding that didn't make me sad that I'd been doing this all my life, this epiphany did the opposite and made me smile. I had recognised what I had previously done and I could see everything for what it is - just a mental condition whose purpose was to distract me. Without consciously trying to, I understood a cycle that has harmed me and my relationships since my early childhood and I was able to break it. That insight helped me get to a place where I would enter any future relationships for the right reasons and not to escape.

That was very early in my practice and since then I've had quite a few insights into what I've been doing with my life. About two years ago I was having negative thoughts quite regularly. If I was still in the depression-anxiety loop, the last few months of that year would have

Mindfully Saving Myself – One Moment at a Time

probably led to a relapse. But my practice has meant I recognised what was happening and I've stuck to mindfulness. Around that time my sleep had been pretty bad for months and I felt in some ways I had slipped slightly backwards. I could have become despondent and like I'd got everything I could have got out of mindful living and let my practice go. Instead, I kept my faith with the process and continued to go to the cushion every day for my daily sit.

Despite my faith in the practice I started to have doubts. I wondered if I had learnt everything about myself that there was to learn. I questioned whether I would have any more insights again. There were darker thoughts that whilst internally my life had improved, my external life was still pretty much the same. I wondered whether I'd not made the most of the insights I'd been given. Had I wasted my practice?

It was a bit of an onslaught but I knew that what was going on in my mind were just thoughts, ideas and opinions - conditions of the mind to be witnessed, and I maintained observation of their comings and goings.

One night I woke up at 2am, which had been normal at that time. This time there was this great anger about something that happened at school - how the school authorities had treated me unfairly. So I lay in bed, trying to not attach to the anger, and asked myself "Why is something from 30 years ago suddenly causing this fury in me at 2am?" Like with the "What is this?" practice, I wasn't looking for an answer I just kept a keen inner eye on all this mental activity.

The question was answered quickly and I saw that my school, especially my year head, had always presumed the worst of me even though I continually proved them wrong. After years of fighting the school I became jaded with everything to do with it. My reaction to the school's treatment of me was why my self-confidence collapsed and was when my depression and anxiety, along with all my behaviours to escape, had started to escalate. The school wasn't the root cause, my reactions were.

I realised it was the lack of care by people who should have cared. They should seen that I was fragile. Most importantly was my attachment and reaction to that treatment set off a chain of events that had affected my life ever since. Everything I did to escape the pain actually took me closer to the hurt. I also came to understand that my reaction to school may have been different.

This insight came within seconds of me asking the question which led me to ask another. "How can I learn to accept what has happened, to let it go, and use this insight for growth?" I asked the question and just observed what was happening without any anticipation of being presented with an answer. I found that just the knowledge of how everything was interconnected meant I could come to accept the anger that had visited me that night. The realisation that I had always been reacting and those reactions were what hurt me the most. With acceptance, the rage evaporated. For me this was a huge breakthrough. I fully awakened to the fact that my pain was caused by me reacting to life, and that I was completely responsible for my own hurt.

When I first meditated I just did it to help with my depression and anxiety. I just wanted to find peace, to be able to separate myself from the mess that was my mind. I never expected or sought more from it. Yet, without expecting or wanting to, I had realisations that have helped me learn about who I am, what has driven me. I am able to use that knowledge, that wisdom, to make a better life for myself. I now understand that I was right to have faith in this wonderful practice. That there is more to learn about this thing we call life and the more we learn and the more we become present, the less we suffer.

Mindfully Saving Myself – One Moment at a Time

To reiterate, these are my experiences. Practicing does not mean that the same will happen for you, so watch out for any grasping within you for outcomes. Accept that you are practicing for no other reason than to practice. If you gain benefits from the practice then great. But accept them without judgement. If insights rarely, or never, come then also accept that without judgement. The impact of mindfulness on your life is powerful only when you don't expect anything. Just practice and see where it leads you.

Stephen McCoull

Using the Inevitable Backwards Step as a Tool

You've been meditating for a while and life is starting to get better. You're less reactive and often spot that you're getting into a thought spiral and you now have the ability to allow that to happen but not engage with it. You feel chilled out more often than not and life is good. You've got this mindfulness thing down to a tee. You may feel life is always going to be better now because you've developed knowledge about what has been driving your unhelpful behaviours for years. You've got new skills that you can deploy to help you ease your negative thought patterns.

If you've managed let go any expectation of an outcome you might still fall into the trap of believing that your mindfulness practice means that you can and will be mindful most of the time. Perhaps you've had some bad times that you handled mindfully, and you start to think that nothing will badly affect your mental state. That if something bad does happen then you won't attach to any negative thoughts and emotions and everything will be mentally peaceful. Or that there is always going to be some level of calmness within you whatever is going on.

Not that I felt smug but I got to that stage and I felt comfortable with this new way of living. I had been meditating daily for about a year and things had been quite stable. I suppose I got lulled into

Mindfully Saving Myself – One Moment at a Time

a false sense of security that because things were calm within me, generally they would remain that way as long as I had a daily practice. However, I was ignoring something very important - the law of impermanence.

I was reminded about that law one Friday, when I was reviewing my finances. My mind started to fill with angry thoughts about the unfairness of my divorce settlement and I was caught up in that emotion. Now this isn't about whether the settlement was actually fair or not, that's not a topic, but the feeling it was unfair was there. Anger arose and despite initially trying to untangle myself from what was happening I ended up following it. Rather than witnessing the whirlwind, I got livid about the way my ex spoke to me. I felt that there was often emotional cruelty that I received from my ex-wife when communicating with her both pre and post-divorce. I got even more frustrated as I remembered how she would often try and turn the situation on its head and accuse me of being abusive, after her attempts to manipulate me resulted in me snapping back.

The flood gates were open, and I was unable to distance myself from the feeling of resentment that she had so many people who support her, when she's this way with me, and I have very few. Out of nowhere there was annoyance and anger at my parents for how they behaved when I was growing up, how they've acted towards me in the last decade but especially in the couple of years before and during my divorce and various breakdowns. I'm not saying they should have behaved any differently than they did, I know they love me dearly, but those were the thoughts that filled me that day.

Then my focus returned to finance and I started to ruminate on the small amount of money I did get out my divorce, how it looked like it was set to be lost because I'd invested it in a flat that I couldn't even afford to rent out and that was losing value as the housing market had imploded. I started to think that I might as well have not worked a single day of the last 24 years because everything I'd worked for was gone.

I started thinking about how, as an adolescent, I lacked confidence in myself and was so shy. I had resentment that I rarely made decisions and exasperation that I didn't realise that I had never been living in the present moment and how I had been ruining my life one day at a time by my attempts to escape the now. I thought about how I never got the most out of me in terms of talent and how that affects me, even to this very day.

Boom! Boom! Boom! The peace was gone. There was a lot of rage in my mind and it all started from a completely rational consideration of my financial situation, and ended with the usual thoughts like "I'm not good enough". Since starting my mindfulness practice back in early 2016 I'd not experienced anything quite like that storm.

What I just described is the biggest step backward I've made, but you can be sure that there will be steps back towards unmindful behaviour on occasions. We're all human, you can't avoid it and if we wished it another way we'd just be adding another layer of suffering and we don't need to do that. As ever, acceptance is key.

What matters most is how you handle that step backwards. That is the true indicator of whether you are living mindfully or not. If you've succumbed to reactivity, to anger or some other strong emotion you may think that you've not learnt anything. If you're still as reactive as before after all these months or years of meditation and mindfulness practice, what is the point? You're still mindlessly attaching to thinking so why bother? You're no good. You might as well give up right now as it's not working. Now old me, the non-mindful me, would have done exactly

Mindfully Saving Myself – One Moment at a Time

that. Let's give up and go and have a beer or five in a pub beer garden in the sun.

The following day I was still reeling with these thoughts and my younger son, who was probably 11 at the time, was a real pain about something and was very upset and shouting. At that age when he got like that he could be hard to deal with. Well, if I'm honest, he was probably very easy to deal with if I had just handled the situation in the right way. With all these angry thoughts swirling around, his moody behaviour wasn't what I needed. The old me would have probably shouted at him, telling him off. The situation would have escalated, and no one would have benefitted. I was close to shouting but instead of reacting I went downstairs, focused on my breath, then on the soles of my feet and how the floor felt beneath them for a minute or two and grounded myself. I observed my anger about my son, accepted that I had it, didn't judge myself for it and then it slowly vanished. I went back upstairs and spoke to him calmly, allowing him space to talk to me. He calmed down and the situation was resolved without much drama. I had mindfully stopped the anger levels growing, there was peace in the house and hopefully my son felt heard that day.

My parents were due to pop over to my house on Sunday morning of the same weekend. When I have guests coming over, especially my parents, Marta and I cleaned the house a bit to try and make it look respectable. As I tidied the house in preparation for them coming over, all the anger about them, that I had felt earlier in the weekend, appeared again. There was rage, very raw rage. But instead of reacting to it and being annoyed at myself for feeling what I was feeling I observed my feelings acknowledged its existence, and focused on my breath again, on the soles of my feet, grounded myself, just as I had the previous day. My parents arrived and there was no internal animosity towards them, it was pleasant enough time and they left without issue.

I then sat with my other thoughts about my ex-wife, my finances, my flat losing value and all the acrimonious views that had taken me over that weekend, and one by one I recognised them, examined them, and accepted that they existed. Most importantly, I didn't evaluate whether the thoughts were true or not, good or bad, and I didn't judge myself for any of it.

I still had some thoughts which I still had to work on and over the months I continued to practice with them. You will likely find that you may also need to revisit previous difficult emotions which have taken you over more than once before you truly find peace with them.

My take away from that weekend was that not once did this myriad of angry and negative thoughts which had flooded me cause issues with the people I was with. I didn't let those emotions spread outwards and I don't think anyone noticed anything amiss, even if internally it felt like a blast of emotion. They didn't notice not because I ignored what was going on but because I had slowly managed to give space to all these strong emotions, sit with them and observe. That's not to say it was easy. Far from it. But instead of beating myself up and deciding that mindfulness is a crock of brown stuff that doesn't work for me, I took away from it that my new lifestyle had changed me for the better. I learnt more about myself as I faced all my experiences and continued along the path.

Those aren't the only step backs I've taken of course and there's been a few more since then, although none as dramatic. I know that in the future there will be other ones as well but when these setbacks happen, I accept them without judgement and that there is further

Mindfully Saving Myself – One Moment at a Time

opportunity to learn about myself and learn to be at peace with whatever I find.

One of the main things that you need to keep in mind when something like this happens to you, is that mindfulness can help us see that thoughts exist but they are not us and, better still, that they are impermanent. With this in mind while on the mindfulness path you can then appreciate that it's ok to have a bad hour, day, week or even month. If we accept that we are having a demanding time but don't react to it with aversion and try to push it away, then we can sit with this experience right now with acceptance. We enable ourselves to just let the chaos run its course without effort to get rid of it. That's how we find the peace within the storm.

Stephen McCoull

What's Outside Doesn't Give You Peace

On this mindfulness journey I've occasionally wondered what my life looks like to an outside observer. You might think following worries about what others think about you is the opposite of mindful living and I'd completely agree with you. Caring what other people think is yet another condition of the mind to investigate and learn from. But the reason I considered the external view was out of curiosity rather than ego.

Whilst I share my meditation journey with lots of people online, it's not something I mention too much in my day to day existence outside of online mindfulness communities I'm involved with. I have talked about it in some detail with my partner, Marta, and I've mentioned it to a few people, including my parents and sister as well as people I volunteer with, but generally I don't make a big deal about it.

Yet, when I contemplated what it looks like, externally, I wondered if the people who are aware of my practice see my life as a contradiction now? Often before work I will meditate and then go through posts on the Daily Calm online Community and try to respond to a few as mindfully and helpfully as possible. If I have time I may read

Mindfully Saving Myself – One Moment at a Time

a few pages of a book by a Buddhist monk or a mindfulness teacher or some other kind of spiritual person that resonates with me. When I'm at work I will get a tea and mindfully walk to the tea room with my focus in my feet.

Whilst not always, I can often feel quite peaceful and remove myself from whatever comes up without reactivity. When thoughts do arise I will frequently contemplate what it is and why it has happened, as well as the drivers of my actions. When I do that I am trying to assess the causes of former suffering so I can learn. I am living mindful now and most of the time I feel great peace. Most of the time . . .

At my job I work with Excel and occasionally will find problems and I still tut, grumble or mutter to myself as I attempt to find the solution. I still swear if the issue isn't resolved quickly, and I still whoop with delight when I finally fix the problem. To the outside observer does it look like I am still reactive, still wound up by what I am doing with my work?

I still listen to noisy bands, like Muse, on a very high volume as a backdrop to my mutterings when Excel formulas misbehave. I occasionally crank up the volume in my car and listen to dance music whilst nodding my head, often badly mistimed, to the music's beats. I'm still also very vocal and passionate, when it comes to politics. I can be quite forthright when I give my opinion on whatever political and international situation people are discussing.

I wonder whether, with my music taste, my mutterings as I work and my political stance, some people would say I'm anything but calm. Maybe they think not much has changed with my life. I'm older, I do a different job at my company than I did a few years ago, but essentially I'm still the passionate and sometimes emotional person that I've always

Stephen McCoull

been. I've never asked, but maybe others still see me in the same way they've always seen me?

However, that is the point. The outside does not matter. What people see isn't important because change doesn't come from outside, the change that occurs on this journey happens inside you. It's your relationship with the content of life that matters. Yes, you might get a new job because you overcame fear to leave your old employer, or you may stop drinking so much or you may start volunteering for a charity, but none of that means you will find peace. Unmindful people can also make all of those changes. External change doesn't automatically lead to peace inside.

When you are mindful you can continue to be as interested as you were in your old pursuits. I still love Knights of Cydonia by Muse, but now, when I listen to it, I don't go into some fantasy about being on stage, being the singer in front of huge crowds of people that are amazed at my vocal skills (anyone who's heard me sing will know that will never be possible). Neither do I treat the music as the backdrop to some other fictional life event I'm making up in my head that excites me but separates me from reality. Instead, I listen to the music and I really hear it. Externally, I'm still just listening to Muse, but inside I'm experiencing the music in ways I've never done before, with little or no mental interruption, appreciating it for all its intricacies. Sometimes, when I really listen to music mindfully, I find things within the music, subtle sounds, that I have never noticed before. Occasionally, I realise a certain bit of music is way more beautiful than I'd ever recognised before. It's amazing when that happens.

When I'm mindful I can still swear when my Excel spreadsheet crashes before I have a chance to save my work. I may curse more than once if it happens a second time, but inside I'm not screaming at myself

Mindfully Saving Myself – One Moment at a Time

that these things always happen to me. I'm not overcome with rage about my laptop because this only happens to my laptop. I hear the words, the complaint, but that is it and I go back to the task at hand, often, with no further negative thoughts. I choose not to make the thoughts inside my head my identity. Externally I am still swearing at Excel, but inside way more than before I am just calm.

When you are mindful you can still engage in debates about politics or whatever floats your boat. You can still present your arguments in a strong way and question the other side's position. It may look the same on the outside, but that doesn't matter because internally you're not swearing at them for their stupidity or wondering why they can't understand the obvious point you're making repeating yourself for the fourth time. Inside, you consider their views, try and challenge them in a logical way and if that doesn't work you just accept it and appreciate that they think differently from you. You understand that you cannot expect everyone to think the same as you, so you let it go without any anger directed towards them. Incredibly you may see that, despite having opposing views, ultimately we are all the same. Additionally, responding in this way could make the other person feel heard, making for a better relationship from which everyone gains when none of us gain from the opposite (as most social media interactions demonstrate).

Living mindfully has meant that, whilst I am still interested in or enjoy similar activities to what I liked before I discovered mindfulness, the amazing thing is I'm not grasping after them in the way I was or using them as a means of escape from myself. I am not generating another layer of suffering. I enjoy my activities in life in a much more healthy and nourishing way that ultimately leads me to live in the moment way more often than I did before.

Stephen McCoull

Yes, there are parts of my life that, externally, don't look like they've changed, but however it looks on the outside everything has changed. Absolutely the whole shebang. For most of my life I rejected who I was and hurled hate at myself inside my head. Through investigating myself mindfully I have grown to like, accept and be at peace with who I am right now in this very moment. How cool is that?

What happens outside doesn't ultimately matter but if you change internally it is likely something will also change on the outside. It may not be your job, or your hobbies but something will. For me being aware in this moment has led me to stop drinking or following other behaviour patterns to escape my life. I can now sit down and write, I can engage with others to help them on a similar path to what I am on which is something I could have never done before.

Whilst I still have the odd bad day, like anyone, my mental health issues have subsided to such an extent that I now volunteer to support people who have difficulties in life like I had once had. I may still swear at Excel or occasionally get upset in my car but many people have told me that I seem much calmer and happier with my life than I had before and more importantly that is exactly how I feel. We don't follow this path to change how we appear on the outside, we live this way because we will learn to have peace with what is, no matter what it is. Yet if you follow the mindfulness path you might look different in some way, maybe you just smile a lot more, because you will have changed for the better.

Throughout this book I have shown how mindfulness has helped me change for the better but only you can find out how it will change you by taking your first step on this incredible journey. We are all different and our journeys will be too but peace is peace whatever else we find.

Life is What We Make it

I want to end by saying that this journey is not easy which is why most people in the world do not dare take it. But if you are to find a calm inner life you first need to battle through the storms that you might have been avoiding for so long. You cannot evade the squall because evasion is the opposite of mindfulness and in the end that will lead you away from peace.

It may take time but once you are able to face everything within you, examining each thought without judgement, with curiosity and an open heart, and continue to do so each day you will eventually finally find peace within yourself. Whilst you cannot always be happy, it's impossible as negative life events are unavoidable, as long as you continue to practice you will always feel a certain harmony, or will be close to returning to it, even when there is sadness in life.

This is the journey of a lifetime, one present moment at a time. Once you discover you are the awareness behind the thoughts, and not the thoughts themselves, your learning will never stop. You must remember that none of us will be perfect meditators, but we will practice

Stephen McCoull

and continue to learn about ourselves and grow ever more mindful until the day that we die. Our ability to be the awareness of what is will stop a bad minute becoming a bad hour, or a bad hour becoming a bad day, or a bad day becoming a bad month. We just need to follow the path without expectation.

I'll share one final thought. This practice reminds me of physics lessons in which we were taught that everything before us seems firm and solid. The desk in front of me is made of wood. I can bash it with my hand and it will maintain its form - a solid object. Yet, when we look at the desk at an atomic level and observe an atom from the desk it is mostly empty space. Each atom of the desk is like that, a vast energetic void, so the desk is really made of lots of empty space despite how amazingly solid it appears. It is almost as if everything in the universe is a mirage.

Like the desk, emotions and feelings in our mind appear so strong and unmovable that throughout our lives they have dictated our actions, as we endlessly react to them and try to flee them. Yet, these apparently solid mental conditions change when we bring our attention to them and really observe what is happening without any aversion. Like the desk, what happens in our mind isn't what it appears to be. Under our brave and direct gaze we come to realise that the constant stream of thoughts in our minds holds no weight at all. The more you unswervingly watch those thoughts and emotions, the weaker they become until their power is lost and they vanish before us. We realise they were made of nothing after all and that we are the awareness behind them rather than their prisoners. We can then step forward into our lives, awake in the present moment for the first time.

Acknowledgements

Becoming aware of what is happening right now, seeing things for how they really are and making that your way of life, may appear to be a solitary pursuit, and indeed there is a lot of inner work, but we're all connected even when working on ourselves. Without certain outside factors I may never have made the alterations to my relationship with thoughts that I've made. I may never learnt to have moments of peace that I never had before. Therefore I have a lot of people, some not so obvious, to be grateful for and to thank.

Firstly there are various friends and colleagues who stuck with me through, what they probably didn't realise, were the worst days of my life. These were people that were there for me, sometimes just for incredibly vital minutes, no matter what else was happening. They didn't try to fix me, they didn't berate me for things I'd done, or whisper seductively that it would all be alright and there was nothing really wrong. They just held space for me in which I could grow. Sometimes the space was a simple word of encouragement, or concern, that may have seem almost like nothing to them but for me it was everything. What fills me with such great faith for humanity is that there's just too

Stephen McCoull

many people to thank one by one and that so many of them were people I never expected support from.

That said I especially want to thank my best friend Mark Sequeria. Mark you never tried to brush anything under the carpet and pretend my life hadn't fallen apart. You were a figurative shoulder to cry on and you were there, on an emotional level, when many were not. You have demonstrated time and time that you are completely trustworthy and loyal and it means so much that you are a part of my life. Part of the reason I survived and then expanded on a mental and spiritual level is because of you. Thank you.

I also want to thank my old mates from my school days who still fill parts of my life. Mark Niles, Tom Charlesworth, Steve Namaseevayum, James Codling and David Chadwick. Whilst we may not always see each other regularly, sometimes not for years, from the very start you've just taken me as I was and how I now am. In the last six years or so it's been such a pleasure to have you in my life when I'm finally fully awake to our friendships.

It may seem strange but I am also so incredibly grateful for the people who I used to know who weren't there for me. With my safety net of many friendships gone, whilst it nearly broke me, it meant that I had to stop and question everything. And I mean everything. Without that loss of support I may never have realised that I could only find the answer to how to find peace inside of me rather than from the content of life. I learnt so much from that experience, lessons that couldn't have been taught by myself to me, if you had been in my life still.

I am so fortunate that I have taken this journey in the 21st Century. If this had occurred when I was in my early twenties I would have never have found the resources and support from people I did. But I have taken those steps in the modern world and I discovered the Calm

Mindfully Saving Myself – One Moment at a Time

app at the perfect moment. So I want to thank everyone who work and have worked for Calm whose app I hold in the palm of my hands whenever I need it. Your app taught me how to meditate and how to be present. It demonstrated how, through meditation, I could learn to love myself and then the world around me simply by being aware with non-judgemental acceptance of what is. Whilst I offer thanks to all Calm's staff I want to specifically pass on my gratitude to Tamara Levitt for both your guided meditations but also how you are so open and vulnerable with everyone who listens to you. You have made this whole way of being really accessible by showing anyone can do it, no special skills are required. I am forever grateful.

There is the Daily Calm community and all the people who have supported me or passed on their own knowledge there. I am extremely grateful to everyone I've interacted with in the community over the last five years or so. You all know who you are, but special thanks Aleisha, Marion, Jade, Daniel, Christi-an and John for your friendship as well as your extraordinary wisdom.

Due to the internet I've also been fortunate enough to come across the Amaravati Theravada Buddhist Monastery in the UK. At the time I writing I have never visited the monastery but your incredible online resources, both written word and online teachings, have helped deepen my understanding of mindfulness and the dhamma. My practice strengthened in the middle of great storms because of the teachings you provide the world. Whilst there are many great teachers in the monastery I will single out Ajahn Sumedho and Ajahn Amaro. You both impart your wisdom to others in such an accessible manner that it cannot do anything but help anyone who really wants to listen. You showed me that the knowing was already within me, I just needed to access it. Thank you.

Stephen McCoull

I have also learnt a great deal from the podcasts of Tara Brach and Joseph Goldstein who offer regular teachings for free. The thoughts you offer for consideration are really needed by the world right now. They have helped me at times when I've had doubt about myself and I am certain they help many millions of people who want to learn about the inner world. Thank you.

To my parents. I know I was a difficult child, I didn't know how to express myself, and I sought solace in things that ultimately were not healthy for me. I know how confusing the times were when I left my former life and started to try to live differently. I know you didn't know what you should do and so I am sorry for all that upset. Yet even if things were scary you were there for me, whether it was giving me a place where I could have the kids overnight, or feeding me when I didn't have enough money to eat every day. You were there for me. I know you often didn't know what to say or do, beyond the practical, but you offered love even when I wasn't very loveable. Thank you and love you back.

This book has gone through so many drafts, I think I lost track at one point, but Caitlin McColl, who I met through Calm, did a great job on helping me with my final draft. I love the way you didn't force your changes upon me but offered them as suggestions. And also the speed at which you worked. It was incredible how quickly you turned around each chapter. It was great collaborating with you. Thank you and see you around online.

Marta I keep saying I'm a lucky man but really I am a fortunate human being to have you in my life. I never gave up on human relationships, despite my previous experiences, but I did doubt I'd be lucky enough to meet someone who would accept me as I am and allow me to just develop as I have been, without any caveats. But then I met you and that doubt was proved wrong. I always have the mental and emotional space I need. I never understood that was really possible in a relationship. I can never be grateful enough for that and it's quite fortunate that I can do the same for you too. I have never felt such love from another human being. Sharing life with you, whether it's watching TV on the sofa alone or with the kids, or off on some adventure, all of it is just right as it should be.

I really appreciate all your efforts of helping me with my forth draft (or was it the fifth?). You were patient, thorough, and helped me see that it was a project worth pursuing. I kept going because of you. Thanks for everything you've given me.

Finally to my children. Hey I know times haven't always been easy or ideal, I am sure, try as I might, that I can never really understand how my depression and what happened has affected you, but I decided to live and then tried as best I could live well because of all three of you. You give me the reason to sit and watch myself so that I can be present and in the end so that I can be there for you even when I am not physically. You fill my heart with love and, even though I know I'm not the world's greatest father, I hope that you can feel how much I love you all. Thank you for giving me a reason to get better and more importantly thank you for your love. I hope, one day, that you too will find the contents of this book of service to you.

Stephen McCoull
October 2021

Manufactured by Amazon.ca
Bolton, ON